CULTURE AND SOCIETY
IN LATER ROMAN ANTIOCH

Culture and Society in Later Roman Antioch

Papers from a colloquium
London, 15th December 2001

Edited by
Isabella Sandwell and Janet Huskinson

Oxbow Books

Published by
Oxbow Books, Park End Place, Oxford OX1 1HN

© Oxbow Books and the individual authors, 2004

ISBN 1 84217 102 X

A CIP record for this book is available from the British Library

This book is available direct from
Oxbow Books, Park End Place, Oxford OX1 1HN
(Phone: 01865–241249; Fax: 01865–794449)

and

The David Brown Book Company
PO Box 511, Oakville, CT 06779, USA
(Phone: 860–945–9329; Fax: 860–945–9468)

or from our website

www.oxbowbooks.com

Printed in Great Britain by
Information Press, Eynsham, Oxford

CONTENTS

INTRODUCTION

Isabella Sandwell

> Although the fourth great city of the Roman world, Antioch has achieved little or no purchase on the modern imagination. The ancient past remains an overpowering presence in Rome and in Istanbul. For Alexandria, we like to think we can conjure up the ancient city from the poems of Cavafy and the Alexandria Quartet of Lawrence Durrell. Carthage, at least, inspired Flaubert's Salammbô. Antioch though, in its time, an equally vibrant presence, a city of some 200,000 inhabitants situated at the joining point of Asia and the Mediterranean, has always remained strangely out of focus.[1]

Peter Brown makes this comment in his review of the exhibition of finds from Antioch and the accompanying catalogue, which were both entitled *Antioch: The Lost Ancient City*.[2] Brown's assessment and the title of the exhibition reveal the general state of interest in Antioch that existed both among scholars and the wider public until very recently. Although in the academic literature there have been a few major works focusing on the city (in particular by Petit, Liebeschuetz and Downey[3]) Antioch still does not generate the same amount of interest as do Rome or Constantinople, for example. At the same time, Antioch has not penetrated the popular consciousness to the same extent as these other cities have done – in fact probably to a much lesser degree. The present book is part of a trend of new interest in the city that hopes to bring it to the centre of studies of the ancient world. The Antioch Tyche from a set of four from the British Museum (Figure 0.1) hints at the importance Antioch had in antiquity.[4]

This set was found on the Esquiline Hill in Rome and represents the four leading cities of the late Roman Empire, Rome, Constantinople, Alexandria and Antioch. In the ancient world an individual Tyche acted as a personification of the "fortune" of the particular city it represented. Thus the Antioch Tyche can be seen as a form of promotion for the city. But as part of a set of Tyches found in Rome the Antioch Tyche has further significance. Clearly it was seen by someone in the traditional centre of the empire, Rome itself, as being one of most important cities of that empire and as being on the same level as Rome and Constantinople. The place of this Antioch Tyche in a set of four Tyches thus captures well the tension, which will be touched on by various contributions to this present collection, between the local and particular characteristics of Antioch and what was Roman and typical about it. As Kondoleon and Heintz point out, such a set of Tyches had empire-wide significance, expressing both unity in

Figure 0.1 The Tyche of Antioch, the British Museum © Copyright The British Museum.

"emphasizing the geographical breadth of the empire" and diversity, by "depicting the late Roman state as a commonwealth of autonomous urban centres".[5] Thus the Antioch Tyche, on the one hand, shared many visual characteristics with the Tyches of Constantinople, Rome and Alexandria, but on the other was distinguished by the male personification of the Orontes river swimming under her feet. Clearly in the ancient world Antioch was considered important both in its own right and as a leading city of the empire.

Two main reasons emerge for Antioch remaining "strangely out of focus" and for it not having received the attention it deserves in previous years. Firstly there is the lack of physical remains. The classical city either disappeared long ago under mud and silt from the river Orontes and from the surrounding Mount Silpios, or has now been built over by the modern town and is thus inaccessible.[6] Almost none of the major public buildings that we know existed in Antioch has been uncovered, and there is also comparatively little archaeological evidence for everyday life in the city.

What we have instead are the large number of beautiful mosaics from private houses of the elite (like those in the suburb of Daphne), but however impressive these are, they are not representative of life in the city as a whole.[7]

The second set of reasons for Antioch having become a "lost ancient city" has more to do with the changed political and religious context of the area. In antiquity Antioch was a leading city in the province of Syria but the borders have since shifted and modern Antioch (Antakya) now lies in the Turkish Republic on the frontier between Turkey and Syria. As Brown points out, this causes problems for the study of Antioch as the city is now separated by a political border from its hinterland, with which it had a close, dependent relationship in antiquity.[8] At the same time, its presence in the Muslim world, on the borders of Arabic speaking Syria, and the fact that it has been an Islamic city since the end of Roman rule in the seventh century have put up other barriers to western interest.[9] It has perhaps been seen as too inaccessible and exotic really to have penetrated the general public's consciousness in the past. Certainly the city is a little too far off the beaten track for the average visitor interested in the sites of the ancient world, and the lack of large-scale physical remains might make it a disappointing visit for those who do make the effort to travel there. To these reasons we can also add another: it is possible that Antioch has been ignored not only as a result of prejudices of place but also of time. Although Antioch was an important city from Hellenistic times onwards, most of the major sources for the city date to the period between the second century AD and the sixth century AD, the period often labelled as Late Antiquity. And, as it is only in the twenty years or so that this period has really become popular among students of the ancient world, it is possible that the study of Antioch has suffered as a result.

If any further justification or explanation is needed for the new interest in Antioch, then this can easily be found. Of course the most obvious reason is very importance of the city in the ancient world. As metropolis of Syria it was the seat of the governor and the administrative centre of the area.[10] It was also a centre for Hellenic culture and an important focal point on the trade and military routes between the outreaches of the empire in the east and the Mediterranean in the west.[11] Lastly Antioch was an important religious centre, not only having a large Jewish community[12] and strong pagan traditions[13], but also being home to one of the oldest Christian communities and the seat of a patriarch.[14] In fact, it is as a Christian city that Antioch has most usually been recognized as important, especially as it was the place where Christians were first given the name 'Christian' (*Acts* XI.26). As such, students of the New Testament and Early Christianity are probably more aware of it than other students of the ancient world. A recent book on early Christianity recognizes this, pointing out that: "If one wished to pick out one city that represented the temper of the new Christian world, it would have to be neither Rome nor Constantinople (nor indeed Alexandria, so rich a source of theological enquiry) but Antioch".[15] From all this it thus becomes clear that the city was important in all the central fields of study: economic, political, cultural and religious.

At the same time less obvious reasons for a new interest in the city have been proposed. Kondoleon highlights the multicultural nature of the city, that it contained a very mixed population of many nationalities and faiths – Jews, Christians, Greeks,

Romans, Syrians and Egyptians – and suggests that as a result it has a particular relevance to the inhabitants of today's multi-cultural cities who are also concerned with issues of "civic community and diversity".[16] Maas, looking at the issue from a related but slightly different perspective, has suggested that a new interest in the Roman Near East and a reappraisal of Rome's relationship with "Persia and other cultures beyond its eastern frontier" have made necessary a re-evaluation of Antioch.[17] Certainly an increased interest in Syriac, in eastern forms of Christianity, and in the Islamic world and its precursors can only encourage a closer inspection of a city that was one of the centres of eastern Christianity, where Syriac, Greek and Coptic speakers rubbed shoulders on a daily basis.[18] All these reasons, as well as straightforward academic interest, make any new works on Antioch valuable contributions.

Gradually the importance of further study of the city is beginning to be recognised, and Antioch is now at last beginning to receive the attention it deserves. The exhibition entitled *Antioch: The Lost Ancient City*, which was put on by the Worcester, Cleveland and Baltimore art museums in 2001 has played a major role in this process. Using art, artifacts, plans and photographs of the region the exhibition aimed to reconstruct life in the city as far as possible and to reunite finds from the original Princeton expedition of the 1930's – finds which for some time had been dispersed in various museums and private collections. The accompanying catalogue has brought the exhibition to a much greater audience and, through a series of essays, places the exhibits in the context of the history of the city and the written sources. With its high-quality illustrations and colour photographs, this book means that the beauty and excitement of the city and its finds can no longer be ignored. Growing interest in Antioch can also be seen in the three-day conference held in Lyon in October 2001, *Antioch de Syrie: Histoire, images et traces de la ville antique*. This covered all areas of life in Antioch and included papers using both all the major written sources relating to the city and the surrounding area and a variety of material and epigraphic evidence. The breadth of this conference reveals just how much potential there is for the study of Antioch, both in terms of the availability of material (some of it very little studied) and in the possibility of finding new approaches to the more familiar sources.

In fact, it could be said that one of the most exciting aspects of the study of Antioch, and one of the reasons for advocating that further attention be paid to the city, is the amount of evidence that we have relating to it. The three best-known bodies of material are the writings of the orator Libanius and the preacher John Chrysostom and the extensive mosaics found in the city and its suburbs. Of course these have always received some attention, particularly from experts in their field, but recently there have been clear signs of increased activity with new translations of Libanius and Chrysostom being published and new approaches being found to all three major sources.[19] There are other sources which are well known but less often used, such as Malalas, Theodoret and Sozamen (to name just a few), and we can add to this list the writings of the Emperor Julian, who spent much time in Antioch, and Ammianus Marcellinus who was born in the city. Some of these sources will be explored and referred to in the following papers. At the same time, however, they will bring into view additional bodies of evidence and material, some discovered in recent surveys, and will suggest how these can add new dimensions to our study of the city.[20] Part of the distinctiveness of this volume thus comes from the fact that it contains up-to-date research on both new material evidence and new approaches to previously studied material.

This, then, is the context that gave rise to the present book. Most of the papers included here were originally given at a one day conference on Antioch sponsored by the Open University and the Institute of Classical Studies at London in December 2001.[21] This one day conference, although much less ambitious, was partly inspired by the three day conference in Lyon and by the general growing interest in Antioch. More particularly it grew out of the present editors' mutual but very different interests in Antioch and a desire to relate their own work to the broader picture of research being carried out in relation to the city. The aim of the conference was thus to bring together work-in-progress on a variety of topics to do with Antioch and the surrounding region in the late Roman period (the second to seventh centuries AD are covered). Its purpose was to give contributors a forum in which to open up their current research to comment and debate, and so in this collection of papers we hope to give a wider audience access to some of the most recent thinking on Antioch, and to capture something of the liveliness of the original one day event. This means that the contributions are quite varied in content and approach, with some representing initial discoveries and the earlier stages of research and others the final stages of long term projects. In a way it can be seen as a showcase of the kind of projects and research being carried out in relation to the city at the present time: it aims to include as broad a range as possible of views and source material, with Antioch itself providing the unifying theme.

Lieu and Haubold and Miles continue recent interest in Libanius as a source for Hellenic education and the classical tradition in Antioch. Lieu uses an account of Libanius' career to show what it reveals about education in Antioch and the east more generally. He describes the activities – and problems – of sophists, teachers, and some students too, and records some of the changes taking place in higher education at the time. In doing this Lieu is able to bring to our attention some new translations of Libanius' writings on education and to increase our knowledge of one of the most important sources on the subject in late antiquity.[22] Haubold and Miles, on the other hand, look at Libanius' *Oration LXIV In Defence of the Pantomime* to explore his understanding of Hellenism and the relationship between the Hellenic heritage and life in fourth century Antioch. They evaluate the oration both as a piece of rhetoric, comparing it with Aelius Aristides' oration *On the Dancers,* and as a text that relates to the realities of life in the city. In particular they argue that Libanius, in contrast to Aristides (at least as Libanius portrays him), has a very malleable understanding of Hellenism that is able to include the dual identity – both Syrian and Greek – of late antique Antioch. They also suggest that for Libanius dance was an essential part of the Hellenic tradition because, unlike written works, it was "integrative" and open to the whole civic community.

In one of the literary contributions the Christians of Antioch find a voice and religious, rather than cultural, traditions and identities are at issue. Sandwell looks at John Chrysostom's attitudes to the relationship between the Church, imperial rule and city life in order to understand how Chrysostom drew the line between the sacred and secular spheres. She argues that Chrysostom's ideas on these matters were distinct from those of Eusebius and Augustine, whose writings are more usually studied on this subject. In particular she considers the complex ways in which Chrysostom at times marked off the aspects of secular and city life as demonic areas that Christians should avoid and at other times saw them as neutral, or as areas that could or should be Christianized. She goes on to examine how this was related to his attempt to communicate with non-Christians.

Two other contributions also look at issues of Christianization but through material rather than literary evidence. Trombley looks at the Christianization of the *territorium* of late antique Antioch – a subject that has begun to receive some attention[23] – and focusses on the Limestone Massif to the east of the city. He returns to issues first discussed in his *Hellenic Religion and Christianization,* to revise the conclusions he came to there in the light of new evidence.[24] He uses epigraphic evidence to understand how, when, and why Christianity spread into this region. He relates signs of Christianization in the epigraphy to the building of churches and the destruction of pagan temples to argue that the Christianization of the region only really took off in the very late fourth and fifth century, that is seventy to a hundred years later than previously thought. Along the way Trombley makes many interesting points about the persistence of pre-Christian cult, both public and private, into the late fourth and early fifth centuries, the problems of identifying Christian inscriptions, and the particularly Antiochene character of the "One God" inscriptions found in the *territorium* of the city. Vorderstrasse too discusses the Christianization of the region around Antioch, concentrating on two sites in the Amuq plain to the north of the city (a village and a church with monastery) and the port site of al-Mina. Her choice to study this region results from a growing feeling that previously attention has been too narrowly focused on the city of Antioch itself and the Limestone Massif and that this area closer to Antioch deserves more attention. She presents work in progress which looks again at the finds from the 1930's excavations in the region carried out by Oriental Institute of University of Chicago, seeing this as preparation for current excavations and surveys in the region. Working within the limits of surviving evidence and the (at times) haphazard recording and publication of finds, she explores levels of Romanization and Christianization in the locality during the Roman and Late Antique periods.

Similar ideas are behind Casana's contribution. He presents the preliminary results of new work carried out by the Oriental Institute of the University of Chicago in their survey of the region of Antioch and in particular the Amuq Valley, using new surveying techniques. In a wide-ranging account of this work he integrates the archaeological survey and "geomorphological and palaeo-environmental investi-gation" well with the literary evidence provided by Libanius to build up a picture of settlement patterns, canal systems, agricultural production, and economic life in the region. He is also able to show that the new findings of the Oriental Institute challenge the previous assumption that the Amuq Valley in Late Antiquity was only lightly populated compared to Antioch itself and to the Limestone Massif. In general the findings that he records greatly increase our knowledge of the Amuq Valley and challenge the perception that there is no further scope for archaeological expeditions either there or in Antioch itself. They show the potential for further new discoveries and research in the area.

Huskinson and Ellis return to Antioch itself to discuss material relating to some very different aspects of life there. Huskinson gives us a timely review of the previous literature and trends relating to the famous mosaic pavements of Antioch in order to explore some of the most pressing issues relating to the study of these mosaics.[25] She then uses this review as a starting point to explore three main themes. Firstly, she discusses stylistic issues. She charts a shift in emphasis, in the modern historiography, from an interest solely in the style of the mosaics to an interest in the social context of the mosaics and their usefulness as an historical source. Secondly, she considers the subject matter of the mosaics and the areas of life for which mosaics can and cannot productively be used as evidence. Lastly, she discusses questions of cultural influence (Hellenic, Roman and local Levantine and Syrian) on the mosaics. Among these more general issues, Huskinson examines the implications of the mosaics for our under-standing of economic life and levels of wealth in Antioch and she refers to the mosaics as a means by which the educated and wealthy inhabitants of Antioch "expressed their interests". Ellis, also takes up this economic angle but, in contrast, uses archaeological evidence to explore the living conditions of the poorer classes during the late Roman/early Byzantine period, in particular in shops and in sub-divided houses in Daphne, previously occupied by wealthy individuals. He thus challenges the normal image of the city as a wealthy and cultured place – Antioch "the beautiful and great" (Libanius, *Or.* XXXI. 7) and the "gay and prosperous" (Julian, *Misopogon* 343B) as two of our written sources call it.

From these brief summaries of the contributing papers it can be seen that there is a wide range in terms of subject matter and content. However, there are themes that recur and thus reveal some of the central subjects of discussion and the most pressing considerations relating to Antioch. For example, many of the papers dealing with archaeological or epigraphic evidence touch on the city-countryside dichotomy as they discuss the territory around Antioch – both the Limestone Massif to the south-east and the Amuq plain to the north – (Casana, Vorderstrasse and Trombley). This dichotomy is known to be a fundamental matter for discussion in debate about any ancient city as so often cities had a very close relationship with, or were dependent on, the surrounding countryside. Libanius, however, makes this relationship explicit in the case of Antioch. In one of his orations he asks the Emperor Theodosius "to show (his) concern not just for the cities but for the countryside too, or the countryside in preference to the cities – for the country is the basis on which they rest" (*Or.* L. 30).[26] For Libanius this dependence of Antioch on the countryside was in economic terms as the city was reliant on the countryside's agricultural produce, and economics is again a theme that recurs throughout various papers in this collection. The particular issue of the economic dependence of the city on the countryside arises in one of the papers (Casana). Other papers discuss different aspects of economic life, such as levels of wealth of Antioch and its inhabitants (Ellis and, less obviously, Huskinson).

Another theme which comes up in a number of papers in this present collection is that of religious influences, although in each case very different approaches and very different bodies of evidence – archaeological, epigraphic and literary – are used (Vorderstrasse, Trombley and Sandwell). This is not at all surprising for the region of late antique Antioch where it is known that there were mixed populations of pagans and Christians well into the fourth and fifth centuries as well as strong Christian communities living in a context of longstanding pagan and classical traditions. The problem of the religious diversity of Antioch raises questions about the nature of communal life in the city (Sandwell) and reveals 'communality' to be another theme very relevant to the study of Antioch; thus the issue of community versus diversity is discussed in cultural as well as religious terms (Haubold and Miles). Due to the focus on both religious and cultural change, many of the papers collected here also deal with the relationship between the city in late antiquity and past traditions either in the city itself or in literature (Haubold and Miles and Sandwell). With so many changes going on in Late Roman Antioch and with so much interaction between different traditions, a focus on attempts to reinterpret the past and certain aspects of civic life in the light of these changes certainly proves to be very rewarding.

In fact, issues of cultural and ethnic influences and identity arise as crucial themes in three of the contributions. These consider to what extent certain aspects of city life are Hellenic, Roman or Syriac/Levantine (Huskinson, Vordertrasse, Haubold and Miles). There appears to be a real question here as to how far Antioch should be seen purely in local terms and as distinct from other cities and how far it should be seen as yet another Greek or Roman city. This issue of the particular character of Antioch is one that can be seen as relevant to almost all the present contributions in some way, as each – implicitly if not explicitly – considers how far a distinctly Antiochene character shows itself in their field of interest. Thus Sandwell touches on characteristics of Antiochene Christianity that are particular and shared as she relates Chrysostom's attitudes to secular rule and the city to the general context of Antiochene Christianity and theology and to the ideas of Augustine and Eusebius of Caesarea, who are both usually considered more typical of the Roman Empire. Also in relation to religion, Trombley has some discussion of the specific and local nature of the "One God" inscriptions of the Antiochene region. In cultural terms Vorderstrasse considers how far the effects of Romanization can be seen in the material evidence from the Amuq plain while, as has been outlined, Huskinson and Haubold and Miles consider how various aspects of literary and visual culture were touched by Greek, Roman and local influences.

The discussions that arise from this particular uniting theme are thus fascinating for our understanding of how Antioch relates to the Roman Empire, to its Greek traditions, and to Syria and the Far East. Founded in 300 BC by Seleucus I as part of his plan to colonize the area with Greeks, the city had from its inception been home to Greeks, Macedonians, Syrians, Egyptians and many others. Then, from the time of the first Roman influence and intervention in the area (in the early 60s BC when the Romans established client kings there) and particularly after Syria was established as a Roman province in 64 BC, Romanization of the physical appearance, culture and institutions of the city began. Lastly, as Antioch was, in a way, a city on the edge of the Roman Empire being not far from the Euphrates, the city also experienced periods of oriental influence as it was occupied by Tigranes of Armenia in 84/3 BC and by the Parthians in 40–39 BC, and was under the control of the Palmyrian "Empire" in the AD 260s. Add to this the strong Jewish and Egyptian presences and an early Christian community as well as that of the local populations and it is clear that issues of cultural identity are central to the life of the city and our understanding of it.

This, then, is perhaps the most important and new dimension of this present collection – that it will bring into closer focus the multi-faceted and very colourful life of this city and give us a clearer understanding of both its particular nature and its central place in the Roman world. Only then can we truly and accurately compare it with other cities of the Roman Empire. Lastly, this volume will be important because of its focus on Antioch as a late Roman city: if any city can disprove or at least greatly complicate the picture of cities being in decline in the fourth and fifth centuries AD it is Antioch. So this collection of papers will find a place in the re-evaluation of the late antique period and its city life, as well as in the study of Antioch itself. The individual contributions should thus be of interest to many, both students and academics, and even to those who have only a tangential interest in Antioch itself.

Notes
1   Brown, 2001: 43.
2   Exhibition, originating at the Worcester Art Museum October 7, 2000 – February 4, 2001; the Cleveland Museum of Art, March 18 – June 3, 2001; the Baltimore Museum of Art, September 16 – December 30, 2001. The catalogue, C. Kondoleon, 2000.
3   Petit, 1955, Downey, 1961 and 1963, and Liebeschuetz 1972. See also Pack, 1935.
4   Kondoleon, 2000: 118–20.
5   Kondoleon, 2000: 116–7.
6   Brown 2001: 43 and Kondoleon: 2000, 7. Although see Casana in this volume who challenges this traditional view.
7   Brown, 2001: 43 and Kodoleon 2000: 7.
8   Brown, 2001: 43.
9   Maas, 2000: 13.
10 Kondoleon, 2000: 3. See also, Liebeschuetz, 1972 and Petit, 1955.
11 Kondoleon, 2000: 3. See also Norman, 2001 and Liebeschuetz 1972.
12 On the Jewish community in Antioch see, Kraeling, 1932, Meeks and Wilken, 1978 and Wilken, 1983.
13 For general studies of pagan religion in Antioch see, Norris, 1990 and Misson, 1914.
14 On the Christian community at Antioch, see, Wallace-Hadrill, 1982, Mayer and Allen, 2000. On pagan and Christian relations see, Festugière, 1959. On the mixed religious situation in Antioch, see, Kondoleon, 2000, 10.
15 Rousseau, 2002: 191.
16 Kondoleon, 2000: 11.
17 Maas, 2000: 13.
18 For Antioch as a centre of eastern Christianity see Wallace-Hadrill, 1982. For Greek and Syriac speakers in Chrysostom's audience see Chrysostom *Baptismal Sermon* 8.1–2 translated by Harkins, 1963 and the Greek (including that by Theodoret) and Syriac *Lives of Simeon Stylites* collected in Doran, 1992. See also, Brock, 1994.
19 For example, for translations (here just those into English are mentioned, for recent translations into French, German and Spanish see the websites listed below), see Schouler, 1973, Molloy, 1996, Lieu and Montserrat, 1996 and Norman, 2001. For new approaches, See, Schouler, 1984, Petit, 1994, Scholl, 1994, Doukellis, 1995, Seiler, 1998, Malosse, 2000, Allen and Mayer, 1993, Mayer and Allen, 2000 and Leyerle, 2001 (This is just a selection of some of the better known and more obvious works, a full list is not possible here, for a

full list of bibliography on Libanius see http://perso.club-internet.fr/plmaloss/libib.htm and on Chrysostom http://www.acu.edu.au/earlychr).

20 Ellis, Casana, Vorderstrasse and Trombley.

21 We would like to thank the Institute of Classical Studies for its generous hosting of the event and the Arts Faculty of the Open University for some financial support. Papers were also given at the conference by Jim Crow, Aideen Hartney, and Tessa Rajak, but regretfully they were not able to contribute to this publication.

22 Lieu's contribution can thus be seen as a useful addition to Norman's posthumously published work on Antioch as a centre for Hellenic culture, Norman, 2000.

23 Trombley, 1994.

24 Trombley, 1994.

25 Recent, and not so recent, works on the Antioch mosaics include, Cimok, 1995 and Levi, 1947.

26 On the relationship between city and countryside in Libanius see, Doukellis, 1995.

Bibliography

Allen, P., and Mayer, W., 1993. 'Computer and Homily: accessing the everyday life of early Christians', *Vigiliae Christianae* 47, 260–80.

Brock, S., 1994. 'Greek and Syriac in late antique Syria'. In A.K. Bowman and G. Woolf (eds) *Literacy and Power in the Ancient World* (Cambridge), 149–160.

Brown, P., 2001. 'Charmed Lives', *The New York Review of Books* 48 (April 12th) (New York).

Cimok, F., 1995. *The Antioch Mosaics* (Istanbul).

Doran, R. (trans. and intro.), 1992. *The Lives of Simeon Stylites* (Michigan).

Doukellis, P.N., 1995. *Libanios et la terre: discours et idéologie politique* (Beyrouth).

Downey, G., 1961. *A History of Antioch in Syria from Seleucus to the Arab Conquest* (Princeton).

Downey, G., 1963. *Ancient Antioch* (Princeton).

Festugière, A.J., 1959. *Antioche païenne et chrétienne, Libanius, Chrysostome et les moines de Syrie* (Paris).

Harkins, P.W. (trans.), 1963. *John Chrysostom's Baptismal Sermons*, Ancient Christian Writers 31 (London).

Kondoleon, C., 2000. *Antioch: The Lost Ancient City* (Princeton).

Kraeling, C.H., 1932. 'The Jewish Community at Antioch', *Journal of Biblical Literature* 51, 130–60.

Levi, D., 1947. *Antioch Mosaic Pavements* (vols. I and II) (Princeton).

Leyerle, B., 2001. *Theatrical Shows and Ascetic Lives: John Chrysostom's Attack on Spiritual Marriage* (Berkeley).

Liebeschuetz, J.H.W.G., 1972. *Antioch: City and Imperial Administration in the Later Roman Empire* (Oxford).

Lieu, S. and Montserrat, D., 1996. *From Constantine to Julian: Pagan and Byzantine Views, A Source History* (London and New York).

Maas, M., 2000. 'People and Identity in Roman Antioch'. In Kondoleon, 2000: 13–21.

Malosse, P-L., 2000. 'La pratique concrète de l'amplification dans la rhétorique ancienne: l'exemple de Libanios dans son éloge des empereurs Constance et Constant', *Revue de Philologie*, 73, 179–97.

Mayer, W., and Allen, P. 2000. *John Chrysostom* (London).

Meeks, W.A. and Wilken, R.L., 1978. *Jews and Christians in Antioch in the First Four Centuries CE*, Society of Biblical Literature Sources for Biblical Study 13 (Missoula Mont.).

Misson, J., 1914. *Recherches sur le paganisme de Libanius* (Louvain).

Molloy, M.E., 1996. *Libanius and the Dancers* (New York).

Norman, A.F., 2000. *Antioch as a Centre of Hellenic Culture as Observed by Libanius* Liverpool).

Norris, F.W., 1990. 'Antioch as a Religious Centre' In H.Temporini and W. Haase (eds) *Aufstieg und Niedergang der römischen Welt* (Berlin, New York), II.18.4, 2322–2379.

Pack, R.A., 1935. *Studies in Libanius and Antiochene Society under Theodosius* (Wisconsin).

Petit, P., 1955. *Libanius et la vie municipale à Antioche au IVe siècle après J.C.* (Paris).

Petit, P., 1994. *Functionnaires dans l'oeuvre de Libanius: analyse prosopographique* (Paris).

Rousseau, P., 2002. *The Early Christian Centuries* (London).

Russell, D.A. (trans), 1995. *Libanius: Imaginary Speeches: A Selection of Declamations* (London).

Scholl, R., 1994. *Historische Beiträge zu den Julianischen Reden des Libanios* (Stuttgart).

Schouler, B., (trans and Intro) 1973. *Discours Moraux* (Paris).

Schouler, B., 1984. *La tradition hellénique chez Libanios* vols. I and II (Lille).

Seiler, E-M., 1998. *Konstantios II bei Libanios. Eine kritische Untersuchung des überlieferten Herrscherbildes* (Frankfurt and Paris).

Trombley, F., 1994. *Hellenic Religion and Christianization c. 370–529. Religions in the Graeco-Roman World t:* (Leiden).

Wallace-Hadrill, D.S., 1982. *Christian Antioch: A Study of Early Christian Thought in the East* (Cambridge).

Wilken, R.L., 1983. *John Chrysostom and the Jews: Rhetoric and Reality in the Late Fourth Century* (California).

1. LIBANIUS AND HIGHER EDUCATION AT ANTIOCH

Samuel N. C. Lieu[1]

The rhetor Libanius had harboured desires to return to teach at his native Antioch even before he had completed his studies at Athens as he had been in correspondence with the then sophist of the city Zenobius (*Ep.* 16.15). However Fate, as he would call it, took him to Constantinople and later to partial exile in Nicomedia. He regained imperial favour soon after AD 343 or 344 through delivering what Sabine MacCormack terms as the "most boring panegyric extant"[2] in honour of the Emperors Constans and Constantius II (i.e. *Or.* LIX)[3] occasioned by the latter's pyrrhic victory over the Persians at Singara (*Or.* I. 69–74). He was recalled to Constantinople to take up an official appointment with an imperial salary. Although he was reasonably successful at Constantinople and honoured with presents from the Emperor, he was not happy. In the summer of AD 353 he managed to obtain leave to pay a visit to Antioch – the first for nearly two decades.

> "I saw the streets and the gates of which I was so fond, I saw temples and colonnades and the time-worn walls of my home; I saw my mother now grey-haired, her brother not yet with a child, my elder brother already a grandfather. I saw the crowd of my school-friends, some as governors, others as advocates, and my father's friends now reduced to a few; the city seemed strong in the number of educated citizens; I was glad and apprehensive at the same time." (*Or.* I. 86)

His visit was a personal triumph. He could have settled there permanently had not the chair of rhetoric at Antioch still been occupied by his former teacher Zenobius. He returned to Constantinople but his heart was set on his native city. He refused meanwhile to accept the chair at Athens because professional jealousy and competition for the students among the schools there had now erupted into physical violence, not just between gangs of enthusiastic students, but against the teachers. Libanius had heard how his former teacher Diophantus, while on his way to dine, had been set upon by two hired roughs who rubbed his face in the dirt. And:

> how three Paphlagonians, brothers in everything, character, ignorance, insolence and physique, had dragged another professor from his bed, carried him to the well and threatened to throw him in – and would have done so too – if he did not swear to leave town: and leave it he did. He retired to Macedonia, took up another occupation and died there. (*Or.* I. 85–86).

Therefore, as soon as there was the rumour that the chair at Antioch was about to fall vacant and that the incumbent Zenobius was still interested in Libanius as his successor, he was back in Antioch like a shot. As he was still officially paid as a professor at Constantinople, he was strictly speaking on special leave. He had to engage in a good deal of intrigue and to write numerous letters, full of pitiful descriptions of ill health – especially his migraine and trouble with his kidneys – before he obtained the emperor's permission to stay in Antioch permanently. At the same time he was struggling to get pupils as the publicly appointed professorship was not yet vacant. Zenobius had apparently changed his mind about taking early retirement and was immersed in his teaching. (*Or.* I. 99) A first attempt by Libanius to establish a school of his own produced a disappointing fifteen students, mainly those he had brought with him from Constantinople and he knew he could not return to the capital without becoming a laughing stock. Charges of sorcery, which had plagued him before, again resurfaced as he tried to draw students by his oratory.

> "A lad who had earned many a dinner by the service of his person, was influenced by a large bribe to scurry off to the emperor with allegations that I had cut off the heads of a couple of girls and kept them for use in magic, one against Caesar Gallus and the other against his senior colleague (Constantius II). The reward for this lie was to bed with a dancer who obeyed my rival sophist's claque in everything. Whether he got his reward", remarks Libanius, "only he and the dancer can tell, ..." (*Or.* I. 98).

At this point, as Libanius lay in bed full of despondency and "high" on medicines of various kinds, an old gentleman came to him and said that it was no wonder he had no success while sulking in bed. He had to actively market his courses, for only those who were in the media limelight always did best. "If you really want to know how many they are who are thirsting for knowledge", he said "just go to any of the temples." Though Libanius did not follow the advice to the letter, he managed to move his school into a shop on the edge of the market-square and the flood of students began. (*Or.* I. 102–03) Those hectic days of his first year of teaching in Antioch would be recalled in a letter to one of his friends, Aristaenetus which would make a good "Don's Diary" for the *Times Higher Education Supplement*:

> This is the account of what happened to me this winter. 4. I began my class with a prologue and a kind of "argument" (or "competitive passage") against a passage from Demosthenes. The prologue asked Fortune to confirm my stay (in Antioch), the debate was filled with rhetorical variations. I had scarcely taken the chair, when seventeen boys appeared. "Plato, I think, was ill", I mean the good Zenobius (the senior professor of the city). 5. Upon which, I continued my lessons, and "the crowd flocked in", citizens and strangers, wishing to see what I was like at this job as well. Everyone probably agreed that I gave fairly good lectures, but there was something else that they wanted to put to the test. 6. So then, it seemed to some that my teaching was no worse than my discourse, and to others that it was even better, so that in a few days the group of pupils enlarged to fifty. It was no longer possible to have lunch, I had to struggle on until the evening: besides all the rest, the control which I exercised over my appetite was also the subject of admiration. 7. Strategius (i.e. the governor) arrived. I addressed a

speech of welcome to him, short, which I believe is the custom for the one who extends the greeting, but pleasing to the recipient himself and to the others. As for the rival, I give him this name since this is what he calls himself, he threatened to speak: but that was the extent of his public speech: a promise. 8. However, as I could see that the teachers were gaining influence from the trade in pupils, and thus law and order in the schools had broken down, I advised my fellow citizens not to ignore this fact, but to protest about it and prevent such a thing. Whereupon there arose quite a strong surge of anger against the culprits. The rival threatened to defend them: but that was the extent of his public speech: a promise. 9. Zenobius died.[4] On my return from his funeral I gave a monody. A little later, in a longer speech, I delivered his funeral oration, and I was considered to have earned my salary. The rival promised to speak, if his father was going to die but he is alive still. At that moment, those bent on being stubborn, only three instead of an entire scintillating table! ended up by surrendering. 10. I really needed a rest, but it seems that my uncle can never have enough of it. Quirinus also was one of those who would not give up (he entrusts his son to me who quotes both of us, you with regard to my works, and me with regard to yours). 11. I thus found myself delivering one of those public lectures which belong to the fictional genre in our schools: the public were stamping their feet for joy, as if sustained by the thing itself. I was right in the middle of the lecture, when someone asked me to write the antilogy as well, using the same technique. So I wrote it, and returned to lecturing as quickly as possible. This second discourse was no less successful than the first, and the enemy were shaken to the core. 12. Now, afraid of being left defenceless, the rival came into the room to stop the desertions, only to provoke even more of them, which would probably not have happened if he had kept quiet. For no sooner than he began his preamble, he demanded permission to reach his conclusion, and since Quirinus refused to allow him to skip all the rest, he gave himself permission to do so. From that day he has been alone in his school: harangues, pressures of all kinds, obligations, all the means by which he tried to keep his pupils were trampled underfoot and vanished.

13. Whereupon, a letter arrived for me from the Emperor which ordered me to return to Constantinople. My migraine and my backache make their own response, that this is impossible. Having settled this matter, I delivered my discourse *On natural gifts,* in the form of a diatribe, you love those. To conclude it, a second hearing was necessary, which Clematius attended. 14. I cannot describe the emotion it aroused. But what I did say, and it was proclaimed, is that the master of this genre and of all other praiseworthy literary exercices, is (you) Aristaenetus. (*Ep.* 405. 3 ad fin., trans. Vince and Lieu).

Sadly his friend was soon to perish in the great earthquake on 24 August AD 358 which devastated Nicomedia (*Or.* I. 118) The decision to set up school near the Market Place turned out to be a wise move as it led to the desired result of healthy enrolment!

The death of Zenobius did not mean the automatic succession of Libanius to his official stipend. The Chair of Rhetoric had been partially funded by the city through the gift of a substantial estate from which Zenobius had derived an income to supplement his not too generous salary. After Zenobius' death, the Emperor Constantius II insisted that this endowment should now be shared by his four assistants or sophists. In the end the five of them were able to form a school of rhetoric with Libanius as its head receiving the official professorial stipend. Finding the necessary means to pay adequate salaries to his four assistants, however, was no easy task. Libanius, who now enjoyed adequate enrolment in his school (around 50 students but he was quick to point out that not all of them could afford to pay full fees), entered into a type of "enterprise bargaining" with the city council on behalf of these four sophists. The dismal pay and working conditions of his less fortunate colleagues, who had all had distinguished teaching careers prior to coming to Antioch, became the central theme in an oration to addressed the city council (c. 360)[5] asking for special financial arrangement for them. It argued that, as ultimately they were employees of the city, the council should consider using some of the income from lands bequeathed to the council by deceased decurions to top up their salaries. Libanius' highly rhetorical description of their plight has often been cited as evidence of the downgrading of the social status of the pagan sophists in Antiochene society, usually without regard for the special historical circumstances of the appeal. "They do not even have a small house of their own," lamented Libanius, and:

> they have to live with other people in lodgings like those of a cobbler. Those who have purchased houses are up to their eyes with mortgage repayment and are worse off than those who have not purchased. One of them has (only) three slaves, another two and a third not even two and their slaves are insolent and mock them because they no longer have anyone to serve them, so much so that the wretches either do without slaves, or employ worthless ones. The sophist with only one child is considered fortunate, while he who has many children is pitied. The third has to be careful that he gets no children, while the fourth acts the sensible part and avoids matrimony altogether. ... The only orations today's teacher makes are to his bakers, not asking for the bread that has been promised them nor demanding their money, but making excuses for what they themselves owe. ... as a debtor he would like to avoid them (i.e. the bakers), but he must run after them as if starving. (Or. XXXI. 11–12).

He goes on to say that the sophists sometimes forcibly took their wives' jewelry, cursing their wretched profession all the way to the bakery. Gone were the days when they had the luxury of stopping at the shops of the silversmiths – for which Antioch was famous – and commenting on the quality and speed of their workmanship; now their only concern was to be able to sell their wives' trinkets and bangles back to them (– a modern analogy would have been academics who previously had secure positions or large research grants and could swan into computer shops commenting knowledgeably on the performance of the latest laptop computers and the efficacy of data-base software etc. giving the impression that they could easily afford to buy the latest state of the art hard- and software now having to sheepishly try to sell their laptops back for whatever they could get). After lectures the four would hang around the lecture rooms as they had no wish to return to their troubles at home.

> They sit down together and talk over in sorrow their hard lot, and one, thinking his position the worst, hears of even bitterer things from his neighbour. "I" says Libanius, "who am at the head of the school and at the

same time a native of Antioch, hide my head in shame when I see such things". (*Or. XXXI.* 13–14).

Though he might be poorly paid, Libanius was quick to remind his audience in one of his *chriae* (i.e. collection of witty or clever sayings) that the sophist was still generally held in awe by his students:

> 7. In fact think about it. The teacher is established in an imposing chair, like judges are. He seems terrifying, he raises his eyebrows in anger and shows no sign of peace. The pupil must go forward in fear and trembling to give an artistically conducted declamations which he has composed and learnt by heart. If his exercise is badly prepared, there are rages, insults, blows and threats for the future. If everything appears to be worked out to perfection and incurs no criticism, the only thing to be gained is the absence of ill-treatment, the order to do no worse the next time. Even more, a misfortune is in store for whoever fufilled the whole task well: indeed, as soon as one has been judged to have spoken faultlessly one must submit to a heavier burden, for it seems that one might very quickly be ready for more difficult exercises. 8. It is the same for all the rest, it's the teacher's part. As for the pedagogue, by Heracles! he is worse than a slavedriver, always on to you, almost stuck to you, continually goading, rebuking all the time, chastising laziness, ordering one to stick to one's task without any praise for what is good, punishing trivia excessively, following you fully armed as it were, brandishing a stick or martinet in his right hand. 9. "But at least parents are indulgent towards young people". Not a bit of it. Far from being gentler, they are worse than the preceding people. At home there is a second battle which yields nothing to those at school. Instead of sollicitous titbits or a drink, "What work have you done? What progress have you made? What have you gained regarding discourse?" Those are the father's questions. Let us also add the mother's, to whom the child must give an account of himself. 10. If he is reproached for some omission it is an understatement to speak of beatings, he must go without dinner. The arrival of evening, which for some is the end of their toil and troubles, is their increase for others: yes, the night, given to us as a time for rest, becomes, for the pupil, a time of work and of the most terrible reproaches if he has not driven away slumber before having had enough sleep. 11. Therefore, he has no no free time to recover, neither at school nor at home, with neither pedagogue nor parents, nor by night or day, always, always he must toil. For the pupil is not even allowed to enjoy peaceful dreams: even they often contain the prediction of future sufferings (*Or. III.* 7–11, tr. Vince and Lieu).

The students on the whole were worked very hard by their teachers to produce the results to please their fee-paying parents. The chain of pressure would later be referred to by Libanius in one of his orations aptly entitled "On the Slavery of the Teacher":

> 47. Not only is he (i.e. the teacher) the slave of as many masters as he has subjects, he is also the slave of a multitude of pedagogues, parents, yes, mothers, grandmothers, grandfathers. If, thanks to his job, he does not triumph over an obtuse nature, if he does not make the pupil appear to be a son of the gods, though he be made of stone, what a flood of accusations there is of all kinds; he has to cast his eyes down to the ground, not that he

lacks excuses, but he seeks to appease the quarrelsome person by his silence. 48. He is also the slave of the gate-keepers (sc. of the town) and of the class of innkeepers: of the former so that they do not speak ill of him to strangers entering the town, of the latter so that they praise him in front of their customers. For both of these, and others even humbler than them can do wrong to a sophist's classroom. Yes, and furthermore he flatters and coaxes the man who comes from elsewhere and the one who goes from here, the first in order that he does not go and wage war here on the spot and ruin the class, the second so that he does not spread troublesome rumours about the school wherever he goes. 49. But the curia (i.e. city council) is also a very weighty mistress : in a few lines she can elect him and beat him, turn his destiny as she wishes, drive him out if she wishes, set up a crowd of rivals against him, and all the other annoyances which seem small but cause great distress. I suppose that if he wishes to escape he must not fail to carry out his job as a slave. He will spend his time at the doors of magistrates flattering doormen: let them drive him away, he can bear it; let them admit him, how marvellous his gratitude! And if he has to act in this way towards the master of the door, what does he have to do for the supreme governor? 50. Until now, my friends, I have concealed the main point of his slavery, but I wish to present it for your scrutiny. This slavery is continually beneath the constraint of infinite necessities, but it increases and grows when the teacher goes to a public debate. For he needs to be praised, and he must obtain this praise by means of the discourse. The acclamation decides whether this day will be better or worse for him : the longer it is the better the day, the shorter it is, the more unhappy the day. Therefore nobody is useless, neither peasant nor craftsman, soldier nor athlete, neither the pedagogue nor the slave who carries a pupil's books on his shoulders : whoever goes there brings help to the oratorical art with his applause. 51. So at this hour, he is enslaved to any individual with hands and a tongue. Now then, when he himself has increased the flatteries and greetings with right hand, head, eyes and cloak, he goes on his way full of pride, as if he were truly free : he does not realise that from the outset each one of the audience was the master of he who was giving the discourse, by the applause he granted and because he could also give his vote on the words uttered. So therefore, if the pupils are the teacher's slaves, the teacher is also a slave, to a countless number of masters (*Or.* XXV. 47–50, tr. Vince and Lieu).

Though rhetoric was still the passport to many important and often well-paid careers, the increasingly bureaucratic government of the Late Empire needed graduates with more specialised training. Rhetorical schools like those of Libanius which tried to give a general education now had to compete for recruits against teachers of Latin (the administrative language of the Empire) as well as the new law schools, the most famous of which was situated not far away from Antioch in Berytus (modern Beirut) in Phoenicia. Libanius tried to persuade a lawyer to join his teaching staff but without success as he was unable to offer him an attractive salary. (*Ep.* 433). He was deeply disappointed by highly qualified students taking courses in short-hand at the bidding of their parents (*Or.* XXXI. 28) and he certainly did not receive gracefully the introduction of a Chair of Latin Rhetoric in his city under Theodosius. Some of the more able and career-minded students still set sail for Athens. The need to hang on to

1. Libanius and Higher Education at Antioch

Samuel N. C. Lieu[1]

The rhetor Libanius had harboured desires to return to teach at his native Antioch even before he had completed his studies at Athens as he had been in correspondence with the then sophist of the city Zenobius (*Ep.* 16.15). However Fate, as he would call it, took him to Constantinople and later to partial exile in Nicomedia. He regained imperial favour soon after AD 343 or 344 through delivering what Sabine MacCormack terms as the "most boring panegyric extant"[2] in honour of the Emperors Constans and Constantius II (i.e. *Or.* LIX)[3] occasioned by the latter's pyrrhic victory over the Persians at Singara (*Or.* I. 69–74). He was recalled to Constantinople to take up an official appointment with an imperial salary. Although he was reasonably successful at Constantinople and honoured with presents from the Emperor, he was not happy. In the summer of AD 353 he managed to obtain leave to pay a visit to Antioch – the first for nearly two decades.

> "I saw the streets and the gates of which I was so fond, I saw temples and colonnades and the time-worn walls of my home; I saw my mother now grey-haired, her brother not yet with a child, my elder brother already a grandfather. I saw the crowd of my school-friends, some as governors, others as advocates, and my father's friends now reduced to a few; the city seemed strong in the number of educated citizens; I was glad and apprehensive at the same time." (*Or.* I. 86)

His visit was a personal triumph. He could have settled there permanently had not the chair of rhetoric at Antioch still been occupied by his former teacher Zenobius. He returned to Constantinople but his heart was set on his native city. He refused meanwhile to accept the chair at Athens because professional jealousy and competition for the students among the schools there had now erupted into physical violence, not just between gangs of enthusiastic students, but against the teachers. Libanius had heard how his former teacher Diophantus, while on his way to dine, had been set upon by two hired roughs who rubbed his face in the dirt. And:

> how three Paphlagonians, brothers in everything, character, ignorance, insolence and physique, had dragged another professor from his bed, carried him to the well and threatened to throw him in – and would have done so too – if he did not swear to leave town: and leave it he did. He retired to Macedonia, took up another occupation and died there. (*Or.* I. 85–86).

Therefore, as soon as there was the rumour that the chair at Antioch was about to fall vacant and that the incumbent Zenobius was still interested in Libanius as his successor, he was back in Antioch like a shot. As he was still officially paid as a professor at Constantinople, he was strictly speaking on special leave. He had to engage in a good deal of intrigue and to write numerous letters, full of pitiful descriptions of ill health – especially his migraine and trouble with his kidneys – before he obtained the emperor's permission to stay in Antioch permanently. At the same time he was struggling to get pupils as the publicly appointed professorship was not yet vacant. Zenobius had apparently changed his mind about taking early retirement and was immersed in his teaching. (*Or.* I. 99) A first attempt by Libanius to establish a school of his own produced a disappointing fifteen students, mainly those he had brought with him from Constantinople and he knew he could not return to the capital without becoming a laughing stock. Charges of sorcery, which had plagued him before, again resurfaced as he tried to draw students by his oratory.

> "A lad who had earned many a dinner by the service of his person, was influenced by a large bribe to scurry off to the emperor with allegations that I had cut off the heads of a couple of girls and kept them for use in magic, one against Caesar Gallus and the other against his senior colleague (Constantius II). The reward for this lie was to bed with a dancer who obeyed my rival sophist's claque in everything. Whether he got his reward", remarks Libanius, "only he and the dancer can tell, ..." (*Or.* I. 98).

At this point, as Libanius lay in bed full of despondency and "high" on medicines of various kinds, an old gentleman came to him and said that it was no wonder he had no success while sulking in bed. He had to actively market his courses, for only those who were in the media limelight always did best. "If you really want to know how many they are who are thirsting for knowledge", he said "just go to any of the temples." Though Libanius did not follow the advice to the letter, he managed to move his school into a shop on the edge of the market-square and the flood of students began. (*Or.* I. 102–03) Those hectic days of his first year of teaching in Antioch would be recalled in a letter to one of his friends, Aristaenetus which would make a good "Don's Diary" for the *Times Higher Education Supplement*:

> This is the account of what happened to me this winter. 4. I began my class with a prologue and a kind of "argument" (or "competitive passage") against a passage from Demosthenes. The prologue asked Fortune to confirm my stay (in Antioch), the debate was filled with rhetorical variations. I had scarcely taken the chair, when seventeen boys appeared. "Plato, I think, was ill", I mean the good Zenobius (the senior professor of the city). 5. Upon which, I continued my lessons, and "the crowd flocked in", citizens and strangers, wishing to see what I was like at this job as well. Everyone probably agreed that I gave fairly good lectures, but there was something else that they wanted to put to the test. 6. So then, it seemed to some that my teaching was no worse than my discourse, and to others that it was even better, so that in a few days the group of pupils enlarged to fifty. It was no longer possible to have lunch, I had to struggle on until the evening: besides all the rest, the control which I exercised over my appetite was also the subject of admiration. 7. Strategius (i.e. the governor) arrived. I addressed a

his hard won students, especially the ones who had come from other cities, was therefore paramount. Libanius took great trouble to give progress reports to their fee-paying parents in courteous but by no means obsequious letters. Inadequate financial support from parents was a constant source of concern to a responsible teacher like Libanius as poverty was not limited to the teachers. Once when he saw a student in tears because he could not afford to pay for both food and books - an unchanging problem – he wrote immediately to the boy's father:

> If you were a poor man, I would ask you to get contributions from your friends and assist your son, but since fortunately you are one of the foremost men of fortune, my advice is that you spend some of your possessions on the most precious of your possessions. Hunger perhaps is not particularly advantageous for a student either, but the question now is not about the lad's belly but about his books. If he has none, he will be like a man learning archery without a bow. (*Ep.* 428, trans. Norman, LCL, *Ep.* 10, p. 377)

As for students who took to the delights of the metropolis as readily as their books, he had this to say to a friend of the father:

> It was probably the case that Meterius here enjoyed himself a little with us, but he worked most of the time. As for his studies, he feasted on them with me; as for pleasure, he took it with those who govern the city, and the latter often hindered his return. 3. You should therefore praise him for his work, and not frown upon his amusements. Anyway, even old men are not averse to horse-racing, in your town also: and it is better to speak of it in this way than to say all that one could. 4. If his father is inclined not to reproach him in any way, approve of this. But if he thinks that he should scold him, make him change his mind. (*Ep.* 475, 2–3, trans. Vince and Lieu).

To the senior Meterius Libanius also wrote:

> I think that you are rather angry with your son. If you are annoyed because you have not seen him for a long time, you give me cause to rejoice. If that is not the reason for your distress, it saddens me that you should regard it as trivial. If your anger is therefore motivated by absence, it reveals the father, and it pleases me: if you have some other cause for blame, you are deluding yourself. 2. I hope that this letter will be the proof of your son's good behaviour. I could not neglect your son, and from the moment that I took charge of him I was unable to ignore what he was up to: on the other hand, I am not in the habit of praising what I do not find virtuous. 3. Therefore, if by making the most illustrious of friendships one of our boys disgraces his father, then Meterius must justify himself to you, for he has made such friends. And since you yourself would wish that all cities might regard him as highly as his native land, stop your accusations, and rejoice instead with us. (*Ep.* 476, trans. Vince and Lieu).[6]

As for the student to whom physical punishment had to be administered, his report was uncompromising:

> The person who wrote to you about the whip and lashes should also have told you the reason for the strokes: you would not have been as distressed about it as you are now. For it seems to me that you are upsetting yourself

> very much, not because your son has been whipped, but because, as you see it, this would never have happened to him unless he had committed some serious wrongdoing. 2. Then listen to my method of dealing with these matters. If one of my pupils is guilty of one of these offences which it is indecent even to name, I send him away and do not allow him to infect the class with his disease: it is against the pupil who is lazy about studying that I use blows. With the first, I fear the festering sore, and I send him away: The other, I wake up with the whip. 3. I caught your son being lazy. Leaving his book where it lay, he showed how fast he could run: therefore it was on his legs that he was punished, so that in future he would concern himself with another race, that of the tongue. 4. Therefore do not add your anger to this first punishment, and do not think that he is depraved: he is already following his brother's example, he loves you, and perhaps he will prove himself capable of living up to you. (*Ep.* 1330, trans. Vince and Lieu).

Most of the 1554 surviving letters of Libanius are what we would call references in which he tried to use his personal prestige and connection to find jobs, and in one case even a wife, for the increasing number of graduates of his school.

The loyalty that the students showed towards their tutors was not always expressed in subdued obedience. With pedagogues (i.e. tutors) especially they could be much less restrained in their praise or censure. Libanius was appalled to discover how some of his more enthusiastic students "appraised" a pedagogue who had appeared to have incurred their displeasure, probably by working them too hard on their grammatical exercises. Their method of course-assessment has fortunately no modern parallel, at least not yet:

> A blanket is spread out on the ground and held on each side by a varying number of students, depending on the surface area of the blanket itself. Then, in the middle of it is placed the chosen victim of the vilest outrage, and he is thrown into the air as high as possible, and it is very high, in the midst of shrieks of laughter. The circle of spectators also find it amusing, their laughter provoked as much by the unfortunate man's dizziness as by the cries he lets out as he goes up and down. Sometimes the wretched man falls back on to the blanket which is raised up high, sometimes he misses it and lands on the ground: then he goes away with injured limbs, so that this outrage is not without some danger. And the worst of it is that people laugh at it. (*Or.* LVIII. 18. trans. Vince and Lieu).

The climax of Libanius' career as an academic-cum-civic politician was the visit of the Emperor Julian to Antioch (July 362 – March 363) in preparation for his ill-fated Persian campaign. As a pagan, Libanius was overjoyed by the accession to the throne of an Emperor who advocated toleration in religious matters and who was a champion of old civic virtues and an ardent lover of philosophy. "I laughed and danced, joyfully composed and delivered my orations; for the altars received their blood-offerings, and smoke carried the savour of burnt sacrifices up to heaven, the gods were honoured with their festivals which only a few men were left to remember. The art of prophecy came again into its own, that of oratory to be admired....". (*Or.* I. 119) Libanius was particularly pleased by the fact that the emperor was escorted through Cilicia by the provincial governor Celsus who was one of his very first students at Antioch (class of

354) and later met the future emperor while at university in Athens. (*Ep.* 736. 1, cf. Ammianus Marcellinus XXII. 9. 13) Through some administrative oversight, Libanius was left out of an important reception and he used it as an excuse to demand a private audience with the Emperor. Julian duly invited him to lunch but he got the reply that the professor was only in the habit of having dinners – a request with which the emperor complied without delay. The two began to correspond regularly and when Julian was killed fighting in Persia, Libanius composed one of his finest and most moving orations on the occasion of the emperor's funeral in Antioch (= *Or.* XVIII).

Though Julian appeared to Libanius as the champion of the spirit of humanism against the tyranny of Christianity, he was also the first emperor to interfere decisively in Higher Education matters. In a famous (and some would say infamous) edict he accused those who teach the classics but do not themselves believe literally in the existence of the pantheon of Olympian immortals depicted in them for being intellectually dishonest:

> In our view a good education does not distinguish itself by the sumptuous harmony of words or speech, but by the wholesome tendency of reasoned judgement, and by fairness of opinion on good and evil, or beauty and ugliness. Thus someone who believes one thing and teaches his pupils another seems to me to be as far from true education as he is from honesty. For the tongue to disagree with the thought as far as trivia are concerned is certainly wrong, but this error is one of those which can be tolerated up to a certain point. On the other hand, by expounding the opposite of what one believes on the most serious matters, is one not acting like a salesman, or living like these disloyal and unscrupulous people who recommend most highly that for which they have the least regard, enticing and hoodwinking with their praises those to whom, I believe, they wish to hand over their inferior merchandise? (Julian, *Ep.* 42).[7]

Such intellectual hucksters and charlatans, according to Julian, should be debarred forthwith from holding teaching positions; and the decree was followed by a flood of enforced resignations throughout the empire and among the victims was the great Christian Neo-Platonic philosopher Marius Victorinus (Augustinus, *Conf.* VIII. v. 10). Prohaeresius, because of his great prestige as a teacher at Athens, was exempted by special decree but he nevertheless resigned in sympathy with his Christian colleagues (Hieron., *Chron.*, *s. a.* 363, ed. Helm, pp. 242, 24–243, 1). The reception of the decree among pagan teachers was only lukewarm. The implied fundamentalism of Julian went against the spirit of rhetorical training, which entailed the literary, philosophical and "scientific" critique of ancient literature and mythology. Even a staunch admirer of Julian, the pagan historian Ammianus (XXII. 10. 7), felt that this controversial edict "should best be buried in eternal silence."

The anticipated Christian counter-attack did not come immediately. Libanius continued to be an honoured teacher and citizen of Antioch under a succession of Christian emperors until his death circa 393. His last years were plagued by illness and consequently by falling enrolment in his school. His last lectures were attended by a derisory number of students. The counterattack came with a vengeance under the reign of the Emperor Justinian (527–567). Within two years of his accession he formally closed the Platonic Academy in Athens. This was not a solitary attack on an establishment of higher education. In 533, he ordered the closing of all the law schools in the Empire with the exception of those in Rome, Constantinople and Beirut, apparently to keep standards from falling. As far as Justinian was concerned, higher education of the type which was being offered in Athens singularly failed to satisfy one of the most urgent intellectual needs of the time which was the combatting of heresies. The main protagonists in the theological debates in the intervening century and a half had been dominated by churchmen like Cyril of Alexandria, Timothy the Cat, Theodore of Mopsuestia – men of learning who employed their philosophical skills to their best theological advantage. Rhetorical education, still mainly dominated by pagans, was failing to deliver the goods.

Libanius had long foreseen such an utilitarian end to Higher Education and that was why he believed that in the long term it was the governing classes and not the rhetors who had to act as champions of the rhetorical education:

> All arts that are favoured by the emperors lead their students to influence and simultaneously big fortune to their teachers: the services are held to be great, and the rewards are great. However, when any profession, even though intrinsically good, is despised by the ruling emperor, it loses its prestige; and if the prestige vanishes, the rewards vanish along with it, or rather, if they be not entirely lost, from being great they become small. ... Who has ever seen priests held in honour while their temples are being demolished? Or a ship-builder making fortune while far inland? (*Or*. XXXI. 26–28, trans. Norman).[8]

Notes

1   The author would like to acknowledge the facilities of the Ancient History Documentary Research Centre at Macquarie University for the preparation of this study. All translations marked (S.) Vince and (S.) Lieu are unpublished. They form part of a major electronic archive of letters and speeches by Libanius on Higher Education at the Centre. All other translations from the works of Libanius are taken from the Loeb edition of A.F. Norman (4 vols., Cambridge, Mass.: Harvard University Press, 1969–1992) and his posthumously published collection of speeches of Libanius on Antioch, some of which are of great importance to our knowledge of the higher educational system at Antioch. See below, n. 5. Translations are reprinted by permission of the publishers and the Trustees of the Loeb Classical Library from LIBANIUS: VOLUME I, Loeb Classical Library Volume L 478, translated by A. F. Norman, pp. 55, 61, 71, Cambridge, Mass.: Harvard University Press, Copyright © 1992 by the President and Fellows of Harvard College, The Loeb Classical Library® is a registered trademark of the President and Fellows of Harvard College.

2   MacCormack, 1975: 169.

3   Translated by Dodgeon *et al*. in Lieu and Montserrat, 1996: 164–209. For dating see *ibid*. 161–63.

4   Libanius remarked in his *Autobiography* (Or. I. 104) that he died of a double illness – his fever and his chagrin on learning that Libanius, the successor he had rejected, had such a large class.

5   For dating see Norman, 2000: 68–69.

6 On the letters to Meterius see especially Festugière, 1959: 115–16.
7 Trans. Coleman-Norton, 1966: 278.
8 Norman, 2000: 77–78.

Bibliography

Coleman-Norton, P.R., 1966. *Roman State and Christian Church*, Vol. 1 (London).
Festugière, A.J., 1959. *Antioche païenne et chrétienne, Libanius, Chrysostome et les moines de Syrie* (Paris).
Lieu, S.N.C. and Montserrat, D. (eds), 1996. *From Constantine to Julian – A Source History*, (London).
MacCormack, S., 1975. 'Latin Prose Panegyrics'. In T.A. Dorey (ed.), *Empire and Aftermath, Silver Latin II* (London).
Norman, A.F., 2000. *Antioch as Centre of Hellenic Culture as observed by Libanius*, Translated Texts for Historians 34 (Liverpool).

2. Communality and Theatre in Libanius' Oration LXIV In Defence of the Pantomimes

Johannes Haubold and Richard Miles

Introduction

Libanius' *Or.* LXIV *In Defence of the Pantomimes* has provoked intense scholarly debate in the past 100 years.[1] It was probably written in AD 361 in the city of Antioch.[2] Libanius, its author, was undoubtedly one of that city's most famous orators. His letters, speeches and declamations highlight his desire to be seen not only as an exponent of the sophistic tradition but also as the chief representative of Antioch.[3] This article argues that in *Or.* LXIV Libanius takes this dual concern as the starting point for developing a vision of Hellenic culture and its relationship to life in the late antique community.

Much of the controversy about *Or.* LXIV has revolved around the seeming discrepancy between the speech with its support for the dance and its practitioners and the main bulk of Libanius' literary output, which demonstrates thorough and often unqualified disapproval of this theatrical genre.[4]

Foerster in his Teubner edition takes a biographical approach to solve this apparent discrepancy, arguing that something must have happened after AD 361 to make Libanius change his mind.[5] Long before Foerster, Sievers had already tried to circumvent the problem by declaring that the speech was just a 'rhetorical exercise', part of the long sophistic tradition of justifying the unjustifiable.[6] As a reaction to this position, Anastasi and Spadaro have recently wanted to place *Or.* LXIV within the historical context of the emperor Julian's often fraught relationship with the city of Antioch.[7] Julian was very critical of the Antiochenes' appetite for the activities of the theatre.[8] Libanius himself advised his fellow citizens to appease the enraged Julian 'by closing the theatres and abandoning the dancers and the mimes'.[9] For Spadaro and Anastasi *Or.* LXIV should been seen as a subtle attempt by Libanius to mediate between the two parties.

Schouler in an important article has attempted to merge what we might call the generic approach with the more political concerns of Spadaro and Anastasi.[10] Whilst accepting that *Or.* LXIV cannot be read in isolation from the environment that made it possible, he nevertheless insists that the world created within the text cannot be reduced simply to a political message. Schouler's approach provides the methodological starting point for this article. We also see tensions between the rhetorical tradition and the world of fourth century Antioch that we cannot and should not try and resolve. It is these unresolved tensions that provide the main dynamic of the text, tensions between past and present, text and performance and competing constructions of Hellenism. In Libanius' vision of the theatre these issues can be explored without being effaced. As a result the dramatic dance, or pantomime, comes to be seen as a central element of communal life in the late antique city.

ANTIOCH AND THE DANCERS

Theatrical performances of tragedy and comedy seem to have waned and eventually disappeared by the third century AD. However, other theatrical forms, particularly the pantomime and mime, took their place and became increasingly popular. The subject matter for the pantomime, or dance (orchêsis), was mostly taken from tragic myth. The scenes were solos performed by a virtuoso masked actor who was backed by musicians and a chorus. The leading dancer impersonated all the characters, whether male or female.[11]

The popularity of dancing in late antique Antioch is well attested by contemporary commentators. Lucian describes Antioch as 'the very talented city which especially honours the dance'.[12] Libanius himself complains that the Antiochenes care 'only about festivals and luxurious living and their competitions with each other in the theatres'.[13] Although he does not say so explicitly, he must have dance performances in mind. We know of two particular religious festivals, the Maiuma and the festival of Calliopea, which included large scale dancing shows.

During the late fourth century, a period when other theatres in the Greek East are beginning to fall into disuse, the theatre at Antioch – and with it the performance of pantomime dances – was still a major emblem of civic pride to its inhabitants. Libanius proudly points out that within its walls the theatre can fit in 'the multitude of the city, thanks to the abundance of its tiers'.[14]

Christian authors too acknowledge the special status of the theatre and dancing in Antioch, although they are generally hostile to it. For example, John Chrysostom complains that on festival days his church, which was next door from the theatre, remained empty, and that 'their vehement shouts, borne in the air from that place (the theatre) resounded against the psalms which we were singing here (the church)'.[15] However, even for Christian opponents, Antioch's theatre was still a matter of civic pride. Thus, the same John Chrysostom who often dismisses theatrical performances of all kinds, claims Antioch's superiority over Constantinople in 'having a larger assembly and a more famous theatre'.[16]

We have already seen that a similar ambiguity pervades the writings of Libanius.[17] However, perhaps because scholars have often viewed Christian polemic as the force behind new ways of viewing theatre in the late antique city (albeit in a negative sense),[18] the work of Libanius and Choricius in defence of the pantomimes, tends to be bracketed as part of a generic, antiquarian, sophistic treadmill: a body of work which was happy to inhabit its own cultural cul-de-sac.[19] In viewing Or. LXIV in relation to its contemporary society as well as Libanius' sophistic predecessors, particularly Aelius

Aristides and Lucian, we hope to show that this text is part of a dynamic discourse that belongs firmly in the context of the late fourth century AD city.

PAST AND PRESENT IN LIBANIUS, ORATION LXIV

Or. LXIV is cast as a response to a lost speech against the dancers by the second century sophist Aelius Aristides.[20] It is possible that Lucian's *De Saltatione* acted as a source of inspiration, though this is not made explicit.[21] At any rate, the tone of Libanius' speech is very different from that of Lucian's dialogue. Unlike Lucian, Libanius engages directly with his predecessor, creating the fiction of a sophistic debate across time. Libanius thus consciously places his topic – and himself – in the long-standing tradition of sophistic speechmaking. One important result of this manoeuvre, and the first one we propose to discuss here, is that it raises questions about the continuity not only of the sophistic tradition but of Greek culture more generally.

Libanius' fundamental objection to Aristides' views on dancing is that they are antiquated and have no resonance in the present world. The very fact that Aristides addresses his speech to the Spartans shows him to be hopelessly out of touch. The Spartans are no longer a relevant audience. To be sure, at other points of his speech Libanius can make use of the Spartan paradigm just as Aristides does.[22] Libanius, too, is willing to use arguments from the past in good sophistic fashion, at the same time attacking Aristides for doing just that. However, he does not simply show himself to be the more versatile sophist than his predecessor. Rather, in presenting himself as discerning in his treatment of the past, Libanius redefines the very nature of the relationship between past and present.

Aristides is time and again presented in *Or.* LXIV as someone who sees the Hellenic heritage as static, and therefore dictating our present lives down to the most minute detail. By contrast, Libanius not only acknowledges change, but sees the relationship between past and present as fundamentally open-ended, a matter of giving and taking. A typical example of the two approaches can be seen in chapters 6 and 7 of the speech, where Libanius depicts Aristides as someone who takes recourse to the 'ancient syllables' of Lycurgus' laws while he himself points out that 'times have changed'. Aristides wants to make an impact on the present solely by using paradigms of the past. The inappropriateness of his approach soon becomes apparent:

> So, if Aristides wanted to persuade the Spartans that they should throw out the dancers – and here I mean the dancers of today – and based this on a reading of the laws, saying that Lycurgus would not have that sort of thing and that it is not in what he wrote, nor is it what they practise and what is customary for them; perhaps even then I would have something to say in response (*Or.* LXIV.6).[23]

We note first of all the sly use of the word 'today'. Aristides' 'today' is not that of Lycurgus, any more than it is that of Libanius. Indeed, Libanius suggests that a decisive rupture occurred between Lycurgus and Aristides, a rupture, which Aristides has failed to notice. Much of the persuasiveness of Libanius' argument rests on his ability to create a bias for the present. While for Aristides any historical development is a development away from the high point of Greek culture that has to be resisted, Libanius validates his alternative model of historic change by holding out the possibility of progress. He can thus defeat his forerunner on his own grounds:

> Indeed, you yourself claim that you improved the art of speechmaking quite considerably, and by the god, I do not blame you for it; nor do I call it a case of boastful self-advertisement. Let me just say that much: it is hardly fair to regard one's own innovations as improvements to speechmaking, refusing to be impressed by what went before, while making out that any advance of the same kind made in dancing does not comply with what went before and therefore proves that dancing is worthless (*Or.* LXIV. 22).

As often with Libanius, the passage bristles with irony, not least because Aristides' very success as a speaker is made to furnish a crucial argument against his case. By implication, Libanius ought to come out on top, thus continuing the cultural process of which Aristides claimed to be such an important part. More importantly, Libanius points out that once we acknowledge that progress has been made in one field, we can no longer use the past in a straight-forwardly normative way. Lycurgus, for one, has so little to say to the world of today that even the Spartans themselves would not welcome him back:

> The Spartans too have long taken to the disgrace. They like it, they act in a way that is so alien to their customs that if Lycurgus himself made a sudden appearance, they would not stand his sight [*prosopon*] (*Or.* LXIV.81).

We will come back to the striking use of the word *prosopon* in this context: Lycurgus' 'reappearance' is imagined specifically in the form of a theatrical performance. For now we simply note that Aristides' representation of Hellenic culture past and present most disastrously founders on his own chosen audience, the Spartans.

'DANCING SYRIANS' AND THE NEW FACE OF HELLENISM

If Aristides misconstrues the relationship between past and present, he also draws an inaccurate picture of the contemporary world. Sparta is no longer at the centre. What is more, it is no longer a place of any importance. Someone who addresses the Spartans, Libanius suggests, may well end up without any audience at all. Thus, as a paradigm of Hellenic culture and identity, Sparta defeats itself.

In answer to Aristides' claim that he is speaking to the Spartans as the true exponents of Hellenic culture, Libanius points out that Aristides himself did not stay in Sparta to 'set up a rhetorical workshop there', but freely moved around a larger Hellenised world:

> I do not suppose you made Sparta a rhetorical workshop, nor did you send your words flowing down the Eurotas. No, you travelled to the Hellespont, to Ionia, Pergamon, Smyrna, Ephesus and Egypt, the country which first

> gave birth to the evil of dancing, as you yourself say. You have also been to
> Rome where dancing is esteemed highly (*Or*. LXIV. 80).

Libanius sketches out a concert tour from Sparta as the supposed centre of the world
via the traditional divide between Europe and Asia at the Hellespont, to Egypt and
Rome. These are real places, with real audiences waiting to be entertained. By contrast,
Sparta as it was has become entirely a figment of Aristides' imagination. To be sure, in
strictly geographical terms it still existed. But who would want to be there only to
have his words flushed down the Eurotas? The alleged centre of Greek culture turns
out not to be part of Greek culture at all.

This is a far cry from the cultural map drawn by Aristides or even Lucian in his *De
Saltatione*. Lucian's Sparta indeed marks a focal point of a Greek world surrounded by
barbarian fringes.[24] For Libanius, not only has the centre of gravity shifted, but the
very opposition between Hellenes and barbarians has been transformed into one
between more and less parochial forms of Hellenism; on this new map Sparta does not
shine. Indeed, as Libanius points out, it falls short even of the most basic values of a
civilised life that the Greeks have always shared with non-Greeks:

> Prosperity has furthered the growth of many cities and Hellenes and
> barbarians alike assign great value to being wealthy. The Spartans were
> convinced by their laws that poverty is stronger than riches (*Or*. LXIV. 8).

The term barbarian occurs only here in *Or*. LXIV, and it is employed to collapse the
very opposition between Greeks and non-Greeks that it helps to set up.[25] The operative
term in *Or*. LXIV is not barbarian but the more neutral – and more malleable – 'people'
(*ethnos*).[26] Within this new discourse, Sparta has decidedly drifted to the fringes.

We have seen that as an imaginary centre of Greek culture Sparta isolates Aristides
rather than allowing him to harness the cultural forces of Hellenism. One of these
forces is the theatre and dance in particular. Libanius argues that Aristides does not
understand dancing as part of Hellenic culture because he has too limited a perspective
of what Hellenism has become. Thus, when Aristides denounces the dancers as
'Syrians', Libanius, the 'modern-day Hellene', proudly presents himself as precisely
that, a Syrian:

> I would not object if someone thought that the dancers, too, were forbidden
> by law to enter Sparta along with material wealth. But Aristides reviles the
> whole practice. He calls it a disease and a corruption of those watching; and
> he includes the Syrians in his dirty campaign. As a Syrian myself – and one
> who can perhaps speak – it seemed to me almost an act of treason to keep
> silent and not to defend the practice and with it the whole people [*ethnos*]
> from the charge (*Or*. LXIV. 9).

We have already seen that Aristides' Sparta is isolated within the Hellenic world of
the Syrian Libanius. The point of privileging Syria here seems not so much that
Libanius wants to create a new centre of Greekness.[27] Rather, his world of Hellenism
as described in *Or*. LXIV is one of multiple centres and identities. Libanius is Syrian
and can speak (Greek). His is a malleable world in which flexibility, fluidity, an
awareness of multiple identities determines the extent of one's cultural and political
success. We might say that Libanius is more Greek than Aristides, *because* he is Syrian.

TEXT AND PERFORMANCE

As a centre of Aristides' world, Sparta is long obsolete. As part of Libanius' new Hellenic world it is a dead end. But perhaps the most striking characteristic of this city and the way Aristides describes it is that it privileges (written) text. We have already seen that Aristides is happy to dig up the 'syllables' of Lycurgus' laws.[28] Modern-day Spartans, by contrast, would not stand the sight of Lycurgus himself; or rather, that of his *prosopon*, his face or mask.[29] Libanius' choice of word is revealing: Lycurgus has entirely become a figure of written text as opposed to live performance. Not even the Spartans themselves would want his part performed to them.

   Here as in so many other respects Aristides' picture of Sparta can be taken as emblematic of his wider approach to Greek culture. Aristides is portrayed as being oblivious to the role of audiences. As we have seen already, it is Libanius who has to remind him that without the very real audiences of Asia Minor, Egypt and Rome he would not have become the famous sophist he was. Where Aristides does mention audiences, he depicts them as passive recipients:

> Aristides says: '<the dancers> themselves live in disgrace and on top of that they corrupt the spectators by dragging them into what is not right.' Here some think he has a point, but truth speaks against his argument. I shall deal with both points separately, if the audience does not shout me down and continues to behave as I asked it to do at the beginning (*Or.* LXIV. 37).

Aristides depicts the audience as being entirely at the mercy of the dancers who corrupt them and drag them around at will. By contrast, Libanius sees the audience as a proactive element in his own rhetorical, as well as any other, performance ('if the audience does not shout me down ...'). This sits well with his chosen topic: by taking the side of dancing and the dancers, Libanius picks out the one dramatic genre which cannot be recorded in *logos* and therefore demands a live performance situation.[30]

DANCE AND SOCIETY

There is an important social corollary to what we have argued last. Time and again, Libanius stresses the communal nature of the dance as performance. All the city is in attendance. Performances can only be enjoyed by those present, and dance, in particular, demands the presence of the whole community. Libanius admits that the effect of dramatic movement is less long lasting than that of *logos*.[31] This means that dancing does not reach as far, but it also ensures that it does not interfere in the rhythms of civic life. Lucian's dialogue on the dancers culminates in a long digression on the dangers of the dance crossing the boundaries between performance and reality, between the theatre and society.[32] Libanius builds containment into the system. Although he acknowledges that in the dance, as with other forms of theatre, appearances can deceive, he argues that the dancer leads his audience back to reality:

> But above all <the dancer> imitates Achilles playing a maiden. Don't be afraid. He will not here stop the dance. Odysseus comes to the door, and

> Diomedes with the war trumpet; and the son of Peleus shows his real self
> instead of what he seems (*Or.* LXIV. 68).

In cognitive and ethical terms, then, Libanius sees the dance as a largely self-contained exercise. Unlike Aristides and Lucian, he is relatively uninterested in its possible long-term effects on individual members of the audience. Instead, Libanius sees the main function of the dance as theatrical performance in providing society as a whole with a moment of respite. Theatre to Libanius does not offer an alternative to civic life. Rather, it is itself an integral part of it. Attending the dance thus becomes an important segment in the community's life cycle:

> Now, let me turn to the audience. I would say they are not perverted, but
> you argue that they are destroyed. I think they would rightly challenge you
> – first by saying: 'O Aristides, we have wives and bring up children. We
> administer our own affairs and those common to all. We come to the theatre
> to have a break. We sit and see whether the performance has any beauties;
> and if some entertainment comes from dancing and enters the soul through
> our eyes, we go home refreshed and get back to our worrisome tasks; the
> planning, the thinking into the future [*pronoia*], the words, the deeds. Later,
> when we have been weighed down by them, we return to the same
> entertainment. We study how the feet are placed and the hands moved. We
> watch the harmony of the gestures which you criticise and the appearance of
> the whole in all its beauty' (*Or.* LXIV. 57).

This is an extraordinarily rich passage that raises many points of interest. Here we simply draw attention to the repetitive and socially bounded nature of the theatrical experience. There is little emphasis on the psychological impact of the dance, though this aspect is not altogether absent. Nor is the theatrical performance viewed as a unique event or as an activity that falls outside normal life. Rather, it is itself part of the life of the city as a whole, which it helps to structure and sustain: "Later, when we have been weighed down …, we return to the same entertainment."

The communal nature of the dance is further emphasised by the assumption of a plural voice to argue Libanius' case in chapters 57ff. and in the listing of the different sections of the community who are involved in the performance both on stage and in the audience. In chapters 36 and 37 we are informed that those who govern the city, the political elite, all attend the dance. In chapter 71, Aristides is chastised for his fragmentary and divisive view of the theatre and hence, of society at large. Contrary to Aristides' argument, the dance enacts both men and women. Libanius argues that one without the other creates a fatal imbalance, and the dance's integrative potential would be spoiled. What is more, he suggests that leaving men out of the picture would constitute an act of violence:

> What sense does it make that you cut the practice in two [*temnein dicha*] and
> undermine it, emphasising some parts while suppressing others? (*Or.* LXIV.
> 66).

THE DANCING BODY AS SOCIAL METAPHOR

The word *temnein* in the passage quoted last introduces a metaphor that will be exploited at some length in chs. 95ff. Aristides is said to have argued in his speech that persons employed to tap their foot to the dance should have as much of it chopped off as the metal stick was long that stuck out from under their sole and enabled them to make the necessary noise. Libanius' defence of the dancers culminates in a sustained attack on this idea which he takes as emblematic of Aristides' approach to Greek culture and social life. In chapter 27 he already argued against a mutilated form of dancing in very much the same terms [*perikoptô*].[33] At the end of his speech he juxtaposes Aristides' preposterous social and cultural violence with the image of the well-trained dancer. His limbs have been stretched, but not severed. One can bend him full circle and send him rolling along, but that will not do him any harm:

> Once <the trainer> has formed <the dancer's> body into a circle rather like
> the branch of a willow, he moves it along to race like a hoop, and off it goes.
> And moving like that does not do the limbs any harm. For each one of them
> has long been educated to be elastic. The trainer has almost severed them
> [*dioikizô*] from one another, guarding the connection between them but at the
> same time loosening it. As a result, both hands and feet follow to whatever
> other part of the body one moves them, rather like wax (*Or.* LXIV. 104).

The motive of elasticity that has been running through the speech is finally made explicit. In many ways, the body of the dancer whose joints are guarded by the trainer is the perfect emblem of the late Hellenic community that is guarded by its elite.[34] A wrestler may loose an eye in the fight, another one may come away from it with broken limbs.[35] The body of the dancer stands for a social and cultural elasticity which holds society together despite it being stretched. The integrative quality of dancing is spelled out towards the end of the speech in a half comical, half grandiose re-writing of the Platonic-Protagorean myth of cultural progress:

> As long, then, as the race [*ethnos*] of the tragic poets flourished, they went
> into the theatres as joint [*koinos*] teachers of the people. When they went into
> decay, only the better off part of society could share [*koinônein*] the education
> in the Museia while most were bereft of it – until a god took pity on the lack
> of education for the many and introduced dancing as a teaching resource of
> history for the masses. The result is that today the gold smith will not have
> a bad conversation about the house of Priam or Laios with someone from the
> schools (*Or.* LXIV. 112).

There is a good amount of playfulness in this passage. As a piece of sophistic entertainment, *Or.* LXIV remains well within its tradition. Libanius takes the arch-sophist Protagoras and re-writes his already half-serious myth of cultural and political beginnings. Dancing takes the place of the *politikê technê* that a sympathetic god bestows upon mankind to secure social cohesion and hence the survival of the race.[36] It is hard to believe that Libanius is being entirely serious here. And yet, for the flexible Hellene Libanius, the playful, self-conscious, and to that extent we might say properly sophistic, aspects of his speech do not detract from his more serious concerns. Flexibility in tone adds to, rather than blurs, a picture of Hellenism that is fundamentally integrative.

CONCLUSION

In conclusion, we have argued for a reading of *Or.* LXIV which acknowledges its place within the unbroken tradition of sophistic speech-making whilst recognising the importance of its historic setting. Dancing, for the fourth-century sophist Libanius becomes a crucial cultural signifier that can both capture and help to resolve some of the tensions between past and present, Greek and non-Greek, educated and non-educated, that threaten the late antique city. This is not to say that Libanius believed the pantomime to be a good thing at all times. Chances are that he did not. Nor is it necessary to take his encomium entirely at face value. Conceived in a climate of rampant cultural and social experimentation, Libanius' *Or.* LXIV is perhaps best seen as a brilliant thought experiment, one attempt among many others at pulling together some of the divergent strands of life in the late antique city.

A brief comparison with some aspects of Lucian's *De Saltatione* will help to highlight some of our arguments. In Lucian's text the dance is very much seen as an ethical phenomenon. The interlocutors are concerned with its effects on the spectator's soul and character.[37] There is little sign in Lucian of an interest in collective audiences and the question of what dancing performances contribute to communal life in the city.[38] In Libanius, any ethical aspects of the dance are subordinated to an overriding concern with its function as an agent and symbol of social and cultural integration. Lucian expresses his interest in questions of cultural identity by mapping out a Greek world that is surrounded by non-Greeks. The dance can bridge the gap, but in doing so it reinforces the old boundaries in important ways. Libanius' approach is far more radical. Because he is both a Syrian and 'one who is able to speak' (Greek) he can grasp the integrative potential of Hellenism, just as the dancers, being both Syrian and Greek, realise this potential in the life of the city. For Libanius, it is the human dancing form that most powerfully represents the essential communality of Hellenic culture in the city.

Having looked at the implied contrast between Libanius' vision of the dance as developed in *Or.* LXIV and that of Lucian, as we find it in his *De Saltatione*, we must finally return to Libanius' real addressee, Aristides. It is Aristides' view of Hellenic culture as something complete, static, and unquestionably normative that provides the backdrop against which Libanius develops his own vision of the late antique community. Aristides' message, as represented by Libanius, amounts to much more than simply the rant of an unreconstructed conservative. Rather, by privileging the old at the expense of the new, written text at the expense of performance, the laws of Lycurgus at the expense of the realities of life in the late antique city, his message comes to stand as representative of the cultural and social disintegration of the Hellenic community. It is not clear, nor is it ultimately important what Libanius really felt about the pantomimes. What we hope to have shown in the course of this article is that like Aristides and Lucian before him – and Choricius after him – he saw the potential of the dance to act as a powerful cultural signifier. His predecessors concentrated on what they perceived to be the crucial ethical issues. Libanius presents us with a vision of cultural malleability and elasticity that transcends the deadlock of Aristides' static and fragmented world.

Notes

1   This is the revised version of a paper given at the one day Antioch conference put on by the Open University and the Institute of Classical Studies. We would like to thank the audiences for their helpful comments.

2   The traditional date of composition, as established by Foerster, is early in AD 361; see Foerster vol 4, 1908: 406. Spadaro argues for a somewhat later date, with Julian already established in power (late AD 361 – early 362): Spadaro, 1989: 529–49. All translations are by the authors. A recent attempt at translating the speech can be found in Molloy, 1996.

3   See Schouler, 1984.

4   For a typical Libanian objection to the dance see *Or.* XLI. 6–9. Scholars have had similar difficulties with Lucian's attitude to dancing. See Baldwin, 1973: 16 n. 48.

5   Foerster, 1908: 406: n. 3.

6   Sievers, 1868: 11.

7   Anastasi, 1984: 235–58; Spadaro, 1989.

8   Julian, *Misopogon*. 342B and 365D, *Epp.* 84 and 89.

9   Libanius, *Or.* XVI. 41.

10   Schouler, 1987: 273–94.

11   For more information on the late antique mime and pantomime see Molloy, 1996: 40–85.

12   Lucian, *De Saltatione*. 76.

13   Libanius, *Or.* LXI. 7.

14   Libanius, *Or.* XI. 218.

15   John Chrysostom, *On Statues. 15.1*, PG (Migne, *Patrologia Graeca*) 49: 153.

16   John Chrysostom, *De incomp.* 11.1.

17   See above n. 4.

18   See *e.g.* Leyerle, 2001; Miles, forthcoming; Jürgens, 1972; Pasquato, 1976; Baumeister, 1987; Lugaresi, 1994; Barnes, 1996; Green, 1994: 169–71; Vandenberghe, 1955; Garton, 1972: 32–37; Chambers, 1903: 1–22.

19   For Choricius' speech on dancing see *e.g.* Cresci, 1986: 49–66.

20   For a reconstruction see Mesk, 1908: 479–509.

21   For the *De Saltatione* as a first response to Aristides see Baldwin,1973: 31.

22   Libanius, *Or.* LXIV. 16.

23   Libanius, *Or.* LXIV. 6.

24   Lucian, *De Salt.* 10 makes much of the fact that dancing appeals to Greeks and non-Greeks alike; cf. *De Salt.* 8–16 (Greeks) and 17–22 (non-Greeks); also ch. 64, where the dance becomes a means of communication between Greeks and barbarians and ch. 66, where 'a barbarian man' comments that a dancer with five masks has one body but five souls. As becomes clear from these last two passages, Lucian plays with the opposition between Greek and barbarian without challenging it to the same extent as Libanius does.

25   Elsewhere, Libanius is perfectly capable of exploiting the traditional opposition between Hellene and barbarian; see *e.g. Or.* XV and XVIII.

26   *Ethnos* in Libanius can refer to professional as well as ethnic groups, and much is made of the ambiguity in *Or.* LXIV. For the dancers as an *ethnos* see ch. 9; for the tragedians see ch. 112.

27   Contrast *Or.* XI, *In Praise of Antioch*, where Antioch expressly replaces Sparta as the second centre of the Greek world alongside Athens: Libanius *Or.* XI. 184.

28   Libanius, *Or.* LXIV. 6.

29   Libanius, *Or.* LXIV. 81.

30   Cf. chs. 10f. where, unlike Aristides, Libanius expressly refuses to discuss mimes.

31   Libanius, *Or.* LXIV. 72.

32 Lucian *De Salt.* 83f.
33 Cf. also Libanius *Or.* XXX. 42 (destroying the temples of a city is worse than chopping someone's hand off).
34 Cf. ch. 36 on *phulakes* as guardians of the city. On the image of the circle applied to the city cf. Libanius *Or.* XI. 204 and 209.
35 Lib. *Or.* LXIV. 119; cf. ch. 104 for competition between the dancer and the wrestler.
36 Plato *Protagoras* 322.
37 Esp. Lucian *De Salt.* 70–2.
38 With the interesting exception of ch. 76, which is specifically about Antioch.

Bibliography

Anastasi, R., 1984. 'Libanio e il mimo', in *La poesia tardoantica tra retorica, teologia e politica: atti del V corso della scuola superiore di archeologia e civiltà medieval presso il centro di cultura scientifica "E Majorana"* (Messina).

Baldwin, B., 1973. *Studies in Lucian* (Toronto).

Barnes, T., 1996. 'Christians and the theatre'. In W. Slater (ed.) *Roman theater and society: E. Togo Salmon papers I* (Ann Arbor) 161–80.

Baumeister, T., 1987. 'Das Theater in der Sicht der alten Kirche', in G. Holtus, ed., *Theaterwesen und dramatische Literatur* (Tübingen).

Chambers, E., 1903. *The medieval stage* (London).

Cresci, L., 1986. 'Imitatio e realia nella polemica di Coricio sul mimo', *Koinonia* 10, 49–66.

Foerster, R., 1908. *Libanius: opera*, vol. 4 (Leipzig).

Garton, C., 1972. *Personal aspects of the Roman theatre* (Toronto).

Green, J., 1994. *Theatre in ancient Greek society* (London).

Jürgens, H., 1972. *Pompa diaboli: Die lateinischen Kirchenväter und das antike Theater* (Stuttgart).

Leyerle, B., 2001. *Theatrical shows and ascetic lives: John Chrysostom's attack on spiritual marriage*, (Berkeley).

Lugaresi, L., 1994. 'Tra evento e rappresentazione: per un' interpretazione della polemica contro gli spettacoli nei primi secoli cristiani,' *Rivista di storia e letteratura religiosa* 30, 437–64.

Mesk, J., 1908. 'Des Aelius Aristides verlorene Rede gegen die Tänzer', *Wiener Studien* 30, 479–509.

Miles, R., forthcoming. 'Unmasking the Self: Church and Theatre in the Homilies of John Chrysostom'. In E. Theodorakopoulos (ed.), *Attitudes to theatre in European culture* (*NCLS Midlands Classical Studies* 7).

Molloy, M., 1996. *Libanius and the dancers* (Hildesheim).

Pasquato, O., 1976. *Gli spettacoli in S. Giovanni Crisostomo: paganesimo e cristianesimo ad Antiochia e Costantinopoli nel iv secolo* (Rome).

Schouler, B., 1984. *La tradition hellénique chez Libanios*, 2 vols. (Lille).

Schouler, B., 1987. 'Les sophistes et le théâtre au temps des empereurs', *Cahiers du group interdisciplinaire du théâtre antique* 3, 273–94.

Sievers, G., 1868. *Das Leben des Libanius* (Berlin).

Spadaro, M., 1989. 'In margine all' *uper tôn orchêstôn* di Libanio'. In A. Garzya (ed.), *Metodologie della ricerca sulla tarda antichità: atti primo convegno dell' associazione di studi tardoantichi*, (Naples).

Vandenberghe, B., 1955. 'Saint Jean Chrysostome et les spectacles', *Zeitschrift für Religions- und Geistesgeschichte* 7 (Cologne).

Weisman, W., 1972. *Kirche und Schauspiele: Die Schauspiele im Urteil der lateinischen Kirchenväter unter besonderer Berücksichtigung von Augustin* (Würzburg).

3. Christian Self-Definition in the Fourth Century AD: John Chrysostom on Christianity, Imperial Rule and the City

Isabella Sandwell[1]

This article is concerned with the boundary between sacred and secular, and attempts to define these areas in the fourth century AD. It looks at the way that John Chrysostom understood the Church's relationship to imperial rule and city life, and at what this entailed for how he defined the sacred and secular spheres. Before the fourth century the institutions of imperial rule and city life had been inextricably bound up with pagan religion and it is hard to identify any clear cut "secular" sphere that was in opposition to religious institutions. It was probably only Christians who, in the first three centuries AD, could even begin to think of there being a distinction between sacred and secular – signs of it can, for example, be see in Jesus' "Give unto Caesar what is Caesar's" and the suggestion that a Christian could have political allegiance to the emperor but still worship his own God. Conceiving of separate sacred and secular fields thus enabled Christianity to survive as a minority religion under pagan Roman rule. After the conversion of Constantine, however, Christians faced a changed situation in which Christianity could now have a much closer relationship with secular institutions. Of course, this change entailed many benefits for Christianity in terms of imperial support, institutional power and numbers of followers. However, at the same time it could also cause problems for Christians in terms of how they thought about themselves and their identity. As Markus has suggested, before the fourth century Christians had largely defined themselves as a persecuted minority and had, in various ways, maintained relatively clear boundaries between themselves and the rest of society.[2] In the context of the fourth century these boundaries had to be redefined and rethought as Christians were forced to ask how far Christianity could become the religion of empire and of city life and still retain its distinctive characteristics. This, however, was not just a problem of identity, but also a practical problem of who to allow into the Christian community and how far religious practice might be adapted to suit the changed circumstances. Some of these issues will be explored through the thought and writings of John Chrysostom while he was preacher in Antioch in the AD 470's–80's. In the process it will be shown that Chrysostom had ways of dealing with the situation that were particular both to Syrian/Antiochene Christianity and to the social context of Antioch.

CHRISTIANITY AND CHRISTIAN IMPERIAL RULE

The first Christian author that we think of when the issue of Christianity's relationship to imperial rule is raised is Eusebius of Caesarea. He solved the problem by adapting Hellenistic theories of kingship to the Christian rule of Constantine.[3] In his *Panegyric* Eusebius compares Constantine to Christ and presents his rule on earth as the equivalent or image of God's rule in heaven. According to this view Constantine's rule represented the rule of God on earth and the church was able fulfil its destiny on earth through imperial rule in the earthly world. This model has had great impact on the way people think about Christianity in late antiquity – so much so that it has been said that the Church in late antiquity accepted the Eusebeian model almost universally. Dvornik, in a major work on Christian political theory, tries to apply this "universal tradition" to Chrysostom.[4] He says that "Chrysostom, on the whole, followed the teachings on Kingship of Eusebius and the other fathers and that Eusebius' enthusiasm over the blessings of the *Pax Romana* infected Chrysostom as it infected many a Christian writer".[5] However, Dvornik's treatment of Chrysostom is very cursory and he bases his argument on little more than a single quotation.[6] In fact his conclusions do not seem to be the result of critical judgement of whether Chrysostom's ideas really fit the Eusebeian model, but rather they assume this from a superficial reading of some of his comments.

Instead I shall argue that Chrysostom can be seen to be part of an alternative Christian tradition that was less optimistic about the possibility of achieving heavenly rule on earth and more critical of imperial rule. This was a tradition for which the issue of the church's relationship to the state and city were never fully resolved by the church.[7] Apocalyptic ideas, based on the *Book of Revelation* in which the emperor is the anti-Christ and the world outside the church is demonised, were prevalent in some circles even in the fourth century among groups labelled as heretical. There were also less extreme models formed. The most famous of these is Augustine's *The City of God*, which, as Markus states, stands in stark contrast to the Eusebeian model.[8] Early in his career Augustine had largely accepted the Eusebeian model. He saw the extinction of paganism and the Theodosian "establishment" as the fulfilment of God's prophecy and "was prepared to think of conversion to Christianity in institutional terms".[9] However, fifteen years later and after the sack of Rome Augustine had lost faith in the legal enforcement of Christian orthodoxy and no longer saw the Christian Empire as an achievable reality in this world.[10] At the same time his growing emphasis on the doctrine of original sin caused him to be less optimistic about the ability of humans to achieve perfection in this life. According to this view, from the fall of Adam onwards, humans were condemned to living a life of sin and only God's grace in the life to come could change this.

In *The City of God* Augustine makes a distinction between sacred history – history that fulfils Christian prophecies of the path to salvation and the coming of Christ's kingdom to earth – and the rest of history. On the whole, although he does sometimes contradict himself, Augustine sees the period of time since the incarnation of Christ as not being part of the path of sacred history and does not attach "any special significance".… "to the period of the Christianization of the empire" under Christian emperors.[11] The sack of Rome by the Goths, and the resulting pagan criticism of Christianity, led Augustine to question the place of Rome, both the city and the empire it represented, in God's plan and in the development of "sacred history".[12] In *The City of God* Augustine articulates his answer to this problem through the model of the two cities, the heavenly city versus the earthly city or Jerusalem versus Babylon. As Markus says, "eventually in the *City of God* Rome becomes the concrete historical representative of Babylon, the embodiment of the earthly city".[13] Rome became the epitome of a place of sin, continued pagan idolatry and incomplete conversion to Christianity. As such it stood in direct opposition to the heavenly city of which true Christians were members. Chrysostom did not, however, envisage these cities as two separate entities in his own time. Instead, he considered the two to be mixed together in the present world and thus "members of the city of God may be found among the ranks of those serving the state….and conversely, adherents of the earthly city are to be found in plenty within the Church".[14] It was only on the day of judgement that the inhabitants (of Rome and the world) would be divided between the two cities. For this reason, Rome and the Roman State cannot wholly be identified with Babylon, even if Augustine sometimes suggests this to be the case. Instead, at least in this present life, Augustine seems to take any religious significance away from the Roman Empire. As Markus says, for Augustine "it is not an instrument of salvation, but it is not a satanic obstacle either – it is just a historical, empirical society".[15]

The main representatives of Antiochene Christianity, including Chrysostom, can be seen to hold views comparable to those of Augustine, although the theological basis for them was often very different. They too did not accept Eusebius' vision of the Christian age under the joint aegis of the Roman Emperor and Christianity. Wallace-Hadrill argues that this was again partly due to the realities of late fourth century existence.[16] The wars on the borders of the Roman Empire, in particular with Persia in Syria, belied the claim that the Christian rulers of the Roman Empire had achieved universal Peace, as did conflicts within the Church. At the same time, men such as Theodoret of Cyrrhus still saw pagan religion as a threat and as far from overcome.[17] For these reasons it was clear to Antiochene Christians that the Kingdom of God on earth had not been achieved. In fact, they went even further than this and did not even see the achievement of God's kingdom an earth as a desirable goal. Wallace-Hadrill argues that they simply were not interested in secular matters and instead held the total rejection of worldly affairs as the ideal.[18] For example, Theodore of Mopsuestia stated that there were two ages of man – that of the present life and that of the world to come and Christian perfection was only achievable in the latter.[19]

So far this does not seem too different from Augustine's way of thinking. However, the Antiochene Christians did differ from Augustine on some fundamental matters. Firstly, whereas Augustine adhered to the doctrine of original sin and humanity's inability to free itself from this, Antiochene Christians had a strong belief in the free will of individuals to choose good or evil, obedience or disobedience to God.[20] Adam, of course had failed in this, but this had been a choice on his part not an inevitable feature of his human nature. In any case, since the time of Christ, humans had the example of a man, Christ – and the Antiochenes placed great emphasis on his humanity – who had succeeded and made the right use of his free will. This emphasis on the ability of humans to choose good over evil meant that humans could progress along the path to perfection in this life. This led to many Antiochene Christians being accused of Pelagianism but they differed from the views of Pelagius in that they never actually made the claim that perfection could be achieved in this life as Pelagius had done. Instead the progress made in this life could only be an education or form of preparation for the life that was to come. For this reason, Chrysostom and the other Christian writers of Antioch did not see the period of Christian imperial rule to have any religious significance.

For Chrysostom Christian imperial rule was actually a negative development as it contributed to making Christians behave less like Christians. In his *Discourse on Babylas* Chrysostom uses this as an argument for why Christianity was superior to pagan religion, it did not need to be "shored up by human honours" and in fact did better without the support of the emperors.[21] Pagan religion, in contrast, needed the support of pagan emperors. Imperial support and "peace" for Christianity actually caused Christians to be lax while when they were persecuted they were, "more sober minded and kinder, and more earnest…." (*On II Corinthians* XXVI. 4, PG 61. 580).[22] According to the Antiochene school suffering and persecution gave Christians a way to imitate Christ and actually helped to teach them how to use their free will in the right way.[23] The coming of Christian emperors thus deprived Christians of a means of achieving perfection. This is a far cry from Eusebius' triumphalist attitude to Christian rule.

This does not mean, though, that Chrysostom had a revolutionary attitude towards the secular powers. In his sermons on *Romans* XIII.1 he says that Paul made his comment on obeying the powers that be to "show that it was not for the subversion of the commonwealth that Christ introduced his laws" (*On Romans* XXIII, PG 60.615). Secular power is not something evil and completely antithetical to the rule of God but is simply human rule on earth. Chrysostom was thus not in the apocalyptic tradition in which the secular world and imperial rule were seen as the rule of the anti-Christ or of demons.[24] He explicitly rejects the idea that the earthly world has been taken over by demons and objects to "many at this day saying that God takes no care for the visible order of things, but has delegated your affairs to demons" (*On 2 Cor.* II. 9, PG 61.402).[25]

At the same time, though, Chrysostom did not see imperial rule as a natural institution because the emperor did "not reign over his fellow-servants by any natural authority" but was elected, and because his rule was subject to change and to being overthrown.[26] Chrysostom was influenced by some classical ideas as to the nature of political rule. He adapted from Aristotle a comparison with the rule of the lion over the other four-legged animals and the rule of the eagle over the birds, which are natural and unchanging to clarify the elected nature of human rule.[27] Chrysostom saw human laws as unnatural because they were a response to human sin and the inability of humans to live as they should. For this very reason, though, human laws were also useful and necessary. In the passage from sermon XXXIV on *I Corinthians* on the reason for the creation of cities, Chrysostom goes on to say that after the time of Noah:

> Our race ran headlong into extreme disorder, He (God) appointed other sovereignties also, those of masters and those of governors and this too for love's sake. That is, since vice was a thing apt to dissolve and subvert our

race, he set those who administer justice in the midst of our cities as kind of doctors that driving away vice.....they might gather together all in one place" (*On I Cor.* XXXIV. 7, PG. 61. 291).[28]

Secular powers were thus seen as God-given even if they were not natural (*On Statues.* VII.3, PG 49.93 and *On Rom.* XXIII, PG 60.615). In his exegesis of Paul *Romans* XIII.1, Chrysostom quotes "let every soul be subject unto the higher powers, for there is no power but that of God". He then clarifies exactly what Paul means by this. He says that Paul did not mean that every individual ruler was elected by God, but rather that only the abstract or "thing" of the ruling "power" was; it is this abstract of power that Christians are obeying when they submit to secular rule. This should be the case even if the emperor was a "Greek" (*On Rom.* XXIII, PG. 60.618) or a wrongdoer. Chrysostom says: "for do not tell me of someone who makes ill use of the thing, but look to the good order of the institution itself" (*On Rom.* XXIII, PG 60.618).

According to Chrysostom, these secular powers, although not original and natural, had a good function to play in keeping order and preventing anarchy and making humans more civilized.[29] Secular rule balanced out inequalities and helped humans live together as it provided the peace and security necessary for humans to carry out agriculture and life generally and stopped war and plundering.[30] He saw fear of rulers and of law as positive because fear most encouraged good behaviour. Just like fear of hell, it would encourage virtue and was thus a disposition that would make his audience more submissive to God's will.[31] Some people practised virtue simply as a result of fear of God. Others, "who are a duller sort" and think more of the things of the present, needed fear of the emperor or rulers to give their soul "a preparatory turn towards its becoming more suited for the word of doctrine" (*On Rom.* XXIII. PG 60.617).

On the whole, Chrysostom saw Christian law as clearly superior to secular law.[32] This is so much the case that Chrysostom even tried to deter his audience from using secular courts.[33] On the one hand, he argues, Christians were too good to be judged by non-Christians because, as Paul says, in the final days Christians will judge unbelievers.[34] Thus they should not show their problems and conflicts to those who are lesser than they are. On the other hand, Chrysostom saw secular laws as inferior because the magistrates who implemented them were corrupt and because eloquence and rhetoric were more important in secular courts than justice. If there were disputes between Christians then Chrysostom, following Paul, argues that these should be quietly resolved by the priest and should not bring ill repute on the church by being publicised in the courts outside the church.[35] Christians did have their own courts and Constantine, during his reign, had given these official sanctions and we have some evidence that they caused problems for non-Christians.[36] As Libanius tells us, Christian courts could even exceed their sphere of influence and judge non-Christians as well as Christians, as they did when punishing pagan peasants around Antioch for the crime of having sacrificed.[37]

Chrysostom, however, does not always see the distinction between sacred and secular law in terms of the former being right and the latter wrong and to be avoided. There are also times when he conceives of the relationship between the two rules differently. At times he allows for two separate spheres of law, both of which have their own areas of provenance and which, in a way, work together and balance each other out. In his *Homily fifteen on II Corinthians*, Chrysostom discusses the art of ruling. In this he outlines three kinds of rule: firstly, "one whereby men rule peoples and states, regulating this the political life" (*On II Cor.* XV.4, PG 61.507), secondly, the individual's rule of the self and, thirdly, spiritual rule in the church.[38] While political rule was good and necessary, as was outlined above, the rule of the Church "is as much better than the political rule as heaven is than earth"(*On II Cor.* XV.5, PG 61.507). This is because it does not only punish sins but also reveals how they might never be committed in the first place. Thus, Chrysostom criticizes the "temporal ruler" for punishing the adulterer straight away and with death because this neither punishes nor reforms the soul.[39] As Chrysostom says elsewhere: kings and rulers might have the power to punish sinners or to "release them from present punishment; but their sin they do not purge out" (*On I Cor.* XL.2, PG 61.349). The two rules clearly have separate spheres of influence. As he puts it in his depiction of the situation after the riot of the statues: "The judges affright; the priests therefore must console! The rulers threaten, therefore the church must give comfort" (*On Stat.* VI.1, PG 49.81). The rule of the church is seen as more natural because of its gentler methods, which cleanse out sin rather than kill the sinner, and because it encourages the ruled to obey willingly rather than unwillingly.[40]

The balance between the different roles of secular and spiritual rule can be seen if we consider the area of governance of each. As we saw, one of the problems with secular rule was that it did not correct or punish the soul. This marks a big difference between the two rules as "bodies are committed to the care of kings, souls to the care of the priest" (*In Oziam, Vidi Dominum*, IV, PG 56.126).[41] Spiritual rule was concerned with "philosophy", "what a soul is and what the world, and what we are to be hereafter, and unto what things we shall depart hence, and how we shall achieve virtue".[42] Secular rule, on the other hand, is concerned with "contracts and bonds and money" (*On II Cor.* XV.6, PG 61.509). Thus the emperor's "province is the ad-ministration of earthly things, whereas the jurisdiction of the priesthood is derived from above..." (*In Oziam*, IV, PG 56.126). Chrysostom does not give much further comment on this division of labour but it seems that secular rule had control over those things that were a necessary part of life, though unattractive to the true Christian, while spiritual rule deals with higher things. Both rules working together cover all aspects of being human, both the ideal Christian ones and the realistic ones of living in the world. To a Christian preacher the former would always be more important; "Christianity keeps together our life far more than temporal laws" (*On II Cor.* XV.5, PG 61.509). The rule of Christian emperors was not heavenly rule on earth and could not be the means for achieving true Christian piety on earth but was just a practical way for keeping order in the world.[43]

In his exegesis of Paul *Romans* XIII. i ("Let every soul be subject to the powers that be.....") Chrysostom talks in terms of there being two separate communities, a religious one and a secular one. But here also he seems to be submitting the former to the authority of the latter and the rulers of the religious community seem to be under the authority of the rulers of the political community.[44] Chrysostom sees that this interpretation of Paul's words might upset Christians who felt it to be demeaning that they should be subject to secular rule. He says that to counter this Paul makes it clear that in being obedient to secular authorities Christians are actually being obedient to God as it was he who set up these authorities. Thus they should "not suppose that (they) are lowering (themselves), and detracting from the dignity of their own philosophy, if they rise up at the presence of a ruler" because the true hierarchy of God over secular ruler was still in place; in obeying the earthly ruler they were indirectly obeying their own ruler, God. This suggestion, that obeying the emperor's rule was equal to obeying God's rule, does seem reminiscent of Eusebius' model of emperors as God's representatives on earth. However, it becomes clear that this is not how Chrysostom sees the matter. He goes on to give further justification that Christians should be obedient to secular powers. He says:

> If you mean to say, that you are entrusted with greater privileges, be informed that this is not your time. For thou art a stranger and a sojourner (in this world) (*On Rom.* XXIII, PG. 60.618).

He is not saying that Christians should obey secular rule because this is God's rule on earth or because heaven has been achieved in this world. Rather, he is still really asserting the special status of the Christian community. The separate sphere of secular rule must only be obeyed whenever it is "not subversive to religion" and in a way that the rules of the religious sphere maintain their rightful supremacy. At the same time, Christians should not obey secular rule because it is superior to Christian rule, but rather because it is irrelevant to them as it is only earthly rule and will be overturned anyway on Christ's coming. He says:

> A time will come when you shall appear brighter than all.....Seek not your change in this life of accidents (*On Rom.* XXIII, PG. 60.618).

Living a true Christian life was not possible in the earthly life so Christians were not losing anything by submitting to earthly rule. What at first appears to be an acceptance of the submission of the church to secular rule is, in fact, another assertion of the special status of the Christian community. Even when Chrysostom at first appears to adhere to something like the Eusebian model this is not really the case. His view seems to be that in a way secular rule was irrelevant to the Christian as the rulings and judgements of this life were not the ones that really affected him. This is the constant throughout Chrysostom's varied views. It has been seen that Chrysostom said that Christians should certainly not submit themselves to the courts of the gentiles because of their noble race, but that ideally they should not seek justice at all in this world, as they were to get it in the world to come. Here he says that Christians should submit to worldly rule in this life despite their noble race because they will gain true justice, suited to their special status, in the world to come.

Whatever Chrysostom's contradictory attitudes to the Christian state, it is clear that the Christian's real citizenship was in heaven and that he or she would only receive true judgement and reward or punishment in the life to come. This is always the bottom line; whatever else he might have said Chrysostom always in the end reminds his audience not to think about the present life but to refer themselves only to "future things". As he says, for example, "the love of the kingdom has not penetrated us, nor desire of things to come inflamed us, otherwise we should despise all present things"

(*On Stat.* V.9, PG 49.72).[45] The earthly city could, as we shall see below, be Christianized and this may allow the earthly city of Antioch to gain some status as a heavenly city. In reality, however, the heavenly city and the earthly city are distinct from one another and the Christian has to choose to be a member of the former:

> If you are a Christian, no earthly city is yours. Of our City "the Builder and Maker is God". Though we may gain possession of the whole world, we are strangers and sojourners in it all! We are enrolled in heaven and our citizenship is there! (*On Stat.* XVII.12 quoting *Hebrews* XI.10, PG. 49. 178).

However successful Christianization was, however much Christians were to "gain possession of the world," they would still be strangers in it. If Christians tried too hard to be citizens of the world, they would be denied their true citizenship in heaven but as this is their "natural" citizenship, they would also never be able to be at home in the world, however hard they tried.[46] He says:

> But seeing we are by nature sojourners, let us also be so by choice, that we may not there be sojourners and dishonoured and cast out. For if we are intent on being citizens here, we shall be citizens neither here nor there. (*On 2 Cor.* XVI.5, PG. 61.518).

There was a long Christian tradition of envisaging Christians as strangers on earth.[47] It is an idea that was often held by those who adhered to some kind of opposition between the earthly city and the heavenly city. For example, in the second century, the author of *The Shepherd of Hermas* and then Tertullian both talk of the antithesis between two cities and the alien status of the Christian in this life.[48] In the fourth century, Ambrose uses the same language and states that Christians should "withdraw from this earthly city for your city is in Jerusalem on high" (*Ep.* LXIII).

It is clear that Chrysostom did not subscribe to the Eusebeian model of the relations between church and state. He did see imperial rule as bringing the peace necessary for the spread of Christianity and as necessary and useful to humans in their imperfect state.[49] However, this is not the same as saying that Chrysostom saw God's rule on earth as a reality achieved by the emperors of the fourth century. He never talks of the *imperium Christianum* and in fact very rarely refers to the secular rulers of his day at all. He also rarely refers to the rulings of Christian emperors to support the cause of the Christian Church; his recriminations against pagan idolatry and sacrifice are, for example, never backed up by reference to imperial laws against these. In fact, the beneficial aspects of secular rule and the secular institution of the city are, in Chrysostom's work, nothing to do with the conversion of the emperor Constantine to Christianity but go back to the early stages of human history and are inherent in the nature of rule itself. They are not corrective to human sin and not a shadow outline of God's rule in heaven. Chrysostom certainly does not have a triumphalist attitude to the fact that most emperors of his century had been Christian. In his twenty-third sermon on *Romans*, it is clear that he does not take it for granted that all future emperors would be Christian. Here Chrysostom's attitude seems prescient of the older Augustine for whom, at the beginning of the fifth century, "legal establishment of orthodoxy has lost much of its significance" and for whom thus the "idea of an Christian empire as an achieved institutional reality also vanishes".[50]

CHRISTIANITY AND THE CITY

In the previous section we began to see that Chrysostom, as other Christians, used the image of the city and of citizenship to conceptualize membership of the Christian community. In these examples this language of the city was used to deflect Christians from their loyalty of earthly cities and their lives in them. However, the very fact that the imagery of the city was used to do this shows the importance of the idea of the city to Christians. Early Christian communities were usually located in the context of the city. This meant that the idea of the city could not help but be important, or at least relevant to them. As Meeks shows, Christianity's growth and the shape it took were "very closely entangled with the nature of the Greek speaking cities of the Roman Empire" and cannot ever be considered as completely separate from this.[51] However, cities were always problematic for Christians because pagan religious life was so embedded in their institutions and way of life.[52] The fact that, in the first three centuries, Christians were a minority group (or groups) with defined membership meant that at least symbolically and ideally they envisioned themselves as separate from civic life.[53] The fact that pagans thought of Christians as being anti-social helped to maintain these ideas. In the fourth century this situation began to change.

Under Christian rulers pagan religion had begun to become more dislocated from the city as Christianity had become more at home in it. The idea of the city was still very important symbolically but now pagans and Christians had to compete to be the representative religion of the city and for the symbolic capital that went with this. The imperial government was now Christian and among its representatives in Antioch there were both pagans and Christians. Similarly, the city council of Antioch was made up of both pagans and Christians.[54] It was thus no longer possible to identify a particular set of religious ideas and practices unquestioningly with the political centre of the city. Christianity, which had before the conversion of Constantine, defined itself in opposition to the world around, was now establishing a relationship with the powers of state and city. The city was thus an important battleground or point of debate between pagans and Christians at this time. The acceptance of the right of Christians to worship publicly as they now could, rather than privately as they had had to before the fourth century, was, as Baldovin has argued, tied in with their ability to lay claim to the city as a Christian space.[55] At the same time, by using images and metaphors of the city to describe Christianity, Christians could appeal to pagans, and more civic minded Christians, in a language that they would have understood and found appealing.[56]

Of course, to some extent, the city could not help but become more Christian under Christian emperors. Pagan religious buildings were no longer erected and existing ones were sometimes destroyed and the legislation against sacrifice and other forms of pagan worship contributed to the secularisation of public festivals. At the same time, Christian buildings and institutions in the city were gaining increasing financial backing, at least from private if not public finances. The most notable Christian building in Antioch in the fourth century was the octagonal Great Church, or Golden Church, which was started by Constantine in 327 and completed by Constantius in 341. This impressive structure was built on the island in the Orontes near the imperial palace and clearly marked the importance of Christianity both in the city and to the emperors.

The other known Christian constructions made during the fourth century were the cruciform church at Kaoussie built by bishop Meletius in AD 379-80 to be the shrine for Saint Babylas and the Church of the Maccabees in the Jewish quarter.[57] There was also another important church in Antioch, the ancient "apostolic" church, which was in the old part of the city and is thought to have dated back to apostolic times.[58] It was in this last that Chrysostom was thought to have preached normally. There were also many other smaller churches and martyria that although not used for daily worship were the site for the many Christian festivals.[59]

These Christian festivals were increasingly being added to and began to replace existing traditional festivals. Gradually, as Liebeschuetz states, "Christianity was taking over the function of providing citizens with holidays and entertainment" with a calendar of feasts and martyr festivals.[60] For example, on the feast days of the local saints, such as Babylas, Ignatius, Julian and Drosis, there would be processions to their shrines, which were usually situated outside the city, and a service and perhaps feasting there.[61] The most notable new festival was the celebration of Christmas, which was introduced in 376 on the day of *Sol Invictus*.

Such developments have led to the argument that cities had become entirely Christianized by the late fourth century. For example, Baldovin examines the stational liturgies of Jerusalem, Rome and Constantinople, to argue that these public rituals and processions enabled the Christians to make these cities their own.[62] He sees such religious processions as replacing public pagan religious praxis and events in providing "the conceptual framework (in terms of the sociology of knowledge, the common sense basis) for society as a whole".[63] Baldovin is right to emphasise the impact of Christian use of public space on the cities of late antiquity; it is clearly one of the most important arenas in which competition between pagan or classical and Christian took place in late antiquity.[64] Baldovin is also right to focus on ritual as being an essential element in changing the way people conceptualized the world; ritual had been essential to the pagan world and its way of constructing reality. However, Baldovin's conclusions too easily assume Christian victory. In his view Christianity became very closely identified with the city and upheld the "structure of society" as a whole in direct replacement of the role that pagan religious institutions had held.[65] He sees this identification to have been so successful that he can say that, "to participate in civilization and to be a Christian were now one and the same thing" and that "…. (Christian) worshipping was not a specialized activity as much as it was an expression of membership in society itself".[66] Baldovin accepts the Eusebian "more practical solution" to the relationship between church and secular powers over Augustine's negative dislocation of the city of God and the earthly city.[67] It is this view that allows Baldovin to talk of the now "holy civilization" and to refer to the ancient city as "the simulacrum of heaven".[68]

Baldovin is considering the situation from the late fourth century up until the sixth century. For the later part of this period in the cities which he studies these statements might be applicable, but if we apply his general conclusions to late fourth century Antioch they would seem more than a little over-optimistic.[69] They idealize the progress of Christianity and take all the tension out of the church's relationship with political and civic institutions that had once been, and still were to some degree, bound up with pagan cultural and religious forms. From Chrysostom's sermons preached at Antioch it will become clear that the Church actually had a more ambiguous relationship with the city and surrounding society. People may have taken part in Christian processions and have felt that they were having an effect similar to pagan festivals but this does not make the identification of membership of the church and membership of civic society unproblematic. At the same time the fact that there was a strong current within Christian discourse that was antagonistic to the city and its values and which sought to construct the Christian church and community in opposition to civic society also caused problems.

In contrast, Natali has a very different approach to these problems from Baldovin.[70] He argues that at least in Antioch the city and its traditions of euergetism had not suffered the decline so often posited in accounts of cities in late antiquity.[71] Rather, in this view, the largely Christianized senatorial elite were still spending large amounts of money on the great liturgies of putting on spectacles and public feasts motivated by traditional *philotimia* and urban patriotism. At the same time, the other great public gift to the city, public building, although no longer being carried out by the senators was now carried out by members of the imperial bureaucracy both pagan and Christian.[72] Natali then goes on to argue that as a result the religious beliefs of these men was kept entirely separate from their role as active members of civic life. He says:

> Ainsi existent côte à côte sans être tout à fait étrangères l'une l'autre, d'ailleurs, deux organisations, l'une municipale et l'autre religieuse dont seul point commun est ces individus qui adaptent leur attitude à la communauté du moment, citoyens dans l'une, fidèles dans l'autre à la fin du IVe siècle....[73]

For Natali this was possible because civic duties and civic life had been secularized and emptied of associations with pagan religion so there was no *direct* conflict in terms of their religion. At the same time, he argues, this civic life had not been given any Christian associations and so no identity was made between church and polis. This separation of spheres is shown nicely by the fact the officials carrying out public building works stopped putting up pagan edifices such as temples but did not start putting up Christian ones; this was left almost entirely to the ecclesiastical community.[74] What was said in church, in Natali's view, did not have any impact on daily civic life and outside the church itself these men would have existed in a world that was no longer pagan but that was also not yet Christian.[75] Natali goes on to add, in what seems to be a view almost in direct opposition with that of Baldovin, that the reason for this is that the elite of the polis, which was itself largely Christian, did not feel that Christianity was able to act as the "civic cement".[76] As a result they tried to save "la communauté morale, spirituelle et politique de la cité" by keeping local forms of patriotism but in a secularized form. In taking this view, Natali also rejects the triumphalism of Eusebian political theology which "closely aligned the destiny of Church and empire" and which Baldovin took as the basis for his model.[77] Instead Natali argues that at the end of the fourth century the church and empire were still not as one.

Natali's model is certainly more realistic for understanding how the elite in late fourth century Antioch would have experienced the relationship between church and

city. It is clear that throughout the governing classes of the Roman Empire there was
a certain compromise over religious issues in the civic and political context, or at least
an attempt to avoid direct confrontation. Natali's model is how Christians and non-
Christians involved in civic life would have liked things to be. However, the church
and Christian leaders were not always ready to accept such a dichotomy between
religious and political/civic allegiance and wanted to lay hold on the civic world too.
There were many occasions, particularly in times of crisis, when the civic and
ecclesiastical communities competed in representing or together worked towards the
public benefit of the city. The traditional civic liturgies might have continued to be
performed as non-Christian and as secular but the Church introduced good public
works that were most definitely Christian to compete with them. The church also
recognised the symbolic importance of trying to represent the city. I now want to look
at how Chrysostom articulates and mediates these problems of the relationship
between city and Church.

We saw above that Chrysostom argued that the Christians were strangers in this
world and did not belong to any earthly city. In reality, though, Chrysostom did have
to deal with the city and his community's relationship to it. Chrysostom saw the
institution of the city as something created by God as the best form in which humans
could live. He saw humans as not being naturally self-sufficient but as needing the
skills and care of others as was only possible in communal habitation of a city.

> For no other reason either did He suffer all things to be produced in every
> place, that hence also He might compel us to mix with one another. But
> having set us in need of one another, He on the other hand made the
> intercourse easy….Here then is why He founded cities also, and brought all
> into one place (*On I Cor.* XXXIV, PG 61. 291).[78]

Cities could thus not be bad in themselves because they were created by God and
because the community of human living which they allow is natural. However, cities
as they were in Chrysostom's day and as humans had made them, were full of things
that were not suitable for a Christian life. In particular Chrysostom often gives negative
connotations to the imagery of the buildings and spaces of the city:

> Were you to go to the bench of justice, quarrels and contentions are there! Or
> into the council chamber? there is anxious thought about political matters!
> Or your home? Solicitude about private affairs takes up all your time! Or
> were you to go to the conferences and debates of the forum? Everything
> there is earthly and corruptible! (*On Stat.* X.2, PG. 49.112).

These are the places that the ordinary members of his congregation would have
frequented in their daily lives. Chrysostom portrays these physical spaces of the most
important parts of the city as worthless and even dangerous places to be: they were
the cause of corrupting attitudes and ways of thinking which were incompatible with
the state of mind necessary for attending church.[79]

There is thus some inconsistency in Chrysostom's attitude to the city. It was a
necessary human institution installed by God but it could be the cause of spiritual
corruption. This inconsistency can also be seen if we consider how Chrysostom
conceives of the relationship between the church and the city. On the one hand the

church is seen as enclosed space (both physically and symbolically) which should have nothing to do with the city and which, in fact, should be in complete opposition to the city because it is a little piece of heaven on earth. On the other hand, the church is seen as at one with the city, as extending outwards to the city or as representing the true values of the city. In a passage from his sermons *On 1 Corinthians* Chrysostom describes how the church in his time in Antioch had deteriorated from the Corinthian church of Paul's, which "was a heaven then". He first makes a nice rhetorical comparison between Paul's days when the houses were churches and his own day when the church has become like a house but in a negative sense. He then extends this comparison to the rest of the city and describes the deterioration in terms of an invasion of the church by values and activities from the city:

> Here there is great tumult and great confusion and our assemblies differ in nothing from a vintner's shop, so loud is the laughter, so great the disturbance, as in the baths, as in the market, the cry and tumult is universal...... (*On 1 Cor.* XXXVI.8. PG. 61. 313).[80]

As before, the very physical imagery of the buildings and spaces of the city is used to show the opposition between church and city and the way that the two have been wrongly brought together. At another point Chrysostom asks his audience to imagine what it would be like to see the sky opening and to see their dead relatives in heaven. This, he says, was the same feeling that being in church should inspire "for, in truth, the things in this place are also a heaven".[81] The church is heaven on earth and so should be completely separate from the city.

At other times, Chrysostom envisions the relationship between city and church differently. The series of sermons written after the riot of the statues[82] shows a very positive attitude towards contemporary Antioch as a city compared with Chrysostom's other sermons. Chrysostom realised that in the aftermath of the riot there was an occasion in which the Church could lay claim to representing the city and had to deal with the conflicts caused by the idea that Christianity and the Church could be equated with the city. Throughout the sermons *On the Statues* Chrysostom seeks to represent the church as the saviour of the city in troubled times. He presented the Christian Bishop, Flavian, as the one who persuaded the emperor not to punish the city too severely. The church itself is described both as "the mother" of the inhabitants of the city and Christians as the city's "guardians, its patrons and teachers" (*On Stat.* VI.1, PG 49.81).[83] In the sermons Chrysostom often calls on his audience to remember and associate with the "greatness of the city" of Antioch and its past; as he says, "the manners of this city have noble characters from old times" (*On Stat.* II.10, PG 49.37).[84] He recognises Antioch's political status as the leading city of Syria and thus expresses his concern "not for one city only but for the whole of the east" (*On Stat.* III.1, PG 49.47). He also uses very affectionate images to describe the city. For example, he describes how the forum used to be like a happy and busy beehive before the desolation after the riot.[85] This is the same forum that Chrysostom usually warns his audience about so vehemently. That the city is deserted and fearful is, at times, something that Chrysostom considers the greatest sadness as now "she (the city) stands desolate, stripped of almost all her inhabitants" (*On Stat.* II. 3, PG 49.35).[86]

In the sermons *On the Statues,* Chrysostom describes the church and the city as being very close. In a twofold process he describes all the inhabitants of the city coming into the church and the church as extending outwards to the whole city. Whereas before it was seen as negative that the attitudes and behaviour of the city had come into the church, here it is a positive thing that so many people came from the city into the church.[87] At the same time, the suffering caused by the crisis is seen to have many beneficial effects in making the citizens more serious and in taking the attitudes of the church out into the city. This is so much so that they city is described as a monastery and a church.[88] He says:

> For our city is being purified every day, and the lanes and crossings and places of public concourse are freed from lascivious and voluptuous songs...our whole city has become a church, since the workshops are closed, and all are engaged throughout the day in general prayers (*On Stat.* XV.3, PG. 49.154–5).[89]

Of course statements such as these are very rhetorical in nature and it is clear that Chrysostom is making as much as possible out of the riot of the statues for the Christian cause. There was a changed atmosphere in the city that allowed Chrysostom to make such claims and it was natural that in such troubled times more people would have gone to church and prayed to God.[90] Chrysostom takes advantage of this in order to take over the city symbolically and to portray it as a truly Christian place. Chrysostom even used the success of the church in caring for and representing the city as a possible way to persuade pagans to become Christians.[91]

Chrysostom's attempt to take over the city for the Christian cause can also be seen in the way that he describes the monks coming into the city from the deserts and mountain tops around Antioch. The monks usually represent the height of Christian goodness and the antithesis of the city with their solitary living and complete lack of worldly goods and desires. They lived a heavenly life on earth and had almost won the battle against temptation because they lived completely outside the bounds of the city.[92] On the one hand they were physically situated outside the city living, often as hermits, in the mountains around Antioch. On the other hand they did not uphold any of the values that were most central to city life; they did not hold public office or fit into the fixed structures of social status and they reversed expectations of what was considered honourable or dignified behaviour. Their entrance into Antioch thus allowed the city to become its own antithesis "as then might one see the city likened to heaven, while these saints appeared everywhere" (*On Stat.* XVII.3, PG 49.172–3). This is especially so because Chrysostom describes all those who were normally powerful and "held the first offices" in Antioch as leaving for the desert in the exodus of citizens fearing the revenge of the emperor.[93] The monks, the normal inhabitants of the desert, replaced them and became the first citizens of the city. In fact, the monks, and in particular their leader Macedonius, as well as the Bishop Flavian played a pivotal role in securing forgiveness for the city after the riot. This has led Maas to state: "Christian models of authority had taken a grip of the imagination. Antioch's political profile had become Christian".[94]

The transformed city of Antioch could then, like the church itself, gain the status of being heavenly rather than earthly as its Christian credentials made "it a metropolis not on earth, but in heaven" (*On Stat.* XVII.10, PG 49.177).[95] Chrysostom's ideal was that the ascetic lifestyles, disdain of riches, and charitable works that characterised the behaviour of monks would replace *philotimia*, patronage and competition for status so that honour becomes associated with avoiding all worldly things.[96] Chrysostom would like all his audience to live like monks in relation to the rest of the city. He often cites monks and saints as the model for every member of his community and he encourages them to strive to change and perfect their behaviour. This often meant that he wanted his audience to hold attitudes very different from those normally held by inhabitants of the city. He tells his audience that poverty and manual labour should no longer be reasons for shame and he encourages the rich to give charity to all the poor of Antioch rather than to put up buildings for the city purely for the sake of honour.[97] This includes persuading the rich who do carry out charitable acts to go further and to transcend the patriotism that makes them give money to the poor from Antioch alone: they should give to foreigners as well. According to Chrysostom Christian charity should not be confined to euergetism and public works for the city itself.[98] In a sermon on *1 Corinthians* Chrysostom asks his audience to imagine two cities, one inhabited by rich people alone, one by poor people alone. He says that the city of the rich would not be able to survive on its own without poor people to carry out manual work. The city of the poor, on the other hand, would be an almost ideal city that would only be destroyed, and not gain anything, if rich people lived there too.[99]

In answer to classical ideas about the city being equal to its inhabitants, Chrysostom gives a specifically Christian conception of why it is the virtue of the citizens, not any external aspect of the city, that really matters. To do this he uses the Christian language of interior and exterior. Thus he says that a normal encomium of Antioch praising the beauty of the suburb of Daphne was only praise in "an outward sense" and for "the present life" alone. Real praise could instead be found by describing "modest and temperate" inhabitants and their "virtue, meekness and almsgiving; all things that pertain to the "true wisdom of the soul"; that is, in inward qualities.[100] To make this point he then uses the metaphor of the goodness of an individual man. As a man must be considered blessed due to the "beauty of the soul" and not outward "comeliness", so a city must be judged by its inner virtue and not its outward appearance.[101] Thus in another example Chrysostom compares decorating the city for what seems to be a traditional pagan, festival with decorating it with the light of their souls and with virtue.[102] In such passages Chrysostom was attempting to change the significance of the city for his audience.

It would be wrong to dismiss Chrysostom's use of the city/church, city/heaven, city/desert oppositions as mere rhetorical play. Bringing these opposites together actually allowed Chrysostom to manipulate the idea of what the essence of a city was in his preaching to his audience. As Daley says of the use of such language of the city in the Cappadocian fathers: "it was not simply inflated fourth-century rhetoric" but was part of a "drive on the part of these highly cultivated bishops and some of their Christian contemporaries to reconstruct Greek culture and society along Christian lines, in a way that both absorbed its traditional shape and radically reoriented it".[103] That Chrysostom describes Antioch as a "metropolis" and "mother-city" in heaven shows this well in that he takes titles from the secular world but places them in a Christian context.[104] He uses terms and language that his audience would have understood but transforms their meaning by placing them in a different frame of reference. By talking of the city in positive terms he claims for the church some of the symbolic power of the classical idea of the city but at the same time he gives this a Christianized interpretation. Chrysostom followed classical theorists in seeing virtue and the city as inter-linked but he substituted Christian virtue for the virtues normally associated with membership of a city.[105] He gives the city a Christian history and ancestry. He starts from the fact that it was the first place in which disciples took the name of Christians[106] and goes through a list of other good Christian actions related to the city, which could be used in place of any classical ancestry.

Chrysostom's audience did not, however, always accept his attempts at Christianization of every part of their civic lives and complained that Chrysostom was expecting too much from them, saying "but we are not monks".[107] There is a certain amount of tension in Chrysostom's sermons between how he wants his audience to behave and how they actually were behaving. His audience did, it appears, see being a Christian as something separate, which they did not have to carry over into their lives as a whole. However, as a result of the preaching they heard in church, it would not have been easy for Christians to forget that there was an alternative model for their mode of living being proposed by the church.

Chrysostom was clearly aware that because of the reality of the world around him and because of differing ideas about the proper place of the sacred, he could not be too closed off from the outside world. He saw it was necessary to discuss the relationship between Church and city and saw the benefits of gaining some hold over the city for Christianity. At times, then, Chrysostom sought to separate his audience off from the city, at times to identify the church with the city. As we have seen, Chrysostom does give the impression that he has very contradictory ideas about the city. However, it would be better to understand these contradictions as Chrysostom trying to balance his ideals with the reality of living in a city and of preaching to an audience that still identified themselves with the secular world outside. Chrysostom wanted himself and his audience to live the life of heaven on earth but knew that this was not possible in the real world and that to assert his ideal too strongly would only alienate his audience and put off potential converts. During the riot of the statues he describes how "Gentiles and Jews...as well as the barbarians" (or the "Jews as well as the Greeks" as he puts it elsewhere) were eagerly looking" to the bishop Flavian to save the city (*On Stat.* XXI, 4 and13, PG 49.213 and 217). This idea will have affected his portrayal of the Church's relationship with the city. At other times he explicitly states that Christianity's positive, un-revolutionary attitude to secular powers was intended to encourage pagan conversion. He says that Paul told Christians that they should obey secular laws "for in this way he (Paul) was more likely to draw the governors who were unbelievers to the religion" (*On Rom.* XXIII, PG. 60.615). Chrysostom made every effort to present the city as a Christian space and to persuade his audience to treat it as such. Laying claim to the city and presenting Christianity as a civic religion were thus both ways in which Chrysostom could appeal to and debate with non-Christians.

THE RELIGIOUS SPHERE

In the first section of this article I showed that Chrysostom did not see Roman imperial rule as the fulfilment of God's kingdom on earth and did not subscribe to the Eusebian model of church-state relations. Imperial rule should be obeyed because it was a means of keeping order on earth but it had no religious significance or validation. Being a Christian was meant to entail that one saw one's citizenship to be in heaven rather than in an earthly city or state. This could suggest that Chrysostom might allow the city and the secular world to exist as a sphere into which religious interests did not intrude. He did seem to accept that some form of secular rule was necessary and beneficial for keeping order. If this secular rule did not have the potential to be God's rule on earth then it was possible that he might see it as a separate sphere that had its own values and goals. However, in the second section I showed that while this was Chrysostom's ideal, the realities of life at Antioch imposed on Chrysostom the rhetorical and apologetic need to lay claim to the earthly city as a Christian space. For example, the confusion after the riot of the statues gave Chrysostom a chance to show that the church could represent the city as a whole and compete with other more traditional civic institutions to do so. In this we can see Chrysostom adapting Christianity to a more civic model. At the same time, though, Chrysostom's attempt to lay claim to the city also entailed an attempt to transform the city and its values so that it fitted the Christian ideal, of which monastic life was the epitome, more closely. When Chrysostom pushes this model to its logical conclusion he leaves no room for a civic or "secular" sphere that had no religious significance.

Although Chrysostom accepted that it had not yet been achieved, his ideal was that Christian values would permeate the whole of civic life and that, for example, prominent men would want to do charitable works rather than win glory in public office. Chrysostom was trying hard to combat the views of those in his audience who wanted to keep their civic and religious lives separate. In one sermon he uses exegesis of *1 Corinthians* X.31–32 "Whether you eat or drink or do anything else, do all for the glory of God", to make this point. He tells his audience that eating, conversation and going into the market place could all be done thinking of God rather than in a "worldly" way. In fact, for Chrysostom, almost every area of life could be considered sacred in that it had the potential to be either pagan (that is Greek, idolatrous and devil-worshipping to use his language) or Christian depending on the state of mind and inner attitude of the individual.[108] Every activity, however, "secular" it might appear, should be done in a Christian way and thus had the potential for fulfilling the religious ideal.

The corollary of this was that everything that was not, or could not, be done in a Christian way, also had religious significance, but a negative one. Chrysostom often ascribes the practices of his audience and things that happen in the city around him to the power of the devil. This can first be seen in the various activities that Chrysostom labels as pomps of the devil. *Pompe* was originally the Greek word used to refer to processions carrying the idols of the gods at games and festivals but Christians had come to use it in the broader sense of anything that they saw as connected with the realm of the devil. This included going to the theatre and the racecourses and the use of omens and portents.[109] Chrysostom saw all these practices as having power and authority in religious terms but this was a negative power of the realm of the devil. Throughout Chrysostom's writings almost any element of the world outside the church could find itself in this position if Chrysostom had reason to rail against it, whether it be women wearing make-up, the theatre, drunkenness, pride or decorating the forum with garlands.[110] Thus we can see Chrysostom defining the huge areas of life that should be seen in religious terms; the Christian should bring their Christianity into all these areas because otherwise they were under the sway of the devil. In this, Chrysostom was reacting to attempts by ordinary Christians, and pagans, to argue that practices such as these had no religious significance and were compatible with Christianity. This can be seen most clearly in the case of the traditional festivals of the city.

In his sermon on the festival of the Kalends, Chrysostom gives an argument against the festival to Christians who have been attending it.[111] He describes the festival as a time when "demons parade in the agora" and when "diabolical night festivals" take place.[112] In the former he is probably referring to the procession conducted through the agora to the circus in which people carried or wore the images of the gods.[113] The latter is his interpretation of the drinking and celebration that take place during the festival, which he sees as "indecorous", "licentious" and a sin. Unholy singing and dancing takes place and it is an occasion for adultery, debauchery and other moral sins.[114] Such festivals also involved spending too much money on extravagances and the gaudy decoration of the city.[115] Chrysostom also condemned the "impiety" of people who see the Kalends as an omen of good or bad luck for the rest of the year. He reminds his audience that to enjoy such a festival was to enjoy worldly things, which was wrong because they "have registered in the citizenship of heaven".[116] He then goes on to argue to them, quoting Paul, that they "should do all for the glory of God".[117] This first includes "going into the agora or remaining at home". He goes on:

> Again, it is possible to remain at home because of God. How and in what way? Whenever you hear a clamour, diabolical disorder and pomps, the agora full of evil and licentious men, stay at home and be free of this disorder and you have stayed at home for the glory of God (*On Kalends*, 3, PG 48.957).

He then goes on to list a whole variety of activities, from talking and being silent to wearing shoes, that could be done "for the glory of God". Chrysostom's critique of the festival as demonic and pagan leads him into a reminder to his audience that their religious allegiance should permeate their whole lives. Harl argues that in fact all Christian critiques of pagan festivals were made in order to highlight the proper Christian way of life and true Christian festivals.[118] The direct contrast between the pagan and Christian ways entailed that no area should be left between them that was free of religious significance. Meslin sees such representations of the Kalends festival by Christian preachers as a direct answer to those who deny that the festival had any religious significance. He goes on:

> En connotant la fête des kalendes d'une signification démoniaque, en en faisant une manifestation du Mal, l'Eglise révélait clairement sa volonté de n'accepter aucune mitigation, aucune conciliation entre de telles pratiques et la profession de chrétien.[119]

By associating the festival with the devil Chrysostom could make his audience "feel the danger" of attending it.[120]

So how can we understand these views, which impute religious meaning to every part of existence, in relation to the view outlined above that Chrysostom saw secular rule as a simply neutral earthly rule that should be obeyed? Markus noted a similar contradiction in Augustine's *The City of God*. At times, and often in the same sentence, Augustine both refers to secular rule as without any religious significance, good or bad, and also talks of the city of Rome as the "new Babylon" and as representing the rule of the devil, the earthly city in this world.[121] Markus, commenting on this contradiction says that it was largely due to the fact that Augustine was using the "logic of late antique rhetoric rather than modern formal logic". Most interestingly, he argues that the focus on Rome as New Babylon is usually associated with a focus on the continued existence of pagan religion.[122]

The same is true of Chrysostom. His most noteworthy attempts to give the whole of civic and daily life religious significance, whether positive or negative, take place at moments of concern over the boundaries between pagans and Christians. This can either be when he is appealing to pagans across that divide, when he is vilifying practices that he considers to be pagan, or when he is trying to draw clear cut boundaries between the Christian community and those outside of it. At such moments it was particularly important for Chrysostom to assert that there was no neutral, secular space, which both pagans and less zealous Christians could inhabit. This can be explained well by the words of Markus (1990:16). He has argued that it was just when the Church was facing problems of identity due to the conversion of Constantine and the large influx of new converts in the fourth century that it adopted a new polarisation of Christian and non-Christian. He describes this as "a contraction in the scope... allowed to the 'secular'" and "a tendency to absorb what had previously been 'secular' into the realm of the 'sacred', turning secular into 'Christian' or dismissing it as 'pagan' and 'idolatrous'", and demonic.

Notes

1 This paper is taken from a PhD thesis completed in 2001–2 and I would like to thank Professor John North for invaluable comments and guidance during his supervision of this PhD. Translations used throughout the article are based on those either in the Post Nicene Christian Fathers series or The Fathers of the Church series, occasionally with some adjustments by the author. The author is aware that a recently completed PhD covers some of the same ground as this paper: see Stephens, 2001 (unpublished). It was not possible, however, to see this work before going to press. My thanks to Wendy Mayer for pointing this out.

2 Markus, 1990.

3 Barnes, 1981: 254.

4 Dvornik, 1966.

5 Markus, 1970: 53 and Dvornik, 1966: 699.

6 Dvornik, 1966: 695–699.

7 Meeks, 1993: 50.

8 Markus, 1970: 42–3 and 50–53.

9   Markus, 1970: 22–23 and 39.

10   Markus, 1970: 53.

11   Markus, 1970: chapter 1 and 25.

12   Markus, 1970: 37–8, 44 and 47.

13   Markus, 1970: 37–8, 44 and 47.

14   Markus, 1970: 58–9.

15   Markus, 1970: 53–4.

16   Wallace-Hadrill, 1982: 59.

17   Theodoret of Cyrrhus, *Therapies for Hellenic Maladies* and Wallace-Hadrill, 1982: 61.

18   Wallace-Hadrill, 1982: 57–61.

19   Wallace-Hadrill, 1982: 62.

20   For these ideas about the nature of man and the nature of Christ, see Wallace-Hadrill, 1982: 118–125.

21   *On Bab.* 41–2 (PG 50.544).

22   See also, *On I Cor.* XXXVI.7 (PG 61.219).

23   See Wallace-Hadrill, 1982: 155–7.

24   *On 1 Cor.* VII.1 (PG 61.55).

25   See also his three sermons on contemporary attitudes to demons and free will, *That Demons do not Govern the World*.

26   *On Stat.* VII.3, PG 49.93. "Nature" was usually understood to be something fixed and unchanging in antiquity, see Aristotle, *Ethics*, II.1.

27   *On Stat.* VII.3 (PG 49.93). This distinction between natural laws and elected ones is less clear in Chrysostom's exegesis of *Romans* XIII.i. (*On Rom.* XXIII, PG 60.615).

28   This is also Augustine's view of secular powers and law. See *The City of God* XIC, 14–15 and Markus 1970: 84. See also Markus' appendix B, 1970: 197–210.

29   *On Stat.* VI.2, PG 49.82. See also: *Ecloga de imperio*, XXI (PG 63.696). *On Anarchy being Evil*, see *On Rom.* XXII, (PG 60.615).

30   *On I Cor.* XV.4 (PG 61.123–4). See also *On Rom.* XXIII (PG 60.615).

31   See also: *On Stat.* VII.4 (PG 49.94), *On Stat.* XV.2 (PG 60.617).

32   *On 1 Cor.* XII.9–11 (PG 61.102–3).

33   *On 1 Cor.* XVI. 3–10 (PG 61 131–139).

34   *On I Cor.* XVI. 5 (PG 61.132–3).

35   For more on this idea see Chrysostom's sermons *Against Publishing the Errors of the Brethren*.

36   CTh. I.27.1 and Liebeschuetz 1972: 240.

37   See Libanius, Or. XXX.

38   *On II Cor.* XV.5 (PG 61.507).

39   *On II Cor.* XV.5 (PG 61.507).

40   *On II Cor.* XV.5 (PG 61.507–8).

41   See also *On II Cor.* XV.5 (PG 61.509).

42   *On II Cor.* XV.6 (PG 61.510).

43   Markus, 1970: 75–78.

44   *On Rom.* XXIII. PG 60.615.

45   *On 1 Cor.* XV.11 (PG 61.127) and XLII.1 (PG 61.363) and *On Stat.* V.4-5 (PG 49.70–71) and VI.8 (PG 49.86).

46   See Meeks, 1993: 50.

47   On this, see O' Daly, 1999: 53–62.

48   Tertullian, *De Corona*, 13. 1–4. See also, *The Gospel of Thomas* and the *Pseudo-Clementine*.

49   In this he differs from Augustine at least in his darkest moments, Markus, 1970: 52.

50   Markus, 1970: 34.

51 Meeks, 1993: 37.
52 Bruit Zaidman and Schmitt-Pantel, 1989. See pages 233–4 specifically on the Greek city and Christianity.
53 Meeks, 1993: 30, 37, 50.
54 See, Petit, 1994.
55 Baldovin, 1987. See also, Mayer and Allen, 2000: 17.
56 As O' Daly says of Augustine, he "was attracted to discourse about humans in society in terms of the city because it allowed him to engage with pagan critics of Christianity and those who, while attracted to or influenced by Christianity were steeped in Greco-Roman culture….(he) engages in debate with a pagan on the basis of common assumptions about cities, real and ideal". O' Daly, 1999: 23.
57 On the former, see, Lassus, 1938: 5–44 on the latter, see Schatkin, 1987, introduction to her translation, 15 and Downey, 1938: 45–48.
58 Mayer and Allen, 2000: 18 and Eltester, 1937: 36, 251–86.
59 Liebeschuetz, 1972: 176 and Mayer and Allen, 2000: 17–20.
60 Liebeschuetz, 1972: 231.
61 Mayer and Allen, 2000: 18–19. See Chrysostom, *On Saint Julian* (PG 50.672), *On Saint Droside* (PG 50.683) and *On Saint Ignatius* (PG 50.595).
62 Baldovin, 1987.
63 Baldovin, 1987: 231. See also, 238: one of the purposes of the liturgical procession was "to manifest publicly the fact that the Christian faith was the religion which expressed the common-sense faith of the city's populace".
64 This can be seen in Antioch in the battle between Apollo and the martyr Babylas, and the attendant rituals and procession, to represent the suburb of Daphne.
65 Baldovin, 1987: 259 and 263.
66 Baldovin, 1987: 263 and 259.
67 Baldovin, 1987: 258.
68 Baldovin, 1987: 257 and 259.
69 Baldovin does admit almost as much for the example of Rome where, he says, "...Christianity was slow in becoming the "common sense" knowledge of society", Baldovin: 1987, 254.
70 Natali, 1975: 41–60.
71 Natali, 1975: 41–42. See also Liebeschuetz, 1992: 1–49.
72 Natali, 1975: 42–7 and 54.
73 Natali, 1975: 53.
74 Natali, 1975: 54–5. It is notable that while many civic buildings were built during Chrysostom's time at Antioch, a forum, a prison, new baths for example, the only religious building to be put up was the cruciform church at Kaoussie.
75 Natali, 1975: 54–5 and 59.
76 "ciment civique", Natali, 1975: 57.
77 Natali, 1975: 41.
78 See also *On Stat.* XVI.17 (PG 49.172).
79 See also *On Stat.*, X.1 (PG 49.111) and XII.2 (PG 49.127), XV.7 (PG 49.156) and XX.3 (PG 49.199). See also his unfavourable comparison of himself with Basil "who never set foot in the market place" and *On I Cor.* XVI.1 (PG 61.129–30) where Chrysostom refers to Paul's discussion of the problems faced by a Christian living life engaged in the affairs of the city.
80 See also, *On Stat.* II.11 (PG 49.38) "the church is not a theatre" and (*On 1 Cor.* XXXVI.9, PG. 61.314). See also passages where, for example, Chrysostom describes people as thinking about the market while they are praying *On Stat.* XX.3 (PG 49.199).

81 *On I Cor.* XXXVI.8 (PG 61.313).

82 In AD 387 the population of Antioch rioted in response to some harsh tax impositions from the Emperor Theodosius. During the course of these riots they smashed up the imperial statues of the emperor and his family and as a result the city was in fear as to what punishment they would receive. Chrysostom interrupted his normal preaching to deliver a series of sermons to placate and reassure his congregation – the series now known as *On the Riot of the Statues* see the post Nicene Christian Fathers vol. IX. See also Libanius, *Orations*, XI, XX, XXI, XXII, XXIII (Loeb, Libanius Selected Works, vol. II).

83 The earlier Bishop Ignatius, is also described as the guardian of the whole city, *Homily to Ignatius*, 4 (PG 50.596).

84 See also, *On Stat.* III.3 (PG 49.48–9).

85 *On Stat.* II.3 (PG. 49.35).

86 See also *On Stat.* XIII.2 (PG 49.136), XVII.5 (PG 49.174) and XXI.14 (PG 49.217–8). See also Libanius, Or. XXIII *On the Refugees*.

87 *On Stat.* IV.1 (PG 49.59). See also *On Stat.* XXI.2 (PG 49.211).

88 *On Stat.* XVII.8 (PG. 49.175).

89 See also *On Stat.* VI.3 (PG 49.82).

90 Chrysostom describes, for example, the people writing outside the tribunal judging those involved in the riots as on their knees and beseeching God to spare their relatives: *On Stat.* XIII.2 (PG 49.137).

91 *On Stat.* XXI.19 (PG. 49.220). See also *On Stat.*, XX1.13 (PG 49.217).

92 Hunter, 1988: 13–14 and 51.

93 *On Stat.* XVII.5 (PG 49.102–3). See also *On the Stat.* XVIII.12 (PG 49.186).

94 Maas, 2000: 19. On the authority of monks see Brown, 1982: 103–152.

95 See also *On Stat.* XIV.16 (PG 49.154).

96 See Chrysostom's *On Vainglory and the Right way to Bring up Christian Children*. On the association of city life and worldly life with "shame" and of the heavenly life with honour, see Meeks, 1993: 62. See also, Daley, 1999: 431–461.

97 Natali, 1975, 45-with reference to Chrysostom, *On the Gospel of John III* (PG 59.38-45) and *Homily on the Amoneans* (PG 51–2.269–70).

98 Natali, 1975, 45.

99 *On 1 Cor.* XXXIV.8 (PG 61.292).

100 *On Stat.*, XVII.13 and 14 (PG 49.178–9).

101 *On Stat.* XVII. 10 and 13-14 (PG 49.176 and 178–9).

102 *On Stat.* XXI. 20 (PG 49.220).

103 Daley, 1999, 432.

104 As Hunter says, Chrysostom had to "redefine virtue in terms of the heavenly politeia", 1988, 65.

105 As Hunter says Chrysostom, in his works, becomes involved in a debate concerning the whole idea of what constitutes virtue, whether it is the pagan devotion to the traditional gods and the social institutions of the Greek city or the Christian version whereby the earthly city is secondary to the heavenly one, 1988, 65.

106 *On the Stat.* III.3; XIV.16 (PG 49.48 and 153), and *On 1 Cor.* XXI.9 (PG 61.178).

107 See Jedin and Dolan, 1980: 322.

108 See, Kyrtatas, 1988: 365–83.

109 *Baptismal Sermon*, XII.52, (PG. 49.239). See also *Baptismal Sermon*, XI.25 (PG 49.228). Harkins, editor of these sermons, suggests that the importance of the pomps of Satan in the renunciation formulae ["I renounce thee satan and thy pomps..."] in all catechetical texts implies that they originated in the context of the pagan mission; see Kelly 1985.

110 His lists of Pompae of the devil are a first place to look for this attitude, see his baptismal sermons in which we see Christians learning about these pomps and then renouncing them in their initiation into Christianity. For the games and theatre as satanic, see *Contra Ludos et Theatra*, (PG 53.23–270) and also, *On Lazarus*, VII.1 (PG 48.1045).

111 For similar negative descriptions of pagan festivals, see *On Lazarus* I, (PG 48.963–5) and *De Anna Sermo* IV.3 (PG 54.659–660).

112 *On Kalends* 1 (PG 48.954).

113 Gleason, 1986: 109–110.

114 *On Kalends*, 2 (PG 48.954–5).

115 On pagan festivals in Chrysostom, see: *On Bab.* 73 and 77-79 (PG. 50.553 and 554–5); *On Gen.* I.2, (PG 53–4.21) XLVIII.30 (PG 53–4.443), LV.1 (PG 53-5.448); *On I Cor.* XXXIII.5–7 (PG 61.282–4); *In illud vidi dominum* I.2 (PG 56.99), XXII.5 (PG 62.37); *On Lazarus.* I.1 (PG 48.963); *On Stat.* XXI.20 (PG 49.220) and *On the Kalends*.

116 *On Kalends*, 3 (PG 48.956–7).

117 *On Kalends*, 3, (PG 48.956–7).

118 Harl, 1981: 123–47.

119 Meslin, 1970: 97. For the same point, see Harl, 1981: 132.

120 Meslin, 1970: 99.

121 Augustine, *The City of God*, II. 29, see Markus, 1970: 59–61.

122 Markus, 1970: 61.

Bibliography

Baldovin, J.F., 1987. *The Urban Character of Christian Worship: The Origins, Development and Meaning of Stational Liturgy, Orientalia Christiana Analecta 228.* Pont. Institutum Studiorum Orientalium (Rome).

Barnes, T.D., 1981. *Constantine and Eusebius* (Cambridge, Mass).

Brown, P., 1982. 'The Rise and Function of the Holy Man in Late Antiquity'. In P. Brown , *Society and the Holy in Late Antiquity* (London): 103–152.

Bruit Zaidman, L and Schmitt-Pantel, P., 1989. *Religion in the Ancient City*, (translated by P. Cartledge) (Cambridge).

Daley, B.E., 1999. 'Building a New City: The Cappadocian Fathers and the Rhetoric of Philanthropy', *Journal of Early Christian Studies* 7, 431–61.

Downey, G., 1938. 'The Shrines of St. Babylas at Antioch and Daphne', *Antioch-on the-Orontes* II 458.

Dvornik, F., 1966. *Early Christian and Byzantine Political Philosophy: Origins and Background*, vol. II (Dumbarton Oaks Centre for Byzantine Studies, Trustees for Harvard University, Washington, Columbia).

Eltester, W., 1937. 'Die Kirchen Antiochias im IV Jahrhundert', *Zeitschrift für Neutestamentliche Wissenchaft*, 36, 251–86.

Gleason, M.W., 1986. 'Festive Satire: Julian's *Misopogon* and the New Year at Antioch', *Journal of Roman Studies* 76, 106–119.

Harl, M., 1981. 'La dénonciation des festivités profanes dans le discours épiscopal et monastique en Orient chrétien à la fin du IVe siècle', *La fête, pratique et discours: d'Alexandrie hellénistique à la Mission de Besançon*, 123–47 (Paris).

Hunter, D.G., 1988. *A Comparison Between a King and a Monk and Against the Opponents of Monastic Life, Studies in the Bible and Early Christianity*, 13 (Lewiston NY).

Jedin, H. and Dolan, P.A., 1980. *History of the Church*. Vol II (London).

John Chrysostom, 1963. *Baptismal Instructions*, translated and annotated by P.W. Harkins, Ancient Christian Writers, 31 (London).

John Chrysostom, 1983. *Saint John Chrysostom as Apologist (Discourse on Blessed Babylas and Against the Greeks)*, translated and edited by M.Schatkin and P.W.Harkins. Fathers of the Church, 72 (Washington).

Kannengiesser, C., (ed.), 1975. *Jean Chrysostome et Augustine: Actes du colloque de Chantilly* (Paris).

Kelly, H.A., 1985. *The Devil at Baptism: Ritual Theology and Drama* (Ithaca).

Kondoleon, C., 2000. *Antioch: The Lost Ancient City* (Princeton).

Kyrtatas, D., 1988. 'Prophets and Priests in Early Christianity: Production and Transmission of Religious Knowledge from Jesus to John Chrysostom', *International Sociology* 3, 365–83.

Lassus, J., 1938. 'L'église cruciforme', *Antioch-on-the Orontes, II. The excavations of 1933–36*. 5–44.

Liebeschuetz, J.H.W.G., 1972. *Antioch: City and Imperial Administration in the Later Roman Empire*, (Oxford).

Maas, M., 2000. "People and Identity in Roman Antioch". In Kondoleon, 2000: 13–21.

Markus, R.A., 1970. *Saeculum: History and Society in the Theology of Saint Augustine* (Cambridge).

Markus, R.A., 1990. *The End Of Ancient Christianity* (Cambridge).

Mayer, W. and Allen, P., 2000. *John Chrysostom* (including selected sermons) (London and New York).

Meeks, W.A., 1993. *The Origins of Christian Morality: The First Two Centuries*, (Yale, New Haven and London).

Meslin, M., 1970. *La fête des Kalendes de Janvier dans l'empire romain* (Brussels).

Migne, J.P., 1863. *Patrologiae Graeca*, vols 47–64.

Natali, A., 1975. "Christianisme et cité à Antioche à la fin du IVe siècle d'après Jean Chrysostome". In Kannengiesser, 1975: 41–60.

O' Daly, G., 1999. *Augustine's City Of God: A Reader's Guide* (Oxford).

Petit, P., 1994. *Functionnaires dans l'oeuvre de Libanius: analyse prosopographique* (Paris).

Schaff, P. (ed.), 1888–89. *Post Nicene Christian Fathers*, vols IX–XIV.

Schatkin, M., 1987. *John Chrysostom as Apologist. With Special Reference to De incomprehensibili, Quod nemo laeditur, Ad eos qui scandalizati sunt and Adversus oppugnatores vitae monasticae* (Thessalonike).

Stephens, J., 2001. *Ecclesiastical and imperial authority in the writings of John Chrysostom: a re-interpretation of his political philosophy*. (Unpublished PhD diss. University of California, Berkeley)

Wallace-Hadrill, D.S., 1982. *Christian Antioch: A Study of Early Christian Thought in the East* (Cambridge).

4. CHRISTIAN DEMOGRAPHY IN THE *TERRITORIUM* OF ANTIOCH (4TH–5TH C.): OBSERVATIONS ON THE EPIGRAPHY

Frank R. Trombley

An important area of new research[1] on Late Antique Antioch has been the study of Christianisation in its *territorium*.[2] This is a consequence of the large number of public and private inscriptions that survive from the second to seventh centuries AD. Earlier studies have covered the epigraphic record only in part. In the remarks that follow, I will update the discussion in light of new materials that have come to my attention since 1994, when a preliminary study of these materials appeared.[3]

Nothing is known of how Christianity penetrated the *territorium* of Antioch before the second half of the third century. The earliest reference is found in the ecclesiastical history of Eusebius of Caesarea, who mentions the existence of 'bishops of the cities and rural districts bordering them' in connection with the synodal letter of the Council of Antioch in 268.[4] At that time the villages were served by *chorepiskopoi* and *periodeutai*, rural presbyters who made circuit tours of the villages in the *territorium* of Antioch and performed the eucharistic liturgy there. Nothing is known about the existence of churches there before the fourth century, the exception being the somewhat dubious reference to a *martyrion* or martyr chapel 'in Syria at the village of Margaritatum' (*in Syria vico Magaritato*).[5] It is sometimes supposed that Christianity began to take root in a big way immediately after the Edict of Milan and that the First Oecumenical Council at Nicaea somehow guaranteed the expansion of Christianity throughout the Greek Orient.[6] The preponderance of epigraphic evidence does not support such a thesis.[7]

The institutional expansion of the new religion into the countryside was partly a consequence of cultural developments in Antioch and came later.[8] It is worth citing a passage from Theodoret's church history reporting the reaction of the urban crowds in Antioch to the news that Julian the Apostate had been killed in battle during the campaign against Persia in the summer of 363:[9]

> When Antioch heard of Julian's death it gave itself up to rejoicing and festivity; and not only was exultant joy exhibited in the churches and martyr shrines, but *the victory of the cross* was proclaimed even in the theatres and Julian's vaticination held up to ridicule. Here I shall record the admirable utterance of the Antiochenes ... , for with one voice the shout was raised: 'Maximus you fool, where are your oracles now? *For one God has conquered and his Christ.*'

 The acclamations contain two key phrases, the victory of the one God and his Christ, and that of the cross. Both expressions have a theological pre-history, but played an important role in the triumphalist propaganda of the Christian church in post-Julianic epigraphy of the Limestone Massif, a district to the east of the Orontes river where the main sequence of archaeological, architectural and epigraphic finds survive from the fourth and fifth centuries.[10] During this period inscriptions containing these formulae existed up side-by-side with others, some of them reflecting pagan cult, others funerary inscriptions that show no trace of the new Christian dispensation. In what follows, I will interpret the epigraphic evidence for continuity of cult at the pagan temples in the Antiochene countryside and the persistence of a non-Christian population. After this, I will present what I consider to be the circumstances under which the new religion displaced the old both institutionally and demographically.

I. PAGAN TEMPLES AND CULTS

The focal points of pre-Christian religious cult are well-known: Georges Tchalenko identified twenty-one pagan temples or local cults in the Limestone Massif.[11] Most of them were erected in the early centuries of the Christian era, and most probably resembled the typical small Syro-Roman temple, with a rectangular cella and colonnaded porch.[12] The local gods belonged to the Semitic pantheon, but their onomastics and cultic terminology were partially Hellenised. Among the most important of these divinities was the great Baal worshipped atop Mount Koryphe (present-day Jabal Shaykh Bararkat), Zeus Madbachos or Bomos, the 'Zeus of the Altar' which stood in the great temenos at the pinnacle which dominates the Dana plain, in the geographical centre of the Antiochene Limestone Massif.[13] The site was a typical 'high place' where another god, Salmanes, was also honoured with Zeus Madbachos, both of them revered as 'ancestral gods'.[14] Theodoret of Cyrrhus gives us a description, which for reasons that will be seen later belongs after 407:[15]

> There is a high mountain lying to the east of Antioch but west of Beroea. It rises above the surrounding mountains with its highest peak being of conical shape and getting its name from its height. The rustics round about traditionally call it Koryphe ['the peak']. There was formerly a *temenos* of the daemons ['pagan gods'] on that ridge which the rustics honoured greatly.

The cult of Zeus Madbachos was widely dispersed in the region, and it outlasted the death of Julian in 363. We know this from the inscriptions at Touron (present-day al-Husn) near the Orontes valley.[16] Here a temple to the same god was rebuilt in 367/8, during the reign of the semi-Arian Christian emperor Valens whose religious policy was to Theodoret's way of thinking too tolerant.[17] The inscription reads:[18]

> For good luck. The five (?) city councillors of Touron, in completing their duty (?) to the ancestral Zeus, Zeus Koryphaios according to command (?) (a small portion (?)) with their ready hands, restored the propylon and stoa and apse of the doorway and the images in the time of Aurelius Marimineos (?) high priest in the year 416 (of the era of Antioch).

The divinity is here known by the epithet belonging to his central shrine on Mount Koryphe.[19] In another inscription, the same divinity is named again, but this time is called as Zeus Tourbarachos, 'Baal of the blessed mountain.'[20] Some idea of the favours that the Baal granted to its worshippers is evident in the votive inscription of a grain-trader and citizen of Antioch, who evidently bought up agricultural surpluses in the Dana plain (2nd–3rd c.?).[21] The Touron inscription demonstrates that the provincial high priesthoods established by Julian continued to operate after his death. The titles of these priesthoods were not finally abolished until a law of emperor Arcadius given at Constantinople on 7 December 396.[22] It is clear from the epigraphy that continuity of cult existed at Touron until at least 396 when the series of cultic inscriptions comes to an end.[23]

Synchronisms in the epigraphy suggest that the cult of Zeus Madbachos was suppressed in or before 407. An inscription of 407 on a house lintel at Kharab Shaykh Barakat, which adjoins the temenos, proclaims: 'One God and his Christ.' It was erected by a Christian presbyter named Rufinianos who evidently officiated in one of the nearby villages.[24] The temenos is devoid of dated Christian inscriptions; one finds only a fragment with the expression 'Help (Greek cross in circle) Lord!'[25] It is not coincidental that One God inscriptions also appear at three neighbouring villages in 407/8 (present-day Shaykh Sulayman, Burj al-Qas and Surqanya):[26] the synchronism implies that Christian monotheism became a dominant cultural force in the district in consequence of the final closure of the great temenos, with a *terminus ante quem* of 406/7. The initiative for this may have come in the last years of Flavian of Antioch (381–404) during whose patriarchate monks are known to have settled in the slopes of Jabal Shaykh Barakat.[27] Later, in 419/20, another inscription turns up at the village of Teledan (present-day Tell 'Adeh), which lies on a lower slope of the mountain: it contains the anti-Julianic formula on the victory of the cross: 'This (Chi-Rho) conquers'.

Other divinities were worshipped in the *territorium* of Antioch, such as the ancestral gods Seimos and Symbaitylos mentioned in an inscription on the olive press at Kafr Nabu and Qal'at Kaluta: [28]

> The olive press (was made) for Seimos and Symbaitylos and Leon the ancestral gods with the entire construction (supported) by the revenues of the gods, through (the) curators Nomerios and Berion and Dareios and Klaudios the *advocatus*, and through Antonios and Sopatros the marble workers, and Gaios and Seleukos the carpenters. May Dometianos (the) carpenter be remembered! It was completed and consecrated in the year 272 (of the era of Antioch = AD 224). Theoteknos is he who wrote (this).

Temples elsewhere had oil presses and manufactures, such as the great temple at Baitokaike in Phoenice.[29] The identities and functions of these gods are now more fully understood, thanks to a recent epigraphic finds at Qal'at Kaluta in Jabal Sim'an that refer to the first-named divinity as Zeus Seimos.[30] He was quite clearly a Baal, a sky god responsible for bringing rainfall to parched fields, whose epiphany was a *baitylos* or meteoric stone.[31] Symbaitylos is more difficult to classify: she may well have been Seimos' female consort or companion; her name means 'with the *baitylos*' (*syn* and *baitylos*).[32] The Aramaic word *bait* meant more broadly the 'house' of a god, whether it lay in a numinous stone or in a formally consecrated temple.[33] The appearance of their names together on an olive press also associates them with the olive harvest and the agricultural cycle in general, so perhaps Symbaitylos was the local fertility goddess of the soil. It is not known when the public cult of these divinities died out, but it probably has a chronology similar to that of Zeus Madbachos at Jabal Shaykh Barakat, with a *terminus ante quem* near 407. Inferences from the archaeology and inscriptions at other known sites of temples in the Limestone Massif suggest a similar chronology.

Ignazio Peña has pointed to the existence of an oracular shrine at Magharat al-Malaab on a mountain peak in the Jabal Sim'an. He observes:[34]

> It consists of four rooms or halls, carved out of the rock within a spacious enclosure marked off by drystone walls indicating the boundaries of the sacred area. The [hall of sacrifices] … has four windows in the east wall … There is a rectangular cavity excavated in the centre. Because this cavity is shallow, it was probably an altar upon which sacrifices were made in honour of the pagan divinity. A niche in the altar probably held the statue of the deity … The oracular hall consists of a room (perhaps a consulting room) leading into a dark corridor – the *adyton* … The purpose of these rock rooms is not clear. It is more than probable that this was a sanctuary, a pilgrimage centre, administered by a group of priests, specialists in oracular rituals.

The site does not seem to have any pre-Christian inscriptions. In consequence it is difficult to surmise the name of the divinity that was thought to provide the oracles, unless it was the Apollo of Daphne who turns up elsewhere in the pre-Christian epigraphy of the Antiochene.[35]

Most known temples were constructed in the second and third centuries AD, at a time when olive monoculture was becoming an important factor in the economic life of the Antiochene. Some of them remained sites of public sacrifice until the later fourth century. Pagan funerary installations where their epigraphy mentions divinties or other features of pre-Christian cult are included in the following somewhat expanded regional list:[36]

Table I. Temples reported in the epigraphy.

Divinity	Structure	Site	District	Date
Zeus Tourbarachos	votive bas relief	Srir	Jabal Barisha	131
Zeus Seimos	*peribolos*	Qal'at Kaluta	Jabal Sim'an	135
–	temple	Babisqa	Jabal Barisha	143
–	*naos*	Me'ez	Jabal Barisha	157
Tyche	*naos*	Me'ez	Jabal Barisha	157
Zeus Bomos	temple	Baqirha	Jabal Barisha	161
–	temple	Baqirha	Jabal Barisha	162/3
–	temple	Srir?	Jabal Barisha	2nd c.?
Zeus Beleos	altar?	Tell 'Arr	*territorium* of Beroea	2nd c.
–	*naos*	Banqusa	–	213/4
Zeus Bomos	temenos	Burj Baqirha	Jabal Barisha	224

Table 1 continued.

Divinity	Structure	Site	District	Date
Helios	altar	between Brad	Jabal Sim'an & Miyasa	224/5
Helios *et alii*	nekropolis (?)	Dar 'Azza	Jabal Sim'an	235/6
–	temple stoa	Burj Baqirha	Jabal Barisha	238
Zeus Tourbarachos	votive bas relief	Srir	Jabal Barisha	243
Zeus Koryphaios	temple	Touron	Orontes valley	367/8

The connection between pre-Christian funerary practice and cult is suggested by two inscriptions found at Rab'ayta in Jabal Barisha dated to AD 153/4. The second of these indicates that sacrifices to the locally worshipped divinity, in this case Helios, guaranteed the inheritance agricultural and developed land in a will. The suggested restorations in the last clause are provisional:[37]

> In the yea[r] 20[2] (of the era of Antioch) on the 30[th] (day) of Deis[ios]. Apo[ll]as himself consecrated sacrifices to ancestral Helios, in order that the man surnamed Ach(illeus?) and my father should have th[e l]and (consisting of) 32 feet of olive (trees) [on which] the tomb (*mnemeion*) is and that they should have the (land) left untilled in accordance with the same measurement on which I established all the (buildings?) with my (moveable possessions?) for all time.

This paticular landholding appears to have been devoted to olive monoculture.

Temple conversions occurred in the Antiochene Limestone Massif, as they did elsewhere throughout the Mediterranean, during the later phases of Christianisation. At the village level they are an important archaeological indicator of the institutional lapse of a pre-Christian cults. Temple conversions are not always announced in the epigraphy. Often they are indicated by the incorporation of spolia from dismantled pagan temple buildings and altars into dated Christian churches, thereby giving a clear *terminus ante quem* for the end of the worship of the pagan divinity at the site. This is borne out by literary texts which indicate that, in the fourth and early fifth centuries, there was normally continuity of pagan cult in some form straight through until the closure of the temple. Examples include the Sarapaion at Alexandria, the temple of Zeus at Apamea, the rural temples implicitly referred to in Libanius' *Pro Templis* and the Marneion at Gaza in Palaestina Prima. The known examples in the *territorium* of Antioch should be added to F. W. Deichmann's list.[38] They include:[39]

Table II. Temple conversions.

Pre-Christian object	Christian building	Site	District	Date
Spolia	church	Qal'at Kaluta	Jabal Sim'an	c.387
Spolia	church	Touron	Orontes plain	c.396
Funerary inscription	Iulianos basilica	Brad	Jabal Sim'an	399–402
Altar fragment	Iulianos basilica	Brad	Jabal Sim'an	399–402
Spolia	East Church	Babisqa	Jabal Barisha	401
Temenos of gods	house	Kh. Sh. Barakat	Jabal Sim'an	407

The temple conversion at Babiqsa is known from the fact that spolia from a temple were built into the East Church or Markianos basilica.[40] The temenos lying outside the village of Dayr Sayta remained abandoned until the early medieval period, when a small fortress was built on its foundations.[41] The oracular shrine at Magharat al-Malaab was eventually converted into a monastery after a Christian holy man became a hermit there, following the usual practice.[42] The *terminus post quem* for this is the late fourth century:[43]

> The *bama* of Magharat al-Malaab was abandoned at the end of the 4th century and later transformed into a monastery. The funerary chapel, cut in the rock in this second period, is noteworthy … Three of the walls are lined by 28 paired sepulchres, a number that gives an idea of the importance the monastery acquired. On the walls, as on those of the hall of sacrifices and the hall of oracles, are engraved more than a hundred graffiti: crosses, overlapping squares, short Syriac inscriptions, etc., an indication of the passage of Christian pilgrims. In fact, a holy hermit, whose fame and veneration eclipsed that of the pagan gods, lived here, probably in the tower (4 x 3 m) built of irregular stones on a hill some hundred metres east of the oracle hall.

The participants in the pre-Christian religious life of the Antiochene are known mostly from the epigraphy. The media of the inscriptions include house lintels, funerary monuments, sarcophagi and the temple at Touron, which continued to operate as a shrine, like the temenos at Jabal Shaykh Barakat, until at least the end of the fourth century.

II. The Pre-Christian Population of the Antiochene

The end of sacrifices at the temenos sites did not preclude the practice of private ritual by families of agriculturalists, as Libanius' oration *Pro templis* makes clear.[44] This is corroborated by a considerable number of inscriptions, which suggest that the acceptance of Christianity was not immediately universal in the Antiochene. The main sequence belongs to the fourth century but does not come to an end until near the end of the fifth. There is accompanying epigraphic evidence to suggest that adults were being baptised into the new religion until at least the end of the fifth century. Let us consider this evidence by first tabulating the data and then looking at the more detailed texts. Inscriptions of this category in the *territorium* of Beroea-Aleppo and the so-called *limes* of Chalkis (which the editors of *IGLS* designate as the Chalkidike) marked with an asterisk (*):[45]

Table III. Inscriptions without Christian symbols.

Structure	Features	Site	District	Date
Lintel	no cross, onomastics	Brad	Jabal Sim'an	207/8
Sarcophagus	no cross, onomastics	Tell 'Aqibrin	Jabal Sim'an	213
Block	no cross	Wadi Naba	–	219/20

Table 3 continued.

Structure	Features	Site	District	Date
Sarcophagus	no cross, onomastics	Tillokbara	Jabal Halaqa	222
Fragment	no cross	Khirbat Hady	Jabal Barisha	222
Sarcophagus	no cross, onomastics	Silfaya	Jabal Barisha	224
Sarcophagus	no cross, onomastics	Kafr 'Aruq	Jabal Barisha	228
Funerary block	no cross, onomastics	Kfayr	Jabal al-'Ala	230
Andron	no cross	Qalbluza	Jabal Barisha	231
Tomb	no cross	Kuwaru	Jabal Dueili	235
House	no cross	Kh. Sh. Barakat	Jabal Sim'an	236
Lintel	no cross, onomastics	Khirbat Khaldia	Jabal Sim'an	239/40
Tomb	subterranean gods	Qatura	Jabal Sim'an	240
Tomb	no cross	Brad	Jabal Sim'an	250/1
Tomb	no cross	Me'ez	Jabal Barisha	252/3
House	no cross	Simkhar	Jabal Sim'an	272/3
House	no cross	Dar Qita	Jabal Barisha	296/7
House?	No cross, onomastics	Brad	Jabal Sim'an	296/7
House	no cross, onomastics	Kafr Nabu	Jabal Sim'an	308
Tomb	no cross	Burdaqli	Jabal Halaqa	310
Tomb	no cross, onomastics	Dana	Jabal Halaqa	324
Lintel	no cross	Telanissos	Jabal Sim'an	334/5
Pedestal	no cross	Kaukanaya	Jabal Barisha	335
Tomb	no cross, onomastics	Juwaniya	Jabal al-'Ala	340
Temple	'one god' (pagan)	Touron	Orontes plain	351
House lintel	pre-Xn. eight petal cross	Babisqa	Jabal Barisha	352
Tomb	no cross	Darkush	Orontes plain	352
Tomb	no cross	Urim al-Jauz	Jabal Riha	354-444
Tomb	no cross, onomastics	al-Mugharrat	–	357/8
Tomb	no cross, onomastics	Kuwaru	Orontes plain	359
Temple	votive offering	Touron	Orontes plain	364/5
Temple	Zeus Koryphaios	Touron	Orontes plain	367/8
Tomb	no cross, onomastics	Riha	Jabal Wastani	c.386?
Tomb	no cross, onomastics	Riha	Jabal Wastani	386
House lintel	crosses added later	Babisqa	Jabal Barisha	389
House lintel	no cross, onomastics	Qatura	Jabal Sim'an	391
Temple	votive offering	Touron	Orontes plain	395
House lintel	no cross	Khirbat Tazin	Jabal Barisha	402
–	no cross	Fidra	Jabal Sim'an	411
Tomb	no cross, onomastics	Riha	Jabal Wastani	421/2
Porch of villa	no cross	Ruwayha	Jabal Wastani	426?
Stone in wall	no cross	Jibrin*	Beroea / *terr.*	427
Colonnade	no cross	Dar Qita	Jabal Barisha	436
House lintel	no cross	Kafr Nabu	Jabal Sim'an	445/6
Balustrade	no cross	Me'ez	Jabal Barisha	458/9
House	no cross	Qatura	Jabal Sim'an	476
Structure	Features	Site	District	Date
Tomb	no cross, onomastics	Hazra	Jabal Halaqa	462
House	no cross, onomastics	Hazra	Jabal Halaqa	480/1

Table 3 continued.

Structure	Features	Site	District	Date
Lintel	no cross	Sarmada	Jabal Halaqa	482/3
House lintel	no cross	Kfellusin	Jabal Halaqa	487
Tomb	no cross, onomastics	Sughana	Jabal al-A'la	494
Tomb?	No cross, onomastics	Gaboula*	*territorium* of Beroea	512

The inscriptions in the list belong mostly either to burials or house lintels, except those from the temple at Touron. None of them has a cross except a problematical text from Babisqa that has a peculiar eight-petal cross that may or may not be Christian.[46] This stands in dramatic contrast to the sequence of the Christian 'one God' inscriptions that begins in the *territorium* of Antioch in 330.[47] It worth noting the dictum enunciated by the editors of the *Monumenta Asiae Minoris Antiqua* that 'the onus of proof is in every doubtful case on the Christian epigraphist,' if he wishes to show that a particular inscription is Christian when the symbols, theophoric names and other features of the new religion are lacking.[48] The inscriptions without crosses in the present list are difficult to identify as specifically Christian on any ground, except for the fact that they were erected in villages that were becoming Christian in the fourth and fifth centuries. This is not in itself a convincing argument for taking them as expressions of nascent Christianity because they are for the most part non-cultic. It must be recognised that, for local incisers of inscriptions, there may at times have been no particular reason for expressing religious belief, but this would neverthless have been odd in light of vivid Christian views expressed elsewhere. It should be remembered that there are dated inscriptions in other provinces, including Syria II and Phoenice Libanensis where inscriptions lacking Christian symbols and phrases persist as late as AD 540.[49]

The literary sources begin to mention Christianity in the *territorium* of Antioch only in the early in the fourth century. The first known Christian church, a *domus ecclesia*, may have been constructed at Qirqbiza in Jabal al-'Ala before 313.[50] The earliest known Christian inscription dates from 326/7, a lintel on which 'Jesus Christ' appears in the vocative case.[51] If this date is taken as a diachronic 'caesura', it is possible to make some generalisations about the cultural *koine* expressed in the pre-Christian inscriptions in the list. This is particularly important, because, as has been recognised, many of the conventions found in these texts were carried over to and persisted in the Christian epigraphy during the fourth century.

III. ONOMASTICS AND ADHERENCE TO CHRISTIANITY

Onomastics in the *territorium* of Antioch pose a particularly difficult problem. The epigraphy of this period abounds in Semitic, unusual, orthographically degraded, or peculiar Greek and Latin names that seem at first sight to be out of place in the early Christian and bilingual Greek-Syriac environment. The existence of Latin names can be explained by the settlement of Roman veterans on lands in the Antiochene.[52] There is a bilingual inscription of this type in the Limestone Massif, at Qatura (Jabal Sim'an). The *nomen* Flavius gives the inscription a pre-Constantinian date, probably in the second century AD:[53]

> Titus Flavius Iulianus a veteran of the VIII Augusta legion consecrated his perpetual tomb to the subterranean deities and to the daemons of himself and his wife for his heirs and their offspring, in order that no one should be able in any manner to alienate the tomb. And you.

At Burdaqli there is a funerary inscription of AD 310 from the time of the Tetrarchy: '[Date] Oualerios Rhomyllos a veteran who was brought back from Upper Pannonia made a sarcophagus, with his wife'.[54] The inscription implies that the man came originally from the village. Veterans thereafter disappear from the epigraphy of the Antiochene. The inscriptions in Cagnat's selection give a predictable idea of the types of Latin and Semitic names that were common among army veterans in Syria and Arabia,[55] whose children were then given varieties of Greek, Latin and Arabic names.[56] Many typically Syrian and Syro-Latin names appear in Cagnat's sample, including Alexandros, Bassos, Magnos, Maior, Malchos, Markos, Maxeimos and Roufeinos. Quasi-Jewish names sometimes appear in pre-Christian contexts. There is always the possibility that these Semitic names, which resemble Christian names of biblical origin, are purely a consequence of local onomastics and have nothing to do with the spread of Christianity or Judaism. Select examples from the epigraphy of the Antiochene will clarify these points.

1. At Riha (Jabal Zawiya), a burial of AD 386 was made in a shared tomb that also has a second monotheistic inscription that lacks a cross. A house builder named Sekoundinos completed both tombs. The seemingly pagan inscription runs: 'The sons of the brothers Pamanos, Theoteknos and Artebanos completed the tomb.'[57] Two of the names are of Iranian origin. It is hardly possible to accept W. K. Prentice's conjecture that the 'brothers' were monks; instead we have to reckon with the possibility that interregional migration explains the unusual personal names. It is difficult to attach a Christian significance to the onomastics in this instance.
2. At Babisqa (Jabal Barisha), a house lintel inscription of April 389 has an assortment of crudely cut Christian symbols that overlay part of the text: two Chi-Rho ligatures, a cross-inscribed in a circle and an eight-petal cross in a square. They were clearly added later, to advertise the conversion of a family or its son to Christianity. The inscription contains a peculiar mixture of Semitic, Greek and quasi-biblical names: 'Cherillos son of Gabronos, Eusebis the architect and Athenis, in the year 437 (of the era of Antioch) on the seventh day of the month of Xandikos. Jacob son (of Cherillos).'[58] There were no other Christians in the village before this time, so it is difficult to read the text as having originally been Christian before the symbols were added.
3. The villages in the north-eastern part of Jabal Sim'an have a large proportion of Greek, Latin and Semitic names. In some instances there is continuity in onomastics straight through into the Christian period. The sites in this cluster, specifically

Batuta, Brad, Burj al-Haydar, Fafirtin, Kafr Antin, Kafr Nabu, Qal'at Kaluta and Shaykh Sulayman, are cases in point. House lintels without crosses persist as late as 444/6. The onomastics in the inscriptions arranged in diachronic sequence look like this:[59] (see Table IV). Few other districts have the 'critical mass' of inscriptions to allow a survey of this type. The decisive shift in local onomastics took place between circa 363 and 487. The 'One God' formula, crosses and other Christian names and symbols began to appear on inscriptions at the beginning of this period, a sign that particular individuals were entering the Christian catechumenate. The disappearance of the peculiar Latin personal names occurred during the third century except for Romanos, which had spread broadly into the Syrian Christian *koine*. The decline of culturally pre-Christian names like Antiochos and Seleukos took longer, until the late fourth century. The Semitic names in this sample were a product of the post-Julianic period, from 363 onward, when the large-scale penetration of Christianity into the *territorium* seemingly acted as a catalyst in liberating submerged local cultures. Names associated with eastern Mediterranean saints, particularly Damianos, Ioannes, Kosmas, Sergios and Symeon, became common. The transitional period between the first Christian and last pagan inscriptions overlaps for a stretch of 82 years, between 363–445/6, and is consistent with the wider pattern indicated in Table II.

It is unknown precisely what local circumstances brought about this change in the north-eastern parts of Jabal Sim'an. Symeon Stylites the Elder ascended his pillar at Qal'at Sim'an only in 409, near the mid-point of the period in question.[60] His presence does not explain the beginnings of Christianisation, which had been in progress since at least 372 when Marianos the *periodeutes* or rural presbyter built the church at Fafirtin.[61] The next important date is 399–402 when the Ioulianos basilica was constructed at Brad. It may well have become the focal point of the nascent Christian communities in the north-eastern parts of Jabal Sim'an. This was finalised in an institutional sense with the permanent closure of the great temple of Zeus Madbachos on Jabal Shaykh Bararkat not later than 407 when 'one God' inscriptions begin to appear in the nearby villages.[62] In contrast to this pattern, it seems unlikely that Christianity made early inroads at Kafr Nabu, where it has been supposed that St. Acheos was an important figure in getting the villagers to accept the new religion sometime in the early to mid-fifth century.[63] The degraded orthography of his Greek name (Acheos < Achaios) is characteristic of the period down to 445/6.[64] H. C. Butler dated the village church there to the fourth century on stylistic grounds, but this is problematical in light of the epigraphy at Kafr Nabu, which took a conventionally Christian configuration only in the early sixth century, over a hundred years after the other villages in the north-eastern parts of Jabal Sim'an.[65] It is significant that the Sergonas named in the gateway inscription of 496 at Brad is characterised as 'newly created' (νεόκτιστος), a term that can reasonably taken to signify recent baptism.[66]

4. The inferences drawn about the emergence of Syriac culture find corroboration in the village of Burj al-Qas (Jabal Sim'an) where there is a bilingual 'one God' inscription in Greek and Syriac of AD 407. The Greek reads: 'One God and his Christ who helps all', whereas the Syriac reads simply '(cross) God the lord (cross)'

Table IV. Onomastics in northeastern Jabal Sim'an

PRE-CHRISTIAN PERIOD

Brad:

Lintel (AD 207)	Ourbikos, Andronikos and Markos, sons of Longinos
	Antonios and Sopatros, brothers
	Kassandros, from the village of Rhezitha
	Zebinos from the village of Kapro[---]
	Sopatros, stonecutter and inscriber

Qal'at Kaluta:

Temple (c. AD 224)	Aphrodisios, villager

Kafr Nabu:

Oil press (AD 224)	Nomerios, Berion, Dareios and Klaudios, curators of the village
	Antonios and Sopatros, marble workers
	Dometianos, Gaios and Seleukos, carpenters
	Theoteknos, inscriber
House (AD 308)	Seleukos, builder
House (AD 445/6)	Kyrionos

CHRISTIAN PERIOD

Batuta:

House (?) (AD 363)	Marianos and children, villagers
	Mariades and Saakonas, architects

Fafirtin:

Church (AD 372)	Antiochos, villager (?)
	Maris, *periodeutes*

Brad:

Block (4th–5th c.)	Theodotos and household, villagers

Kaluta:

Lintel (AD 387)	Antiochos and Theophilos, villagers

Brad:

Lintel (AD 400)	Ioulianos, housebuilder
	Marinos

Shaykh Sulayman:

House (AD 407)	Martyris and children, villagers

Brad:

North Church (5th c.)	John son of Malchion, George son of Sergios, Zokota son of Eutychios, villagers

Brad:

Gateway (AD 491)	Argyrios son of Pelagios, builder or householder
	Kosmas, artisan
Gateway (AD 496)	Kosmas and Symeonos, artisan
	Sergonas, newly baptised
	Romanos, Ioannes, Eustathios, villagers
	Sergios, inscriber

Table IV. continued.

Burj al-Haiydar:
Doorway (AD 487)   Simeo(n), villager

Kafr Nabu:
Building (AD 504/5)   Acheos, local saint

Kafr Antin:
Building (AD 523)   Damianos, builder

Kafr Nabu:
Martyrion (AD 525/6)   Abha, presbyter (in Syriac)

(*'alaha' mara'*).[67] The difference in phrasing between the texts confirms the supposition that the 'one God' formula was more a product of the culturally Greek elements in Antiochene rural society and was a consequence of the anti-Julianic focus that the patriarchate of Antioch acquired in the later fourth century. The onomastics at Burj al-Qas combine the new and the old in greater extremes than was seen in the villages in the north-eastern parts of Jabal Sim'an. A Greek lintel inscription of AD 493 gives a list of names: '(Chi-Rho) [date] In the time of Raboulas, Barapsas, Bardas, Kosmas and Leonidas'.[68] The classical 'Leonidas' is a sign that Atticising Greek names still enjoyed some currency in the later fifth century. Its religious significance is moot, however; all one can say is that it is synchronous with the last elements in the sedentary population the *territorium* of Antioch accepting Christianity.

5. A similar pattern is apparent at Baqirha (Jabal Barisha). The gate of a temple was dedicated to Zeus Bomos in AD 161. The dedicants have a combination of Greek theophoric and pre-Christian Aramaic names: Apollonios, Apollophanes, Chalmion and the family of Marion.[69] A sarcophagus bears the names of Apolinarios (*sic*) and his son on a sarcophagus that may also be of second-century date.[70] In the Christian period, Hellenized Syrian names prevail, some them with unusual orthography. A house completed in May 384 has the names Diakon and Mikalos on its lintel (?).[71] Unusual names still prevailed in the late fifth century: the lintel of a cloister gate completed in either 491 or 501 mentions Symeones the presbyter, Symeones son of Berlos and Symeones son of Maron.[72] One might suppose that the onomastics here reflect the influence or ownership of the monastery by that of Symeon Stylites the Elder at Qal'at Sim'an. For example at Jibrin in the *territorium* of Beroea this saint is depicted on a column whose inscription reads: 'Abraames (cross) son of Azizos. Saint Symeones' (late 5th-early 6th c.).[73] Abraames was the local stylite at Jibrin, and Symeon was known as 'Symeones' in the nearer desert steppe, a fact also reflected at a fairly distant site, Palmyra in the eastern part of Syria II, where a funerary inscription of AD 535 mentions a 'Symeones'.[74] The threefold recurrence of the name 'Symeones' at Baqirha can therefore only be understood as the effect of the famous stylite on Greek onomastics. There were many other monasteries in the Dana plain and surrounding hills, but little is known of them.[75]

6. Jabal Halaqa consists of the high ground surrounding the Dana plain to the north and west. It has one of the earliest known 'one God' inscriptions at Sarmada,[76] and one of the latest inscriptions without a cross at Harza: '[---] to all in the year 530 (of the era of Antioch). Herodis the artisan built it'.[77] The latter is found on a lintel and dates from AD 480/1. It seems not to be Christian, for another inscription apparently mentioning the same builder has been emended to give him a pagan theophoric as his patronymic Ph-s-lona, which may be derived from the divine name Aphlad.[78] The absence of a cross, coupled with Herodis' classical Greek name and Aramaic patronymic, suggest that he was not a Christian. It is quite possible that the man came as a migrant labourer from another locality.

7. The inscription at Sughana runs: 'In the year 543 (of the era of Antioch [= AD 494]) on the second day of the month of Apellaios, Antichianos the artisan made (it). It is the tomb of Markos and Luona'.[79] In the Christian inscriptions, personal names of this type would be extraordinarily unusual at such a late date, when we would expect to find either biblical or Greek and Syriac theophoric names. Markos falls into this category but Luona does not.

8. The latest example was found in the dry salt lake of Gaboula (present-day al-Jabbul) and dates from AD 512 and runs: 'In the year 824 (of the Seleucid era). [Ba]rsagaris [and] Sergis sons of Masika. Seventeenth (day) [in the month of] Dystros.'[80] The men named in the inscription seem to have been Arabs. The name Sergis was normally a Christian one by this early sixth century, but its use by pagan Arab pastoralists living on the desert fringe cannot be excluded.

It will only be through the critical analysis of this corpus of theologically ambiguous inscriptions that final conclusions can be drawn. It is the working hypothesis of this paper that most of these texts will eventually be shown to be pre-Christian.

There is circumstantial evidence that adult pagans were accepting baptism all through the fifth century. This is evident from the construction of baptistries between the late fourth to mid-sixth centuries, and by references to newly baptised adults in the epigraphy. The inscription on a gateway built at Brad (Jabal Sim'an) in 496 refers to one of its builders as Sergonas the 'newly created' (νεόκτιστος), a clear reference to adult baptism.[81] There is a similar expression found in the epigraphy of the Syrian diaspora, the term *neophōtistos* or 'newly illuminated', which invariably refers to persons newly baptised.[82] It occurs in the inscriptions of migrants from the villages of Syria II in the town of Iulia Concordia, which lies directly west of Aquileia, the provincial capital of Venetia et Histria in north-western Italy.[83] The inscriptions are undated but appear to belong to the late fourth and early fifth centuries. A baptistery at Apamea, the provincial capital of Syria II, is referred to in a mosaic inscription of AD 455 or 470 as a φωτιστήριον or 'place of illumination',[84] as is another of unknown provenance from the earliest phase of Christianising the countryside in the archiepiscopate of Markellos of Apamea (c. AD 380–90), who showed excessive zeal in this task.[85] It suggests that baptisteries were normally built only where a large college of presbyters and deacons was in place:[86]

> When the most pious Markellos was (arch)bishop (and) in the days of the most worthy presbyters Palladios and Eusebios, the church was built from

the foundations up with the baptistery (φωτιστήριον)and reliquary chamber (μαρτύριον), including all the ornamentation, by the exertion of Euphrasios the deacon and *oikonomos* and of the other deacons.

The plausibility of adult baptisms in the later fifth century is reinforced by epigraphic evidence from Tiaret in Mauretania Caesariensis, where two inscriptions use the formula *acceptus est* (*apud deum*), which could refer to baptisms administered at the point of death. One of the deceased, Propertia Gududia, has a Punic cognomen.[87]

IV. CHRISTIANISATION

In turning to the Christianisation of the *territorium* of Antioch, I will begin by commenting on the sequence of inscriptions containing triumphalist phrase 'one God and his Christ'. It seems quite doubtful that it was ever intended to express a specific position on either Arian or Christological questions, for the simple reason that the phrase was in continuous use over too long a period of time for it to apply to any particular controversy. Another difficulty is the fact that Eusebius of Caesarea occasionally uses the phrase in his life of Constantine and church history in contexts designed to contrast the Christian belief with the polytheistic *mentalité* of religious behaviour in the Tetrarchic period. Finally, there was the Christian usage of the 'one God' phrase as a liturgical feature of temple conversions during the fourth to sixth centuries, where its anti-polytheistic polemical force should be reasonably obvious.[88]

A central question is when, where and how what became the anti-Julianic phrase 'one God and his Christ' was used, and what its significance was *vis-à-vis* the acclamation 'one God only'. These expressions and many similar turns of phrase may have originated in or have been inspired by letters Constantine the Great sent to the provincial bishops, of whom Eusebius of Caesarea was one. The latter mentions a letter dispatched not long after the destruction of Licinius in 323 in which Constantine 'eloquently exhorts his subjects to acknowledge the God over all things, and openly to profess their allegiance to *his Christ* as their saviour' (λογιώτερον τοὺς ἀρχομένους προτρέπων, τὸν ἐπὶ πάντων Θεὸν γνωρίζειν αὐτόν τε τόν Χριστὸν αὐτοῦ διαππήδην ἐπιγράφεσθαι σωτῆρα)[89] Elsewhere Eusebius observes that '[Constantine] truly maintained a continual testimony to *the Christ of God*' (ὁ Χριστὸς τοῦ Θεοῦ)[90] who had appeared to him in a dream on the eve of the battle of the Milvian bridge.[91] In the latter instance, which is based on a conversation that took place between Constantine and Eusebius, and was confirmed by an oath, 'Christ of God' (from which 'his Christ' is derived) seems to have been emperor's own phrase.

Whether these were the actual words of the emperor, as seems probable, or were instead ideological structures configured by Eusebius' desire to 'invent' a Christian empire, the phrases found an important place in the Greek Christianity of the Antiochene. The absolute *terminus post quem* for these acclamations to have got in circulation would have been 337–339, when the final recension of Eusebius' life of Constantine was published. Other phrases abound such as 'the one and only God' (Θεὸς ὁ εἷς καὶ μόνος) when Eusebius comments on Constantine's Tricennalia.[92] This question is clarified to some extent by a tabulation of the dated instances in which it appears in the Antiochene Limestone Massif, and also in the parts round Beroea-Aleppo and in the so-called *'limes* of Chalkis' or Chalkidike. The last named are marked below with an asterisk (*). It is of particular significance that Flavius Eusebius the imperial *singularius* who erected the first Christian inscription at Dar Qita in 350 used the expression 'one God and his Christ, be a helper.'[93] It has been observed that[94]

> Eusebius evidently accepted Christianity during the later years of Constantine the Great in the East and took the fashionable *praenomen* Flavius as the sign of his politics and religious faith, and then brought it with him to Dar Qita as its first Christian citizen.

The expression 'one God' runs like a leitmotif though Eusebius' life of Constantine and, it would seem, became one of the key acclamations of rural Greek Christian vernacular culture, along with the use of the Chi-Rho, the victory symbol par excellence.

It should be remembered that the expression 'one God and his Christ' had a particular signification in Antiochene Christianity. Its flexibility was so great that it could be used allusively, as when in 358 Constantius II exiled Liberius patriarch of Rome (my italics). Theodoret of Cyrrhus remarks:[95]

> The edict of the emperor was read in the circus, and the multitude shouted that the imperial ordinance was just; that the spectators were divided into two factions, each deriving its name from its own colours, and that each faction would now have its own bishop. After having thus ridiculed the edict of the emperor, they all exclaimed with one voice, *'One God, one Christ, one bishop.'* I have deemed it right to set down their precise words. Some time after [the] Christian people had uttered these pious and righteous acclamations, the holy Liberius returned...

The acclamation 'one God and his Christ', from which the circus factions had mockingly derived their own acclamation, had been in circulation in the Antiochene already from at least 341/2, to judge from the house lintel inscription at Sarmada given below.[96] In the fourth-century context treated by Theodoret, the expression was 'pious', that is anti-Arian and anti-imperial; in the contemporary context of his ecclesiatical history, it was proto-Chalcedonian and therefore 'orthodox', for otherwise he would not have quoted it in this work, whose date of composition has a *terminus post quem* of 440.

The expression 'one God only' may go back to the time of Constantine the Great, appearing for example in Theodoret's hagiographic narrative about the conversion of the royal family of Iberia c. 333:[97]

> [The queen] made known to [the king] the *power* of that God whom the captive [woman St. Nina] adored, and besought him to acknowledge the *one only God*, and to erect a church to him, and to lead all the nation to worship him.

The 'power of God and Christ' is celebrated in a Christian funerary inscription at Kaukanaya in Jabal Barisha in 384.[98]

The inscriptions of the Antiochene have one other connection with Constantine's religious views that has so far been overlooked: the prayer prescribed for the soldiery to recite on Sunday (τοιαῦτα κατὰ τὴν τοῦ φωτὸς ἡμέραν ἐομοθέτει πράττειν τὰ στρατιωτικὰ τάγματα) uses key phrases that also turn up in the inscriptions: 'We know only you as God. We acknowledge you as emperor. *We call upon you as helper.* From you we received *victories* ...'(σὲ μόνον οἴδαμεν Θεόν· σὲ βασιλέα γνωρίζομεν· σὲ βοηθὸν ἀνακαλούμεθα· παρὰ σοῦ τὰς νίκας ἠπάμεθα).[99] Christ is frequently referred to as 'helper' in the inscriptions, normally with the present active participle, and different species of victory formulae appear as well. This may go back to the settlement of veteran soldiers on lands in the Limestone Massif, men who had the same ideological predilections as Flavius Eusebius the imperial *singularius* and landowner of Dar Qita in Jabal Barisha. For the present the epigraphic data come down only as late as the reigns of Galerius, Maximinus Daia and Licinius, the last of the pagan Tetrarchs, but it should be remembered that Constantine was the last and greatest exponent of the Diocletianic system.

These acclamations undoubtedly differed from the range of meanings the expression 'one God' had, for example, in Palestine I, II and III, where it was neither 'typically Christian' nor necessarily always of Jewish origin.[100] The different parameters have to be carefully considered, as with the building complex at Qana in South Arabia where a 'one God' inscription of possibly Jewish outlook has been discovered.[101] The 'one God' inscriptions of Syria I include:[102]

Table V. Dated 'One God' Inscriptions.

Formula	Epigraphic context	Site	Date
One God who is capable of all things	stone	Balqis-Zeugma*	325
One God.	capital	Qarqaniya	330
Christ of God help! One God only.	house lintel	Qatura	336/7
One God and his Christ.	house lintel	Sarmada	341/2
One God only.	–	Kaukan	349
One God ΙΧΘΥΣ	house lintel	Simkhar	349/50
One God and his Christ, be a helper.	agora	Dar Qita	350
One God who helps.	gate	Dar Qita	355
ΙΧΘΥΣ Logos.	medallion	Baqirha	360/1
One God only. ΙΧΘΥΣ	tomb	Kuwaru	361/2
One God and his Christ, help of the unfortunate man.	sarcophagus	'Arshin	363
One God and his Christ who helps Marianos and his children.	–	Batuta	363
One God and his Christ who helps.	church	Fafirtin	372
One God who helps those who fear him.	–	Juwaniya	374
One God only.	near pagan tomb	Urim al-Jauz	376/7
One God and his Christ.	house	Kaukanaya	378
One God only who helps.	block from pagan tomb	Ruwayha	384/5
One God only.	tomb	Riha	386
One God who helps us and his Christ.	baptistery	Babisqa	390
One God and his Christ who helps.	house lintel	'Arshin	392

Table V: continued.

Formula	Epigraphic context	Site	Date
One God and his Christ who helps Eboulos.	lintel	'Arshin	392
One God only who helps all his friends.	tomb	Juwaniya	398
One God and his Christ.	church	Kfar Dar 'Azza	399/400
One God who helps all.	church	Babisqa	403/4
One God and his Christ and the Holy Spirit	–	Shaykh Sulayman	406/7
One God and his Christ.	house?	Surqanya	406/7
One God and his Christ.	house	Kh. Sh. Barakat	407
One God and his Christ who helps all.	–	Burj al-Qas	407
One God against the whole [cosmos?]	monastic cell	Burj Za'rur*	410/11
One God who helps all.	lintel	Dayr Sayta	411 or 412
One God and his Christ and the Holy Spirit.	Church of Paul and Moses	Dar Qita	418
One God and his Christ.	door frame	Fidra	421
One God and his Christ and the Holy Spirit.	church courtyard	Dar Qita	431
God a helper	–	Banqusa	436/7
ΙΧΘΥΣ, Chi-Rho	lintel	Rafada	439
One God and his Christ	lintel	Dar Qita	456
One God and his Christ.	House XI	Dar Qita	452
One God and his Christ.	lintel	Dar Qita	462
One God and his Christ and the Holy Spirit help(s).	church lintel	Dana	483/4
One God and his Christ.	house	Dar Qita	485
One God and his Christ.	church	Kaluta	492
ΙΧΘΥΣ helps	tower	Zarzita	500
One God and his Christ, help the cosmos.	baptistery	Dar Qita	515/6
One God	lintel	Kaukaba	540/1
One God & his Christ & the Holy Spirit help.	Church of St. Sergios	Dar Qita	537

This survey, which is not entirely complete because of absence of undated inscriptions, is highly suggestive. It demonstrates that the acclamation shouted by the crowds in Antioch had been in popular use since 341/2.[103] In one instance, a former civil servant, Flavius Eusebius a *singularius*, an employee of the Praetorian Prefect, used it when he completed building the agora at Dar Qita in 350.[104] The formula is repeated twice in 363, the year of Julian's death, at Batuta (Jabal Sim'an) and 'Arshin (Jabal Barisha).[105] The largest cluster of inscriptions using the expression is concentrated between 390–407, when it turns up eight times. As should be apparent from Table II, this cluster of 'One God and his Christ' inscriptions corresponds closely to the period of temple conversions in the Antiochene, whose *termini* are AD 387–407. This is also the period during which other types of Christian inscriptions first begin to appear in the villages of the Limestone Massif. Down to the reign of Julian the acclamation was used mostly in private contexts, on house lintels, private building projects and even burial inscriptions. As late as 363 a man could use it in a very personal way, 'One God and his Christ, help of the unfortunate man [in death]'.[106] There were alternate ways of expressing the same general concept, as for example with the acronym ΙΧΘΥΣ, which is apparent in the dated inscriptions between the *termini* of AD 349/50 – 500.[107]

The use of the formula 'one God and his Christ' became a regular feature of the epigraphy at Dar Qita and accounts for a sizeable part of the overall number of Christian inscriptions there, appearing in AD 350, 418, 431, 452, 456, 462, 485, 515/6 and 537, and becoming a fixed feature of local culture.[108] It has been supposed that Dar Qita became the estate of a monastery or of the patriarchate of Antioch, resulting from a legacy of the family of Flavius Eusebius the *singularius*.[109] Whether this can be definitively shown to be the case or not, the *termini* AD 418–537 may well correspond to the protracted final phase of Christianisation in the Limestone Massif, as suggested in the list of inscriptions without crosses in Table III, with the flow of converts declining to a trickle in first quarter of the sixth century, a phenomenon symbolised by the construction of a baptistery at Dar Qita in 515/6.[110] An undated law (*inter* 472–529) published in the *Codex Iustinianus* in 534 required the baptism of all Roman citizens and slaves.[111] The disuse of the 'one God and his Christ' formula after 537 at Dar Qita may well be an expression of confidence *ex silentio* that the last of the sedentary residents of the Dana plain and Jabal Barisha had all become baptised Christians. Its apparently official or semi-official use at Dar Qita and other villages between 350–537 casts doubt on the supposition sometimes mooted that the formula has a reference point in the Trinitarian or Christological controversies; it transcends these issues because of its long use, and is monotheistic pure and simple.

Christian inscriptions make use of pagan acclamations as paradigms for monotheistic concepts. One sees this in a window lintel inscription at Radafa in Jabal Halaqa. The inscription runs: 'Jesus the Nazoreos (*sic*), the son of God begotten of Maria. He dwells here: nothing that is evil shall enter!'[112] The acclamation is a Christian transformation of an acclamation of the hero Herakles: 'Herakles the splendidly victorious child of Zeus dwells here: nothing evil shall enter!' Christ had become the 'new Herakles'. The personal name Herakles survived among pagans in some parts of Syria until the early fifth century, as we learn from an inscription of AD 409.[113]

This began to change with the demise of Julian, after which 'One God and his Christ' became a public expression of militant monotheistic religious fervour. The phrase began to be used particularly on the baptisteries constructed at Babisqa in 390 and at Dar Qita in 515/6,[114] making them the architectural symbols of the Christian victory over Hellenists like Julian and the theurgist Maximus of Ephesus, and in due course a symbol of final victory over the ancestral cults in the *territorium* of Antioch when the temenos of Zeus Madbachos was suppressed not long before 407. The baptistery built at Dar Qita in 515/6 is significant as part of the liturgical *koine* of the church of Antioch during the last stages of Christianisation in the countryside; its lintel was laid in the same year as the now famous inscription of the *martyrion* of St. George in Zorava in the province of Arabia, the first Christian building in the town.[115]

V. BAPTISTERIES

Baptistries were an important institutional symbol of the existence of Christian belief, especially as they were the focal point of the liturgical expression of the abandonment of pre-Christian belief and practice.[116] Baptisteries with dated inscriptions are quite rare in the Antiochene Limestone Massif. In addition to the buildings listed below, baptisteries have been identified at Qirqbiza in Jabal al-'Ala, and at Dahas (c. 500), Kasayjba (c. 414?) and Qasr Iblisu (431?) in Jabal Barisha.[117] The chronology of the epigraphically dated baptisteries corresponds to the middle and later phases of the appearance of the 'one God' inscriptions, after Christianity had achieved a clear institutional presence and the main sequence of baptisms was in progress:[118]

Formula	Symbols	Site	District	Date
One God and his Christ help us	Chi-Rho	Babisqa	Jabal Barisha	390
One God and his Christ	crosses	Dar Qita	Jabal Barisha	515/6
–	cross	Bashmishli	Jabal Barisha	536/7
The gate was built	cross	Dar Qita	Jabal Barisha	566/7

It is significant that the baptistery at Babisqa was constructed in 390, a decade before East Church was built between 401–406/7.[119] This suggests that the patriarchate of Antioch saw its first task as getting the rural congregations baptised; the remainder of the institutional framework could wait until additional funds and personnel could be found. It is far from clear that the presbyter and architect Markianos Kyris who supervised the construction of the two buildings was a permanent resident at Babisqa between 390–407/8,[120] for he is also named in a mosaic in the basilica at Brad (Jabal Sim'an)[121] and in another inscription of unknown provenance:[122]

> After making a vow, Markianos, together with his wife and child and Eusebia his daughter-in-law (?) laid the mosaic for the basilica with the apse at the time he was the most holy presbyter.

It therefore seems likely that Babisqa became a regular site for baptismal liturgies involving catechumens from all the villages surrounding the Dana plain in the decades after 390.

The construction of the later installations goes down to the time of the programme of Christianisation initiated by Justinian the Great and reported by John of Ephesus.[123] There is nothing in the epigraphy to suggest the continued presence of pagans in the Limestone Massif, but it cannot be excluded that these monumental buildings were being used as central shrines where Arab pastoralists came in from the desert steppe to the east of the Limestone Massif to receive baptism, as happened in the first quarter of the fifth century at Qal'at Sim'an.[124] They may well have been attracted to villages like Dar Qita where there was a small basilica dedicated to St. Sergios, a martyr specially revered by the Christian Arabs, and where a college of five presbyters existed, some of whom may have been Arabs to judge from the onomastics (John, Sergios, Danos, Bachchos and Rhamlys), when a second baptistery was erected in 566/7.[125]

VI. CHRISTIAN FUNERARY INSCRIPTIONS

Christian funerary inscriptions are not as frequent in the *territorium* of Antioch as building inscriptions, but begin at a relatively early date. When analysed with the 'one God' inscriptions tabulated above, they indicate settled communities with buildings and clear funerary customs.[126]

Table VI. Dated Christian Funerary Inscriptions.

Formula	Symbols	Site	District	Date
Alpha-omega	–	Kuwaru	Jabal Dueili	359
One God only	ΙΧΘΥΣ	Kuwaru	Jabal Dueili	361–2
Eusebios Christianos	crosses	Kaukanaya	Jabal Barisha	369
One God only	six-point cross[127]	Urim al-Jauz	Jabal Wastani	376/7
Power of God and Christ	–	Kaukanaya	Jabal Barisha	384
One God only who helps	–	Ruwayha	Jabal Wastani	384/5
Jesus (?) one God only	–	Riha	Jabal Zawiya	386
One God only who helps all his friends	–	Juwaniya	Jabal al-'Ala	398
Place (topos) of Alexandros	cross	Riha	Jabal Zawiya	422
–	cross	Kfar Lata	Jabal Wastani	449

It is noteworthy that the first known Christian burial at Riha in August 422 came only a year after the last pagan one in 421/2.[128] There was an earlier Christian burial in 386, but the same *heroeion* also accommodated what appears to be a pagan burial near the same date.[129] It may therefore be the case that the village was divided on matters of religious belief for a period of perhaps 35 years. Some Christian funerary inscriptions, although undated, require comment because of their use of florid and sometimes poorly spelled Greek. Most of these are situated in Jabal Zawiya, which was somewhat separated from the rest of the Antiochene Limestone Massif and susceptible to different cultural influences to judge from the onomastics. One such inscription is found at Urim al-Jauz in Jabal Zawiya (4th–5th c.?), which amongst other symbols has palm fronds and a Chi-Rho and Alpha-Omega inscribed in a circle:[130]

a. He built the (*heireon*) of Asterona(s) on behalf of the salvation of himself and of (his) brothers, and (he built) this tomb (*mnemeion*) as long as (?) theirs.
b. You are exalted, Aristonas, you have (Chi-Rho) made these (*sic*) tomb (*heroeion*), while your brothers are in death.
c. One God who helps all. Exalt (?) the better. Light. Life.

Sometimes Christians took over pagan funerary temples, as is the case with a burial mentioned in an inscription of 384/5 at Ruwayha:[131]

> One God only who helps. On behalf of the salvation and remembrance of the living. Bassimas and Mathbabea built (it) in the year 433 (of the era of Antioch).

These sites will require further study in light of recent archaeological exploration.

VII. CONCLUSION

The analysis given above was necessarily brief, and has to some extent simplified complex cultural processes that can be fully understood only through a careful analysis of the other categories of evidence, like the non-narrative data found in the extensive architecture of the Limestone Massif. It can be seen, however, that as historical evidence the epigraphy has more important uses than simply dating buildings. It is the one vehicle through which the religious consciousness of the ordinary rural people of the Antiochene can be reconstructed. Inscriptions are in every respect vernacular documents from which it is evident that the acceptance of Christianity was often a distinctly personal decision that flew in the face of the local loyalties to the cults of the ancestral gods and to the publicly perceived need to propitiate the divinities that brought rainfall and fertility to the soil. The intelligent variation in the way the epigraphy makes use of everyday Christian symbols and phrases is proof of the agriculturalists' sagacity in their choice of monotheism.

APPENDIX I.
PRE-CHRISTIAN RELIGIOUS CULT IN PHOENICE LIBANENSIS DURING AND AFTER THE REIGN OF CONSTANTINE (AD 306–337)

Christianity spread at a typical and sometimes optimal rate in the *territorium* of Antioch. It is therefore useful to identify comparative data in the epigraphy of the other Syrian provinces. There is already a preliminary study of the Apamene.[132] It is difficult to discover clear signs of a decline in the temple cults in the second half of the third century, particularly where certifiably Christian inscriptions are absent. The latter begin to appear only in the decades after Constantine's victory over Licinius in 323, which gave the Christian emperor control of the Roman Orient until his death in 337. We should therefore expect to see 'business as usual' in the temple cults.

    This is precisely the picture that emerges in the epigraphy. Four examples will suffice to prove that the old cults were living religious systems during the fourth century. A fifth cultic inscription from the province of Arabia is included as well.

1. *SEG* 39, 1565. Brahliya, Phoenice Libanensis (AD 321/2)
    'In the year 663 (of the Seleucid era), Anianos son of Heliodoros with his brothers and friends made a vow and dedicated an altar to Zeus Aktipegeos[133] and Apis Ouranios, at the time when seven springs broke forth, fostering children and mothers, when Herophilos was archon.'

2. *SEG* 18, 615. 'Arne, Phoenice Libanensis (AD 330)
    'On 25 Peritios in the year 641 (of the Seleucid era), the temple building of the god Zeus of the village of Ornea and (its) rooms [—], with the (other temple) precincts of the village were ornamented from the (funds) of the god himself.'

3. *SEG* 18, 612. Rakhle, Phoenice Libanensis (AD 360?)
    'In the year 570 (of the local era)[134] on 5 Loos, after Moithos the child of the goddess was besprinkled. A[..]aias son of Amaros, Ropalios son of Zabdas,

Moith[os] son of Abudaanas, Netioro[s] son of Silouanos, Sym[eon?] (and) Thole<m>os (?), the (board of) six (and) Am[....] son of Mabbogaios (and) O<b>baa[s] the administrators.'

4. *SEG* 18, 613. Rakhle, Phoenice Libanensis (c. AD 360 ?)[135]

'For a blessing of the goddess Leukothea during the headship of Be[elk]amos, through the administrators Mnaseas son of Ptolemeos and [..]na[.] son of [Theu]das and Amateos son of Beelibos and Sobeos [and Aeia]vo[s] sons of Beeliabos and Beeliabos son of Aeianou[s and ...]s son of Beelkamos and Phaleos son of Amreos [—].'

5. *SEG* 7, 1169. 'Orman, Arabia (AD 517)

'Zaidos, Klimos (and) Mokeimos of the tribe of Konenoi[136] attended to the purification, in the year 412 (of the province of Arabia).'

Appendix II.
Epigraphic Collections

The largest corpus of evidence on the *territorium* of Antioch is found in the reports of the Princeton University expedition to Syria in 1899, 1904–5 and 1909), and all subsequent studies have used these materials as a starting point, since they frequently provide photographs of the stones and offer contextual comments that sometimes affect the interpretation of the inscriptions. The volumes containing the Greek and Latin inscriptions of the *territorium* of Antioch were compiled and edited by W.K. Prentice (*AAES* III and *PAES* III B), and were in every respect a pioneering work. Prentice was working in the pre-modern age of Late Antique epigraphy, when there were few canons for interpreting the titulature and abbreviations for Late Roman imperial and ecclesiastical officials. Prentice's editions were updated, improved and reprinted in the early volumes of *Inscriptions grecques et latines de la Syrie*, edited by L. Jalabert and others (*IGLS*). New inscriptions were added to those found in the volumes of the Princeton Expedition, but no supplements were issued for *IGLS* volumes I–III that cover the Antiochene. One therefore has to turn to *Supplementum Epigraphicum Graecum*, which normally gives a transcription and brief historical analysis of inscriptions found since *PAES* and *IGLS*. (J. Jarry's editions of inscriptions discovered in the 1960's were not, however, given the attention they deserved in *SEG*, probably because they appeared in a Near Eastern Studies journal, *Annales islamologiques*.)

Notes

1   I have endeavoured, where possible, to employ the accepted English system of transliteration for Arabic placenames. This has involved changing many of the previously accepted transliterations, including those used in my own books and published papers. I cite only the epigraphic editions from which I actually transcribed the inscription.

2   The discussion began in Liebeschuetz, 1977: 485–508; Liebeschuetz, 1979: 17–24. See also Harnack, 1924: 660–676.

3   Trombley, *HRC* 247–283.

4   Eusebius *HE* 7.5. Noted by Harnack,1924: 672.

5   Harnack, 1924, 673.

6   Peña, 1997: 51–2, 64. It is not easy for me to see how the theological polemics of the post-Nicaean decades and the impasse over the Arian controversy should have contributed to the expansion of Christianity, particularly in Oriens where the anti-Nicaean party prevailed until the 370's.

7   Elsewhere, Peña, 1997: 95 puts 'the mass conversion of the rural population in the fifth century'. I have argued elsewhere against the idea of 'mass conversions', suggesting an articulated process based on the personal decisions of urban and rural people, a view that I find is in agreement with Peter Brown's: Trombley, *HRC* I, 244; II, 382–385.

8   Trombley, *HRC* II, 134–173, 246–279.

9   Theodoret, *HE* 3.21, adapted from *NPNF*, Series 2, III, trans. B. Jackson, p. 107.

10 Tate, 1992.

11 Tchalenko, 1953: pl. VII.

12 Tchalenko, 1953: pl. VIII.

13 *AAES* III, 100–108a. *IGLS*, 465–475. no. 43. Jarry, 1967: no. 43. See Millar, 1993: 251–256. Trombley, *HRC* II, 254–55.

14 Jarry, 1967: 163–64, no. 41.

15 *Historia Philotheos* 4.2, translated in Trombley, *HRC* II, 145.

16 Trombley, *HRC* II, 275–278.

17 Trombley, *HRC* I, 110, n. 46.

18 *IGLS*, 652.

19 The cult seems to date at least from the Seleucid period. *IGLS*, 1184A, line 3.

20 Jarry, 1967: no. 44.

21 Jarry, 1967: no. 41.

22 *Codex Theodosianus* 16.10.14, in *Theodosiani Libri XVI cum Constitutionibus Sirmondianis*, edd. Th. Mommsen, P. Krueger and P.M. Mayer, I–II (Berlin, 1905).

23 Trombley, *HRC* II, 275–278. Cf. *SEG* 7, 59.

24 *PAES* III B, 1126 = *IGLS*, 477.

25 *AAES* III, 109 = *IGLS*, 475.

26 Trombley, *HRC* II, 253–55, 260–61.

27 The chronology of the event is similar to that of the closure of the Marneion and other urban temples of Gaza in Palaestina Prima. The temples were closed to cultic use by an imperial rescript in 398 and destroyed at the request of the bishop in 402, according to the chronology worked out by Henri Grégoire. Trombley, *HRC* I, 210–213.

28 *PAES* B III, 1170. *IGLS* 376. Trombley, *HRC* II, 258–260.

29 *SEG* 32, 1446 = *IGLS* 4028 = *IGRR* III, 1020.

30 *SEG* 47, 1922–1924.

31 Another Baal was Zeus Hadad. *SEG* 28, 1336 (Nikopolis, Euphratesia, 2nd–3rd c. AD).

32 Trombley, *HRC* II, 258f. and note.

33 *SEG* 26, 1652 (*territorium* of Tripolis, Phoenice, AD184).

34 Peña, 1997: 203–4, with plan.

35 E.g. *IGLS*, 991, 1184A-B. There is a votive inscription at Europus in Euphratesia dedicated to 'Apollo the most holy' that may belong to the time of the Tetrarchy. Its square uncials are of 2nd–3rd c. date. *IGLS*, 133.

36 *PAES* III B, 1092. *IGLS*, 556, 569, 581. Jarry, 1967: 39, 40, 44, 45. *SEG* 20, 344; 32, 1447; 47, 1922.

37 *SEG* 32, 1425, 1426.

38 Deichmann,1939, 105–136. Trombley, *HRC* I, 108–147, 207–222; II, 134–143, 159–161.

39 *PAES* III B, 1092, 1097, 1126. *IGLS* 477, 556, 557. Tchalenko, 1953: pl. XI; III, nos. 1,3, 7. *SEG* 20.328, 329. Trombley, *HRC* II, 258f., 270f., 276f.

40 *PAES* II B, 165–169.

41 Tchalenko,1953: III, no. 21.

42 Cf. the case of Thalaleios at Gabala in Syria I. Trombley, *HRC* II, 159–161.

43 Peña,1997: 203.

44 Trombley, *HRC* I, 8.

45 *AAES* III, nos. 20, 89, 117, 269, 279, 283. *PAES* III B, 1069, 1079, 1093, 1104, 1107, 1112, 1125, 1134, 1135, 1138, 1153, 1171, 1175. *IGLS* 264, 359, 375, 420, 437, 444, 447, 476, 483, 491, 496, 497, 505, 523, 539, 554., 600, 612, 660, 665, 681, 688, 690. Tchalenko, 1953: III, nos. 21a. Jarry, 1967: nos. 82, 99, 112, 121. Jarry, 1970: nos. 9, 49, 57. Jarry, 1985: no. 18.

46 *PAES* III B, 1093 = *IGLS* 554.

47 Jarry, 1982: no. 46.

48 *Monumenta Asiae Minoris Antiqua* I, ed. W. M. Buckler (Manchester, 1928), p. xviii.

49 For Syria II, see now *SEG* 43, 1020 (AD 463). For Phoenice Libanensis, *SEG* 18, 607 (Boudai, AD 539), 611 (Mu'allaqat Zakhla, AD 540?). Cf. Trombley, *HRC* II, 156f.

50 Peña, 1997: 62–3 and n. 1.

51 *IGLS*, 594.

52 Tate, 1992: 290–1.

53 E.g. *PAES* III B, 1127 = *IGLS*, 455. It belongs to a much earlier date than was supposed in Trombley, *HRC* 2, 256. The inscription is pre-Constantinian and probably pre-3rd c.

54 *PAES* III B, 1107 = *IGLS*, 523.

55 *IGRR* III, 1007, 1022, 1091, 1104, 1110, 1135, 1159, 1170, 1179, 1183, 1188, 11213, 1216, 1218, 1233, 1234, 1246, 1249, 1265, 1267, 1271, 1298, 1299, 1302, 1305, 1309, 1310, 1313, 1336, 1340.

56 *IGRR* III, 1216.

57 *AAES* III, 278 = *IGLS*, 689.

58 *AAES* III, 66 = *PAES* III B, 1094 = *IGLS*, 555.

59 *PAES* III B, 1167, 1170–1173, 1175-1177, 1179, 1180, 1199, 1201, 1202 = *IGLS*, 359, 363, 364, 366, 372, 375-378, 389, 391, 392, 404. *PAES* IV B, 52. *SEG* 43, 1025.

60 Trombley, *HRC* II, 185.

61 *IGLS*, 389.

62 See above, Section I.

63 Trombley, HRC 2, 259–260.

64 Cf. the St. Zacheos < Zachaios named on an estampage. *IGLS* 209 (*territorium* of Beroea-Aleppo, AD 504)

65 Trombley, *HRC* II, 253–63.

66 See Gregory of Nyssa, *Or.* 7.15, *PG* 35, 773C, which contains the phrase: '... the newly created soul, which the Spirit has formed anew from water.' Lampe, 1961: 903.

67 *PAES* III B, 1189 = *IGLS* 373.

68 *PAES* III B, 1190 = *IGLS* 374.

69 *AAES* III, 48 = *IGLS*, 569.

70 *AAES* 49 = *IGLS*, 570.

71 *AAES* III, 50 = *IGLS*, 568.

72 *AAES* III, 51 = *IGLS*, 566.

73 *IGLS*, 256.

74 *SEG* 43, 1039.

75 See Tchalenko, 1992, 63-106.

76 *AAES* III, 78 = *IGLS*, 518.

77 *IGLS*, 496.
78 *IGLS*, 497.
79 Jarry, 1970: no. 57.
80 *IGLS*, 264.
81 *PAES* III B, 1177 = *IGLS* 372.
82 Lampe, 1961: 905.
83 *IG* 14, 2325, 2326, 2334.
84 *SEG* 29, 1589. Cf. Lampe, 1961: 1510.
85 Trombley, *HRC* I, 122-29; II, 283–89.
86 Jarry, 1985: no. 13.
87 *Inscriptiones Latinae Christianae Selectae* I–III, ed. E. Diehl (Berlin, 1925–31), nos. 1533, 1534.
88 Trombley, *HRC* II, 313–315, etc. See Peterson, 1926: 1–46, etc. It is a feature of *formgeschichtlich* method that this work has little to say about the archaeological, political or social context of the 'one God' inscriptions. See below.
89 Eusebius, *V. Constantini* 2.47. *NPNF* Series 2, I, trans. C. McGiffert, p. 512. Cf. Eusebius of Caesarea, *Life of Constantine*, trans. A. Cameron and S.G. Hall (Oxford, 1999).
90 Eusebius, *V. Constantini* 3.2. *NPNF* Series 2, I, p. 520.
91 Eusebius, *V. Constantini* 1.29.
92 Eusebius, *V. Constantini* 1.5.
93 *PAES* III B, 1074 = *IGLS* 542.
94 Trombley, *HRC* II, 269.
95 Theodoret, *HE* 2.14, adapted from *NPNF* Series 2, III, p. 79.
96 *AAES* III, 78 = *IGLS*, 518.
97 Theodoret, HE 1.24, adapted from *NPNF* Series. 2, III, p. 59.
98 *AAES* III, 36 = *IGLS*, 602.
99 Eusebius, *V. Constantini* 4.20.
100 *SEG* 44, 1340.
101 *SEG* 39, 1661 (Qana, AD 350–400?). Bowersock, 1993: 3-8.
102 *AAES* III, 16, 21, 22, 78, 90, 116, 263, 278. *PAES* III B, 1074–1077, 1080–1082, 1084, 1085. 1095, 1126, 1139, 1189, 1192, 1196, 1206, 1210. *IGLS* 373, 382, 386, 396, 400, 425, 432, 443, 458, 477, 490, 518, 535–538, 540, 542, 543, 545, 547, 561, 595, 596, 605, 611, 617, 662, 668, 689. Jarry, 1967: no. 122. Jarry, 1970: no. 31, 34. Jarry, 1982: nos. 2, 7, 46. *SEG* 43, 1026. Mouterde-Poidebard, 1945: no. 15.
103 *AAES* III, 78 = *IGLS*, 518.
104 *AAES* III, 66. *PAES* III, 1074 = *IGLS*, 542.
105 *PAES* III B, 1201. *IGLS*, 391, 621.
106 *IGLS*, 621.
107 PAES III B, 1206. IGLS, 396, 425, 458, 662.
108 *PAES* III B, 1075, 1077, 1080–1082, 1084, 1085, 1089. IGLS, 536–538, 540, 542, 543–545, 547.
109 Trombley, *HRC* II, 268–272. Cf. Peña, 1997: 55f.
110 *PAES* III B, 1085 = *IGLS*, 537.
111 *Codex Iustinianus* 1.11.10.1, 3 and 5, in *Codex Iuris Civilis* II, ed. P. Krueger (Berlin, 1929). Trombley, *HRC* I, 88f.
112 *PAES* III B, no. 1151 = *IGLS*, 424.
113 *SEG* 42, 1334 (Abu Hamsa, Syria II, AD 409).
114 *PAES* III B, 1085, 1095. *IGLS*, 537, 561.
115 *AAES* III, 437a. Cf. Trombley, *HRC* II, 363f.
116 See the remarks of Peña, 1997: 95–104. *Pace* Peña, the first baptistery to be constructed in the Antiochene Limestone Massif was the one in the East Church at Babisqa in Jabal

Barisha, for which Peña gives the date of AD 480 (*sic*). The correct date is August AD 390. *IGLS*, 561.

117 Peña, 1997: 95–97. Peña does not give the epigraphic or stylistic reasons for these dates.

118 *AAES* III, 46, 58, 62, 67a. *PAES* III B, 1095. *IGLS*, 537, 561, 571.

119 *AAES* III, 67–69. *PAES* III B, 1096-1098. *IGLS*, 557–559.

120 Markianos' name appears on the windows of the west façade in an inscription of 403/4. *SEG* 43, 1026.

121 *SEG* 40, 1779.

122 *SEG* 44, 1306.

123 Trombley, 1985: 328–334.

124 Trombley, *HRC* II, 163–167.

125 *AAES* III, 61, 62. *IGLS* 545, 546.

126 *AAES* III, nos. 22, 34, 35, 278, 282. *IGLS* 595, 598, 617, 660, 668, 684, 687, 689.

127 It is impossible to say whether this was used as a Christian symbol or as a Jewish one.

128 *AAES* III, 283. *IGLS* 688.

129 *AAES* III, 278, 279. *IGLS* 689, 690.

130 *IGLS*, 671.

131 *AAES* III, 263. *IGLS* 680.

132 Trombley, HRC II, 283–311.

133 Zeus 'the source of (the sun's) rays.'

134 R. Mouterde, *editor princeps*. The rationale for the date is not explained in *SEG*. If the era system used was the Seleucid, it would give AD 259/60 as the date.

135 See previous note.

136 The men were Arabs.

Abbreviations

AAES III	*Publications of an American Archaeological Expedition to Syria in 1899, Part III: Greek and Latin Inscriptions* ed. W.K. Prentice (NewYork, 1908).
IGLS	*Inscriptions grecques et latines de la Syrie*. Ed. L. Jalabert, R. Mouterde *et alii* 1–7 (Paris 1929–70).
IGRR III	*Inscriptiones Graecae ad Res Romanas pertinentes* III, ed. R. Cagnat (Paris; repr. Chicago, 1975),
NPNF, Series 2	*A Select Library of Nicene and Post-Nicene Fathers of the Christian Church, Second Series*, edd. P. Schaff and H. Wace (repr. Grand Rapids, 1983).
PAES II B	*Publications of the Princeton University Archaeological Expeditions to Syria in 1904–5 and 1909, Division II: Architecture, Section B: Northern Syria*, ed. H.C. Butler (Leiden, 1920).
PAES III B	*Publications of the Princeton University Archaeological Expeditions to Syria in 1904–5 and 1909, Division III: Greek and Latin Inscriptions, Section B: Northern Syria*, ed. W.K. Prentice (Leiden, 1922).
PAES IV	*Publications of the Princeton University Archaeological Expeditions to Syria in 1904–5 and 190. Division IV: Semitic inscriptions, Section B Syriac inscriptions* ed. E. Littmann (Leiden, 1934).
SEG	*Supplementum Epigraphicum Graecum*, ed. P. Roussel *et alii* 1– (London, 1923–).
Trombley, *HRC* I–II	F. R. Trombley, *Hellenic Religion and Christianization c. 370–529, Religions in the Graeco-Roman World* 115 / 1–2 (Leiden, 1993–4; repr. 1995, 2001).
ZPE	*Zeitschrift für Papyrologie und Epigraphik*

Bibliography

Bowersock, G., 1993. 'The new Greek inscription from South Yemen'. In J. Langdon, S. Reinert *et alii*, *ΤΟ ΕΛΛΗΝΙΚΟΝ. Studies in Honor of Speros Vryonis, Jr I. Hellenic Antiquity and Byzantium*, (New Rochelle), 3–8.

Deichmann, F.W., 1939. 'Frühchristliche Kirchen in antiken Heiligtümern' *Jahrbuch des Deutschen Archäologischen Instituts* 54, 105–136.

Eusebius, *V. Constantini* 2.47. *NPNF* Series 2, I, trans. C. McGiffert.

Eusebius of Caesarea, *Life of Constantine*, trans. A. Cameron and S.G. Hall (Oxford, 1999).

Harnack, A. von, 1924. *Die Mission und Ausbreitung des Christentums in den ersten drei Jahrhunderten*, II (Leipzig).

Jarry, J., 1967. 'Inscriptions arabes, syriaques et grecques du Massif du Bélus en Syrie du Nord', A*nnales islamologiques* 7, 139–220.

Jarry, J., 1970. 'Inscriptions arabes, syriaques et grecques du Massif du Bélus en Syrie du Nord' *Annales islamologiques* 9, 187–214.

Jarry, J., 1982. 'Nouvelles inscriptions de la Syrie du Nord', *ZPE* 47, 73–103.

Jarry, J., 1985. 'Nouveaux documents grecs et latins de Syrie du Nord et de Palmyrène', *ZPE* 60, 109–115.

Lampe, G.W.H., (ed.), 1961. *A Patristic Greek Lexicon* (Oxford).

Liebeschuetz, J.H.W.G., 1977. 'Epigraphic evidence on the Christianisation of Syria', *Akten des XI. Internationalen Limeskongresses* (Budapest), 485–508.

Liebeschuetz, J.H.W.G., 1979. 'Problems arising from the conversion of Syria', *The Church in Town and Countryside*. In D. Baker (ed.), *Studies in Church History* 16 (Oxford), 17–24.

Millar, F., 1993. *The Roman Near East 31 BC – AD 337* (Cambridge, Mass.,)

Mouterde, R., and Poidebard, A., 1945. *Le Limes de Chalcis: Organisation de la steppe en haute Syrie romaine I–II* (Paris).

Peña, I., 1997. *The Christian Art of Byzantine Syria* (Madrid).

Peterson, E., 1926. *ΕΙΣ ΘΕΟΣ: epigraphische, formgeschichtliche und religionsgeschichtliche Untersuchungen* (Göttingen)

Tate, G., 1992. *Les campagnes de la Syrie du Nord du IIe au VIIe siècle* (Paris).

Tchalenko, G., 1953. *Villages antiques de la Syrie du Nord. Le Massif du Bélus à l'époque romaine* (Paris).

Trombley, F., 1985. 'Paganism in the Greek world at the end of antiquity: the case of rural Anatolia and Greece', *Harvard Theological Review* 78, 327–352.

5. THE ROMANIZATION AND CHRISTIANIZATION OF THE ANTIOCHENE REGION: THE MATERIAL EVIDENCE FROM THREE SITES

Tasha Vorderstrasse

INTRODUCTION

The archaeology of the Antiochene Region in the Roman and Byzantine periods (64 BC–AD 638) has largely focused on the city of Antioch and the Limestone Massif region: Princeton University conducted excavations at the city of Antioch[1] and Butler, Tchalenko, Peña et al., and Tate have made detailed architectural studies of the Limestone Massif, and some limited excavations have been conducted in Déhès.[2] The excavations conducted by the Oriental Institute of the University of Chicago and Sir Leonard Woolley in the 1930s examined sites closer to Antioch than the Limestone Massif, but these sites have largely been ignored in subsequent studies of the region. This is partly due to the fact that the excavators only retained a portion of the archaeological materials, making a complete reconstruction of these sites difficult, and partly because much of the remaining material remains unpublished. This paper will therefore focus attention on this area closer to Antioch, rather than concentrating on the Limestone Massif . It will examine the three sites of Tell al-Judaidah and Çatal Hüyük in the Amuq Plain and al-Mina, looking at them in both the Roman and late antique periods in order to determine the impact of Romanization and Christianization.[3] In the Roman period the evidence is too limited to determine the nature of the sites, but in late antiquity they were, respectively, a monastery, a village, and a port. The paper will conclude with a summary of the evidence.

EXCAVATIONS

The 1930s were a time of extensive excavations and surveys in the Antiochene region. The Oriental Institute of the University of Chicago conducted a survey of the Amuq plain and excavated the village sites of Çatal Hüyük, Tell al-Judaidah, and Tell Tayinat[4] and Sir Leonard Woolley conducted excavations at the port site of al-Mina.[5] The excavators of the Amuq sites were largely concerned with prehistoric materials and assigned the later objects to the Roman, Early Christian, and Byzantine phases (Phase R-T), but exact dates of these periods remain unclear. Of the objects dating to these periods, only the location of the coins is currently known[6] (Waagé, who studied some of the pottery, mentioned that pieces may have been retained by the Syrian

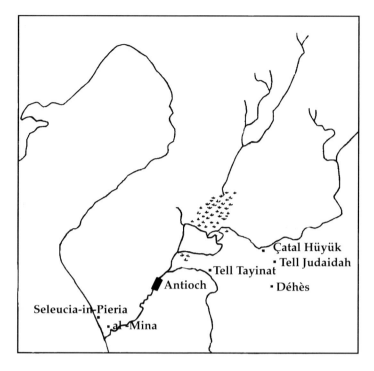

Figure 5.1 Map of the Antiochene Region. After Haines, 1971: pl.1.

government[7]) and only the architecture was ever published, but without any detailed study.[8] Only the sites of Çatal Hüyük and Tell al-Judaidah will be considered here, as Tell Tayinat does not have any architecture or pottery that can be attributed to the Roman or Late Antique periods, and the small number of coins of the Roman period found at the site could easily be strays. Also at the port of al-Mina the excavators did not retain all of the materials found; although they preserved all of the coins, they kept only decorated or large pieces of pottery and glass. Therefore, only a partial picture of these three sites is possible, due to the dearth of material.

THE ROMANIZATION OF THE ANTIOCHENE REGION

After the Roman conquest of the Syria in B.C. 64, the city of Antioch remained an important administrative and commercial centre, as the focus of Roman power in the region.[9] Until recently, the impact of the Roman conquest on the eastern half of the Roman Empire had largely been seen as minimal, particularly when compared to the more dramatic changes that took place in the western half of the empire. Studies have now demonstrated, however, that it did affect the populations of the East, but in different ways. They continued to use Greek and celebrate their Hellenistic identity, while at the same time adapting to various aspects of Roman material culture, including pottery, sculpture, and architecture.[10] Further studies will undoubtedly demonstrate the affects of this impact on different regions in the east.

As Antioch was a major commercial centre one might expect that the three sites examined would yield a large amount of materials from the Roman period. Further, one might expect these objects and the landscape to show some signs of Romanization. In fact, the evidence from these sites is limited, although there is some evidence for the Romanization of material culture (see below). The archaeological materials from the Amuq sites of Tell al-Judaidah and Çatal Hüyük consist only of fragmentary architecture, graves, and a few pieces of pottery. At al-Mina, the evidence is even more limited. Woolley only discovered seven Roman coins[11] and did not report finding any pottery or architecture from the site, leading him to conclude that it was not occupied in the Roman period.[12] Although there is some indication that it may have been occupied in the Roman period, al-Mina will be only considered in the Late Antique period (see below). Despite the problems of the evidence, these three sites appear to be only sparsely occupied under the Romans.[13]

Çatal Hüyük

At the site of Çatal Hüyük, the archaeologists combined phases Q-R (Hellenistic and Roman periods) into a single phase (Level 2)(Figure 5.2). The excavation revealed a

Figure 5.2 Hellenistic/Roman level at Çatal Hüyük. After Haines, 1971:26–27.

square building on the northeastern spur of the mound of about nine meters square, divided into three rooms (here shown by the black outline in the centre of Figure 5.2). In addition to the square building, there were foundations and paving of other buildings that have since disappeared, and a basin. There are also walls that may have enclosed the entire complex, although these are in a fragmentary condition; the inhabitants of the Late Antique village probably robbed out the stones to use in their constructions (see below).[14] The surviving square building was probably part of a larger building complex that has since disappeared.[15] Unfortunately, the simple construction of the building makes it difficult to date specifically to either the Hellenistic or the Roman period, particularly in the absence of large amounts of pottery.[16] But about thirty Roman coins were found at the site of Çatal Hüyük, indicating some activity on the mound in this period.

Five Roman burials (AS 3, 5–8)[17] were found sunk into Level 3, Phase O (1000–500 BC), apparently outside the Hellenistic/Roman building complex, although the fragmentary evidence of the architecture means that the relationship of the burials to the building complex is not entirely certain (Figure 5.3). If the burials were contemporary with the structures, then these would likely be the residents of the building complex. Three of the bodies (AS 6–8) had been buried in what Haines termed as "sausage jar burials" and one body had been buried in a stone cist (AS 3). Four other "sausage jar burials" can also be identified, although no bodies were found inside these graves.[18] Although cist graves are common in the Near East,[19] the sausage jar burials are more unusual. One possible reason for this use of jars is that the population did not have access to a large amount of stone and were forced to use storage jars instead. Other parts of the mound did not yield architectural evidence from the Roman period, but the excavators did discover one Roman grave (BS 13) in Area II on the southeast spur of the mound (see below).[20]

Tell al-Judaidah

The evidence for Roman occupation at the site of Tell al-Judaidah is also somewhat problematic. Again, the excavators were not able to differentiate between the time periods and thus assigned levels to Phases P-R (Syro-Hellenic, Hellenistic, and Roman periods). They discovered a series of very fragmentary levels consisting of refuse pits,

AS 3

AS7

Figure 5.3 Grave types from Çatal Hüyük: cist grave (AS3) and jar burial (AS7) Vorderstrasse, adapted from Haines, 1971: pl. 26.

pavements, walls, and a few rooms of buildings.[21] Less than ten Roman coins were discovered at the site, indicating a limited amount of commercial activity there. Far more evidence, however, can be deduced from the pottery found at the site.

A few pieces of Roman pottery from the site were published in Waagé's examination of the fine wares from Antioch. As the wares were very similar between the two sites, Waagé published all of the pottery together without noting whether or not the pottery came from Antioch or Tell al-Judaidah, except in his study of the Eastern Terra Sigillata A stamps (ESA). Waagé identified three examples (type 426p, type 432k, and one unidentified type), all stamped with the greeting XAPIC.[22] Both 426[23] and 432[24] are common forms that appear at excavations throughout the eastern Mediterranean in the first century AD and imitated Italian sigillata forms. Italian sigillata thus set the fashion for certain forms of ESA.[25] The stamps also imitated Italian sigillata stamps, but unlike western pottery stamps that denote the name of the pottery or the workshop, the ESA stamps primarily depict palmettes or greetings, although the earliest stamps were Latin names written in Greek.[26] Clearly, wares that resembled Italian sigillata pottery in both form and stamps were favoured by at least some of the population.

In addition to the three pieces of pottery published in his study of terra sigillata, Waagé also published several examples of lamps from Tell al-Judaidah and Çatal Hüyük. Unfortunately, he does not specify which site the particular lamps came from, but it is possible to determine this from the numbering of the lamps. The lamps of the Roman period from the Amuq are Types 34, 36b, and 39a-b. Lamps 34, 36b, and 39b are from Tell al-Judaidah, while 39a came from Çatal Hüyük.[27] Type 34 (dating to the first century AD) is fragmentary, but Type 36b (second century AD) can be identified with Broneer Type XXI.[28] Lamps similar to Type 36 have been found at other sites in Syria.[29] Type 39 also dates to the first century A. D. and has been identified by Waagé with Broneer Type XXIb.[30] The scene of two gladiators in combat on 39a[31] and the rosette on 39b[32] is attested on other lamps found in excavations. Broneer argued that the lamps of Type XXI were of Antiochene manufacture, but it is likely that they were made in Antioch following general Italian models.[33] The limited evidence from the lamps accords well with the evidence from the pottery.

The Christianization of the Antiochene Region

The city of Antioch had a considerable Christian community prior to the conversion of the empire. It had been a major centre of Christianity outside of Jerusalem and provided an important base for the emerging church. After the official recognition of Christianity, the patriarch of Antioch became one of the most important Christian offices in the empire.[34] The recognition of Christianity as the official religion of the Roman Empire in the fourth century affected people's needs for art and material culture as individuals acquired a new Christian identity.[35] The objects were created, acquired, displayed, and used according to specific needs and conditions that helped to create a visual sense of Christian identity amongst producers and consumers; and individuals manipulated images in order to renegotiate their identities and social relations in the face of change. Due to the adoption of Christianity as a state cult, a vast number of churches were erected. Some churches were constructed due to the patronage of emperors, bishops, and elites and these were sumptuously decorated. Churches were a place where bishops and priests had the opportunity to preach sermons to large sections of the population. They also became the houses of sacred objects that became the focus of pilgrimage, as well as hostels for travellers.[36]

Tell al-Judaidah

The site of Tell al-Judaidah provides an example of the Christianization of the landscape of the Antiochene region. The site is a monastery that possessed a chapel that served as a focal point for the Christian population and a place of pilgrimage for relics.[37] The monastery of Tell al-Judaidah is a *coenobium* where monks lived a communal life consisting of a daily routine of prayer, work, and meals.[38] The excavators discovered the stone remains of a small church, a house of several rooms, and outlying buildings surrounded by a wall dating to the Late Antique period. Except for the church and its associated structures, only limited signs of habitation were found on the mound from this period. The evidence thus suggests that the site was a small

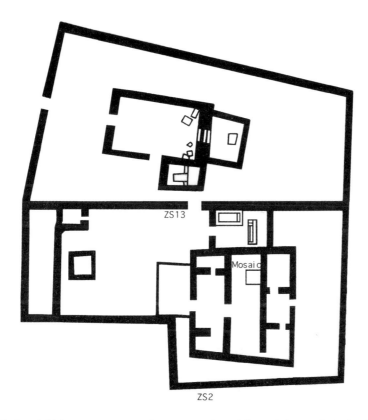

Figure 5.4 Tell al-Judaidah Monastery. Vorderstrasse, adapted from Haines, 1971: pls. 49C, 62, 63B.

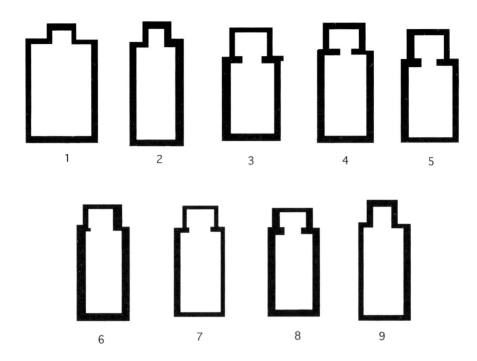

Figure 5.5 Schematic Plans of Chapels in the Calcaire Massif: 1. Bamouqa (Voderstrasse, adapted from Peña, et al., 1987: 54, fig. 34) 2. El-Qabou (adapted from Peña, et al., 1983: 137, fig. 13B 3. Kousik (adapted from Peña, et al., 1983: 187, fig. 28) 4. Serjible (adapted from Peña, et al., 1980: 399, fig. 54) 5. Kafr Deryan (adapted from Peña, et al., 1975, 96, fig. 7) 6. Burğ Heidar (adapted from Butler 1920: 291, ill. 315) 7. Sitt er-Rum (adapted from Butler, 1920: 259, ill. 277) 8. Kefr lab (adapted from Butler, 1920: 287, Ill. 310) 9. Burdjkeh (adapted from Butler, 1920: 329, ill. 373).

monastery without an associated village. This fits in well with the coin evidence: only about ten Late Antique coins were recovered from the site and one would not expect that the monastery would be the focus of considerable commercial activity. Braidwood identified the site in 1938 as a sixth-century monastery,[39] but Haines ignored this attribution and presented the architecture without any analysis. Thus, the studies presented here are a result of my own work.

The church consisted of a rectangular nave paved with red bricks and a square sanctuary that was smaller than the nave. A small room had been built against the southern wall of the church containing a tomb, perhaps that of the founder of the monastery. In addition to the church, there was a building nearby that may have been the residence for several monks, consisting of a few rooms, including a large central room with a small geometric mosaic. Two stone sarcophagi, again probably of important monks, were located between the building and the division wall. Other features in the monastery included a basin, two burials, and a cistern beyond the enclosure wall.[40] Two burials (ZS2 and ZS 13) appear from the plans to be simple pit burials located in the area around the church.[41] The sex of these two burials is not known, but it is likely that they are of monks from the monastery.

This church and its associated buildings are comparable to monasteries in the nearby Limestone Massif, that usually consisted of a small chapel, collective tomb, associated buildings, and an enclosure wall. Similar monasteries included those of Burğ Heidar and Qasr ed-Deir that consisted of a church and a small building for the monks.[42] Scholars have largely neglected these small monasteries and chapels,[43] with the exception of Peña, Castellana, and Fernández, who studied monasteries and other religious buildings of the fourth to the sixth century in the Jebel al'Ala, Jebel Wastani, and especially the Jebel Baricha regions of the Limestone Massif. They divided the monasteries into three categories: small (housing about 7 monks), medium (housing about twice that number), and large (housing 30 monks).[44] Thus, based on this evidence, Tell al-Judaidah is typical of other small monasteries found in the region, housing only a small number of monks. In addition, several chapels similar to Tell al-Judaidah have been identified in the Limestone Massif. Peña, Castellana, and Fernández identified four : Bamouqa (dated to the fourth century),[45] el-Qabou (fifth or sixth century),[46] Kousik (sixth century),[47] Serjiblé,[48] and Kafr Deryan (sixth century).[49] Butler also identified four similar chapels: Burğ Heidar,[50] Sitt er-Rum,[51] Kefr lab,[52] and Burdjkeh,[53] all dating to the sixth century (Figure 5.5).

In the course of the excavations at Tell al-Judaidah, the excavators also found two stone reliquaries with lids and a fragment of another, at the eastern end of the church near the steps leading to the sanctuary. The reliquaries were gabled and had crude acroteria at the corners; the two complete examples were pierced by holes in the top of the box and had a horizontal drain at the bottom.[54] Reliquaries of this type are common to the region in the fifth and sixth centuries, attested in the excavations at Antioch, the surveys of the Limestone Massif, and in the excavations at Apamea. Although some could be ornately decorated, most examples, like those at Tell al-Judaidah, were plain. These reliquaries would have held the bones of saints that were venerated at a particular church or shrine. The holes in the lid allowed oil to be poured into the reliquary and the contact with the remains gave the oil special healing qualities. The enriched oil was then released through a hole near the bottom of the box, bottled, and taken home by worshippers to be used for healing.[55]

Çatal Hüyük

At the site of Çatal Hüyük, the archaeologists discovered remains on the northeastern spur of the mound that they partly dated to the Late Antique period, but the lack of pottery evidence makes it impossible to confirm this. The site consists of a walled settlement with small blocks of buildings (including domestic residences and stables) and streets paved with pebbles.[56] In Area II, where they had already found one Roman burial, they found twelve graves (BS 10–12, 14–16, BS20, BS 25–28, BS 32) with similar orientation, suggesting a Late Antique cemetery on the site in this period.[57] About fifty coins were found at the site dating to the Late Antique period, a number that does suggest some occupation, but we do not know its true extent, due to the lack of pottery evidence.

There are also signs of Christianization in two lamps published by Waagé in his study of lamps from the Antioch excavations; but unfortunately he does not give them a specific number, making it impossible to determine whether they came from Tell al-Judaidah or Çatal Hüyük. These horn-handled lamps were both of Type 53, dating to the fifth and sixth century, and both had crosses on them, although one is rather faded.[58] Similar lamps have been found elsewhere in Syria, suggesting that this is a regional type.[59] Interestingly, the two lamps found at Déhès closely resemble the two lamps found in the Amuq.[60] Due to the presence of the crosses on the lamps, it is tempting to assign them to the monastery of Tell al-Judaidah, but unfortunately this is unclear. What is evident, however, is that the population of the region wished to use objects with Christian symbols on them in order to demonstrate their religion visually.

Al -Mina

The evidence for Christianization is less obvious at the port-site of al-Mina than at Tell al-Judaidah. At al-Mina, the Late Antique level consisted of several large buildings and fragments of others, in addition to a small graveyard. The graves were inhumations roofed with tiles and the excavators found no sign of grave goods.[61] As the graves were never published, it is impossible to determine the character and nature of the burials: the lack of grave goods could indicate Christians or, equally, members of the population too poor to afford grave goods. The only overt sign of Christianity at al-Mina is a column found re-used in the Early Islamic period with a double cross on it.[62] A total of forty coins were recovered dating to the Late Antique period at al-Mina, suggesting some commercial activity during this period.[63] Unfortunately the excavation selectively retained only the decorated or large pieces of pottery (two pieces of Phocean red slip ware and one red slip imitation) and large pieces of glass.[64]

CONCLUSION

This study has shown that the settlements in the Amuq Plain and the Orontes Delta offer some pointers to the Romanization and Christianization of the Antiochene region, although evidence that is limited and largely unpublished. The three sites examined in this paper were all different: an inland village, a monastery, and a port. The evidence from the pottery and lamps from Tell al-Judaidah and Çatal Hüyük does point to some Romanization of the population, and provides an indication of the desirability of objects imitating Italian forms, but the small number of objects makes it impossible to speculate further. The evidence from the Late Antique period is far more detailed and there are signs of Christianization at the sites. The evidence in the Plain of Antioch is biased in favour of the church at Tell al-Judaidah, simply because the excavators recorded more information about it than the village at Çatal Hüyük, making it possible to reconstruct more of the history of the site. Excavations at smaller sites in both the Amuq Plain and the Limestone Massif might yield further comparisons to the Tell al-Judaidah church and the Çatal Hüyük village. More categories of evidence have been published from al-Mina, but the amount of pottery and glass retained by the excavators was unfortunately small. This material will form a basis for the current investigations in the region by the Oriental Institute of Chicago, including the various surveys currently being conducted there, and will amplify our understanding of the region in this period. It will also allow us to situate these older excavations in their context and will provide ideas for future avenues of research.

Notes
1 Elderkin, 1934; Stillwell, 1938; R. Stillwell, 1941; Waagé, 1948; Waagé, 1952; Lassus, 1972.
2 Butler, 1920; Butler, 1929; Tchalenko, 1953-1958; Peña, Castellana, and Fernández, 1975; Sodini, Tate, Bauvant, Bauvant, Biscop, and Orssaud, 1980; Peña, Castellana, and Fernández, 1980; Peña, P. Castellana, and R. Fernández, 1983; I. Peña, P. Castellana, and R. Fernández, 1987; I. Peña, P. Castellana, and R. Fernández, 1990; Tate 1992.
3 The material presented from al-Mina is based upon research for my Phd. dissertation: *A Port of Antioch under Byzantium, Islam, and the Crusades: Acculturation and Differentiation at al-Mina, A.D. 350–1268*, Ph.D., University of Chicago, forthcoming. See also my forthcoming article that will appear in the proceedings of the October 2001 Lyon Colloquium *Antioche de Syrie: Histoire, images et traces de la ville antique* to be published in *Topoi*.
4 Haines, 1971.
5 Woolley, 1937: 1, 3–4; Lane, 1938: 19–78; Woolley, 1953: xii, 153; Winstone, 1990: 200.
6 I will publish the coins of the Amuq excavations from the Achaemenid-Islamic periods in a catalogue and circulation discussion tentatively titled *Coins from the Plain of Antioch*.
7 Waagé, 1948: 7.
8 Haines, 1971. Haines only published the architecture and stone objects.
9 Downey, 1961: 11–12; Grainger, 1990: 34, 48, 58-59, 125–126, 162.
10 Bowman, 1990: 121, 124, 135; Dodge, 1990: 188; Bowman and Rathbone, 1992: 108; Alcock, 1993: 1–2; Woolf, 1993–1994: 116–117, 120, 125–128, 131, 133, 135; Gawlikowski, 1997: 46, 52; Schmidt-Colinet, 1997: 157, 159–162, 165, 167, 170, 174; Woolf, 1997: 1; Smith, 1999: 89; Bowman, 2000: 180.
11 Robinson, 1937: 193–194.
12 Woolley, 1937: 5; Lane, 1938: 19; Woolley, 1953: 168, 180.
13 Sparse occupation in the Middle Roman period has been attested elsewhere, see Kendrick, 1978: 147; Kendrick, 1981: 440; McClellan 1999: 20. Kendrick suggests that the reason for the lack of fine wares in the Middle Roman period is either depopulation or a decline in living standards that forced the population to exclusively use coarse wares. As Kendrick admits, neither explanation is satisfactory. McClellan suggests that the gap may be due to the inability of archaeologists to recognize pottery from this period.
14 Haines, 1971; 16.
15 Tchalenko, 1953–1958: 12, pls. XXI–XXII.
16 Hirschfeld, 1995: 289. Hirschfeld notes that the simple construction of houses means that they are often difficult to date.
17 Krogman, 1949: Tables III–IV.
18 Haines, 1971: 9, pls. 5, 26. Haines does not illustrate the sausage jars and the one photo of the jars was taken at an angle, making an accurate reconstruction of the jars impossible. A very small line drawing on the map of Level 3 suggests that the "sausage jars" were actually storage jars with small ends and pointed handles.

19 Cist graves are attested at a wide variety of sites for different periods. See Moorey, 1980;
    7, 9, and accompanying bibliography. See also Stucky, 1983: 19, 34; Boehmer, Pedde, and
    Salje, 1995: 155.

20 Haines, 1971: 16.

21 Haines, 1971: 31, 34, 36.

22 Waagé, 1948: 7–8, 33–34, pl. V. 426 and 432 are Hayes, 1986: 30–31, Forms 37 and 36
    respectively. For stamps see Iliffe, 1938: 47–48; Comfort, 1938: 30, 45; Iliffe, 1938: 30, 45;
    Slane, 1997: 334.

23 For Syria-Palestine see Crowfoot, 1936: pl. IVa; Horsfield and Horsfield, 1942: 192–193;
    Waagé, 1948: No. 426, pl. V; Cox, 1949: 12, Group VIb, no. 67; Jones, 1950: 242, no. 385, pl.
    192; Kenyon, 1957: 296, Form 14b, fig. 79.19–21; Baly, 1962: 283, Shape F3–4, pl. XLIV;
    Dothan, 1971: 44, fig. 15. 18; Johansen, 1971: 100, nos. 141a-c, fig. 39; Kenrick, 1981: 445,
    Type 32; Stucky 1983: 133, Type 14, no. 239; Hayes, 1985: 190, nos. 4–7, pl. 53; Reynolds,
    1997–1998: 38, fig. 2; Slane, 1997: 307, TA23, pl. 16. For Africa see Kendrick, 1985: 235, 237,
    B332, fig. 68.6.19–20; Kadous, 1988: 128, no. 10. For Greece see Robinson, 1959: 24, no. G8,
    pl. 60; Slane, 1990: 47–48, fig. 5.90.38. The form may also be attested in Pompeii, see Pucci,
    1977: 19, Table IX. He lists the form as Samaria Form 14, which could refer to either 426 or
    432 (see below). As he does not illustrate the type, it is not possible to determine the type
    referred to here.

24 For Syria-Palestine see Crowfoot, 1936: 21, no. 16; Horsfield and Horsfield, 1942: 192–193,
    no. 399, fig. 53 and no. 467, fig. 55; Waagé, 1948: no. 432, pl. V; Cox, 1949: 12, Group VIb,
    nos. 66–67; Jones, 1950: 242, no. 386, pl. 192 and possibly no. 394, pl. 192; Kenyon, 1957:
    296, Form 14b, fig. 79.17–18; Johansen, 1971: 100, no. 14.1d, fig. 39; Negev, 1974; 38, no.
    148, pl. 27; Kendrick, 1978: 151, Type 31, fig. 13.31; Kendrick, 1981: 445, type 31; Stucky,
    1983: 133, Type 14; nos. 238, 240–241; Negev, 1986: 24; Hayes, 1985: 190, no. 3, pl. 53;
    Slane, 1997: 307, TA23, pl. 16. For Africa see Kendrick, 1985: 235, B331. fig. 79.17–18;
    Kadous, 1988: 128, no. 10. For Greece see Loeschcke, 1912: 360, Type 1, taf. 1; Robinson,
    1959: 24, no. G10, pl. 60; Schäfer; 1962: 787, no. 17, abb. 1; Hayes, 1973: 451–452, nos. 127–
    128, pl. 85; Unterkircher, 1983: 180, abb. 2. 8.3; Meyer-Schlichtmann, 1988: 151, T31a. For
    Italy see Guzzo, 1970: 45, no. 116, fig. 22 and possibly Pucci, 1977: 19, Table IX (see note
    above).

25 Slane, 1997: 273–274.

26 Hayes, 1986: 11; Zorolu, 1989: 573; Slane, 1997: 334.

27 Waage, 1948: 71–72; Krogman, 1949: 409. Waagé lists the excavation numbers of all the
    lamps, making it possible to determine those that came from the Amuq excavations,
    although he does not identify them to a specific site. Krogman, however, notes the
    numbering system for the excavations, making it possible to identify the lamps with Çatal
    Hüyük and Tell al-Judaidah.

28 Broneer, 1930: Type XXI, pls. VII–IX; Waagé, 1941: 55–57, 60–64, fig. 77.

29 Broneer type XXI is attested at various sites throughout the eastern Mediterranean, but for
    close parallels see Amy and Seyrig, 1936: 262, pl. L, nos. 4–5; Baur, 1947: 13, no. 22, fig. 6;
    Goldman and Jones, 1950: 92, group XI.

30 Broneer, 1930: Type XXIb, 73; Waagé, 1941: 64, fig. 77; Kennedy, 1963: 72–73. Similar
    lamps have been found at Tarsus, see Goldman and Jones, 1950: 104, Group XIII that they
    identify with Broneer, Type XXIII. Although the form is similar to Broneer Type XXIII, it
    does not have a handle.

31 Heimerl, 2001: 196, nos. 150–153. These fighting gladiators are similar, although not
    identical to the those on 39a.

32 P. Bruneau, 1965: no. 4610, pl. 30; Bailey, 1985: c407, pl. XI; Heimerl, 2001: no. 37, pl. 1.

33 Bronneer, 1930: 75; Waagé, 1934: 62. Slane, 1990: 11–12, n. 21.
34 Downey, 1961: 272–316; Harvey, 2000: 39–49; Maas 2000: 17–20.
35 Scherrer, 1995: 1.
36 Peña, Castellana, Fernández, 1983; Elsner, 1998: 7–8, 28, 50, 138–139, 141, 230.
37 Sheehan, 1985: 219.
38 Vööbus, 1960: 159–160, 167; Sheehan, 1985: 209; Hirschfeld, 1992: 23.
39 Braidwood, 1937: 6.
40 Haines, 1971: 30–34.
41 Haines, 1971: 34, pl. 62.
42 Tchalenko, 1953: 170; Sodini, 1989: 389, 351.
43 Butler, 1929: 74. He noted that a large number of small churches are in the region.
44 Peña, 1983: 327–328; Peña, Castellana, and Fernández: 9, 19, 31–32; Peña, 1990: 560–561.
45 Peña, Castellana, and Fernández, 1987: 54, fig. 34.
46 Peña, Castellana, and Fernández, 1983: 137, fig. 13B.
47 Peña, Castellana, and Fernández, 1983: 187, fig. 28.
48 Peña, Castellana, and Fernández, 1980: 399, fig. 54.
49 Peña, Castellana, and Fernández, 1975: 96, fig. 7.
50 Butler, 1920: 291, ill. 315.
51 Butler, 1920: 259, ill. 277.
52 Butler, 1920: 287, ill. 310.
53 Butler, 1920: 291, ill. 373.
54 Haines, 1971: 30–32, pl. 67.
55 Delehaye, 1935: 237, 240–241; Lassus, 1947: 164–166; Tchalenko, 1958: 17, no. 15; Canivet, 1978: 155; Gessel, 1988: 185–188, 190; Sodini, 1989: 353; Kondoleon, 2000: 224, no. 114.
56 Haines, 1971: 9–10.
57 Krogman, 1949: pl. 33.
58 Waagé, 1941: 67, fig. 80, nos. 159–160.
59 Waagé, 1934: 67, no. 31; Waagé, 1941: 67, Type 53; Kennedy, 1963: 87; Orssaud, 1980: 159, Type 1a, figs. 310–312; Touma, 1984: 186, Type V, figs. 150–151. Touma publishes similar lamps from Ras Ibn Hani and Anab al-Safina.
60 Orssaud, 1980: 159. Fig. 311 closely resembles no. 159, while Fig. 312 is similar to no. 160 and no. 31 published in Waagé, 1934.
61 Lane, 1938: 20, 24–25.
62 Lane, 1938: 24–25. Unfortunately, Lane does not publish this drawing or picture of this cross, making it impossible to date.
63 For the coins from the first season see Robinson 1937, p. 193–194.
64 Lane, 1938: 27–28, 62–64.

Bibliography

Alcock, S.E., 1993. *Graeca Capta: The Landscapes of Roman Greece* (Cambridge).
Amy, R. and Seyrig, H., 1936. 'Recherches dans la Nécropole de Palmyre', *Syria* 17, 229–266.
Bailey, D.M., 1985. *Excavations at Sîdi Khrebish Bengazi (Berenice) Volume III. Part 2: The Lamps* (Supplements to Libya Antiqua V, Tripoli).
Baly, T.J.C., 1962. 'Pottery'. In H.D. Colt (ed.) *Excavations at Nessana. Volume I* (London), 270–303.
Baur, P.V.C., 1947. *The Excavations at Dura Europos Final Report IV. Part III. The Lamps* (New Haven).

Boehmer, R.M., Pedde, F., and Salje, B., 1995. *Uruk. Die Gräber* (Uruk-Warka Eindberichte Band 10, Mainz).

Bovon, A., 1966. *Lampes d'Argos* (Études Péloponnés V, Paris).

Bowman, A.K., 1990. 'Classical Architecture in Roman Egypt'. In M. Henig (ed.) *Architecture and Architectural Sculpture in the Roman Empire* (Oxford University Committee for Archaeology Monographs no. 29, Oxford), 121–137.

Bowman, A.K., 2000. 'Urbanisation in Roman Egypt'. In E. Fentress (ed.) *Romanization and the City: Creation, Transformations, and Failures* (Journal of Roman Archaeology Supplement No. 38, Portsmouth), 173–188.

Bowman, A.K. and D. Rathbone, 1992. 'Cities and Administration in Roman Egypt', *Journal of Roman Studies* 82, 107–127.

Braidwood, R.J., 1937. *Mounds in the Plain of Antioch: An Archaeological Survey* (Oriental Institute Publications 48, Chicago).

Broneer, O., 1930. *Corinth IV. Part II. Terracotta Lamps.* (Cambridge, MA).

Bruneau, P., 1965. *Expédition Archéologique de Délos: Les Lampes* (Paris).

Butler, H.C., 1920. *Publications of the Princeton University Archaeological Expeditions to Syria in 1904–5 and 1909. Ancient Architecture in Syria.* (Leiden).

Butler, H.C., 1929. *Early Churches in Syria Fourth to Seventh Centuries.* (Princeton)

Canivet, M.T., 1978. 'Le reliquaire à huile de la grand église de Hurte', *Syria* 55, 153–162.

Comfort, H., 1938. 'Supplementary Sigillata Signatures in the Near East', *Journal of the American Oriental Society* 58, 30–60.

Cox, D.H., 1949. *The Excavations at Dura Europos. Final Report IV. Part 1. Fascicule 2. The Greek and Roman Pottery* (New Haven).

Crowfoot, G.M., 1936. 'The Nabataean Ware of Sbaita', *Palestine Exploration Fund Quarterly*, 14–29.

Delehaye, H., 1935. 'Saints et reliquaires d'Apamée', *Analecta Bollandiana* 53, 225–307.

Dodge, J., 1990. 'The Architectural Impact of Rome in the East'. In M. Henig (ed.) *Architecture and Architectural Sculpture in the Roman Empire* (Oxford University Committee for Archaeology Monographs no. 29, Oxford), 108–120.

Dothan, M., 1971. 'Ashdod II–III. The Second and Third Seasons of Excavations 1963, 1965, and Soundings in 1967', *'Atiqot* 9–10, 1–219.

Downey, G., 1961. *A History of Antioch in Syria from Seleucus to the Arab Conquest.* (Princeton).

Elderkin, G.W. (ed.), 1934. *Antioch-on-the-Orontes 1: The Excavations of 1932.* (Princeton).

Elsner, J., 1998. *Imperial Rome and Christian Triumph: The Art of the Roman Empire AD 100–450* (Oxford).

Gawlikowski, M, 1997. 'The Syrian Desert under the Romans'. In S. Alcock (ed.) *The Roman Empire in the East* (Oxbow Monograph 95, Oxford), 37–54.

Gessel, W., 1988. 'Das Öl der Märtyrer. Zur Funktion und Interpretation der Ölsarkophage', *Oriens Christianus* 72, 183–202.

Goldman, H. and Jones, F.F., 1950. 'The Lamps'. In H. Goldman (ed.) *Excavations at Gözlü Kule, Tarsus. Volume I. The Hellenistic and Roman Periods* (Princeton), 84–134.

Grainger, J.D., 1990. *The Cities of Seleukid Syria* (Oxford).

Guzzo, P.G., 1970. 'La Campagne 1960-1962 dell Soprintendenza al Parco del Cavallo'. In *Atti dell Accademia Nazionale dei Lincei. Notize degli Scavi di Antichità. Supplemento III* (Roma), 24–73.

Haines, R.C., 1971. *Excavations in the Plain of Antioch II: The Structural Remains of the Later Phases: Chatal Hüyük, Tell al-Judaidah, and Tell Ta'yinat* (Oriental Institute Publications 95, Chicago).

Harvey, S.A., 2000. 'Antioch and Christianity'. In Kondoleon, 2000: 39–49.

Hayes, J.W., 1973. 'Roman Pottery from the South Stoa at Corinth', *Hesperia* 42, 416–470.

Hayes, J.W., 1985. 'Hellenistic to Byzantine Fine Wares and Derivatives in the Jerusalem Corpus'. In *Excavations in Jerusalem 1961–1967. Volume 1* (Toronto),181–197.

Hayes, J.W., 1986. 'Sigillate Orientali.' In *Enciclopedia dell'Arte Antica. Atlante Delle Forme Ceramiche II. Ceramica Fine Romana nel Bacino Mediterraneo (Tardo ellenismo e primo impero)* (Roma), 1–96.

Heimerl, A., 2001. *Die Römischen Lampen aus Pergamon* (Pergamenische Forschungen Band 13, Berlin).

Hirschfeld, Y., 1992. *The Judean Desert Monasteries in the Byzantine Period.* (New Haven and London).

Hirschfeld, Y., 1995. *The Palestinian Dwelling in the Roman-Byzantine Period.* (Jerusalem).

Horsfield, G. and Horsfield, A., 1942. 'Sela Petra, the Rock, of Edom and Nabatene. The Finds', *Quarterly of the Department of Antiquities in Palestine* 9, 105–204.

Iliffe, J.H., 1938. 'Sigillata Wares in the Near East. A List of Potters' Stamps', *Quarterly of the Department of Antiquities in Palestine* 6, 4–50.

Iliffe, J.H., 1942. 'Sigillata Wares in the Near East II', *Quarterly of the Department of Antiquities in Palestine* 9, 31–76.

Johansen, C.F., 1971. 'Les terres sigillées orientales'. In A.P. Christensen and C.F. Johansen, *Hama. Fouilles et Recherches 1931–1938. III. 2. Les Poteries Hellénistiques et les Terres sigillées orientales* (Kobenhavn), 55–204.

Jones, F.F., 1950. 'The Pottery'. In H. Goldman (ed.) *Excavations at Gözlü Kule, Tarsus. Volume I. The Hellenistic and Roman Periods* (Princeton), 149–296.

Kadous, E.Z.H., 1988. *Die Terra Sigillata in Alexandria. Untersuchungen zur Typologie* der *Westlichen und oestlichen Terra Sigillata des Hellenismus und der Fruehen Kaiserzeit.* (DPhil. Thesis, Universität Trier).

Kendrick, P.M., 1978. 'Hellenistic and Roman Fine Wares', *Iraq* 40, 147–162.

Kendrick, P.M., 1981. 'The Fine Wares of the Hellenistic and Roman Periods'. In J. Mathers (ed.) *The River Quoeiq, Northern Syria and its Catchment. Studies Arising from the Tell Rifa'at Survey 1977–1979* (British Archaeological Reports International Series. S98 (ii), Oxford), 439–458.

Kendrick, P.M., 1985. *Excavations at Sîdi Khrebish Bengazi (Berenice) Volume III. Part I: The Fine Pottery* (Supplements to Libya Antiqua 5, Tripoli).

Kennedy, C.A., 1963. 'The Development of the Lamp in Palestine,' *Berytus* 14, 67–116.

Kenyon, K.M., 1957. 'Terra Sigillata'. In J.W. Crowfoot, G.M. Crowfoot, and K.M. Kenyon, *Samaria-Sebaste III: The Objects* (London), 287–305.

Kondoleon, C., 2000. *Antioch: The Lost Ancient City* (Princeton).

Krogman, W.M., 1949. 'Ancient Cranial Types at Chatal Hüyük and Tell al-Judaidah, Syria from the Late Fifth Millennium B.C. to the mid-Seventh Century A.D.', *Belleten* 49, 408–477.

Lane, A., 1938. 'Medieval Finds at Al Mina in North Syria', *Archaeologia* 87, 19–78.

Lassus, J., 1947. *Sanctuaires Chrétiens de Syrie: liturgique des édifices du culte Chrétien en Syrie, du IIIe siècle à la conquête musulmane* (Bibliothèque archéologique et historique 42, Paris).

Lassus, J., 1972. *Antioch-on-the-Orontes V: Les Portiques d'Antioche* (Princeton).

Loeschcke, S., 1912. 'Die Arbeiten zu Pergamon 1910–1911. V. Sigillata-Töpfereien in Tschandarli', *Mitteilungen des Deutschen Archäologischen Instituts Athenische Abteilung* 37, 344–407.

Maas, M., 2000. 'People and Identity in Roman Antioch'. In Kondoleon, 2000: 13–27.

McClellan, M.C., 1999. 'Hellenistic and Roman Pottery from 'Ain Dara'. In E.C. Stone and P. Zimansky (eds) *The Iron Age Settlement at 'Ain Dara, Syria: Survey and Surroundings* (British Archaeological Reports International S786, Oxford), 19–22.

Meyer-Schlichtmann, C., 1988. *Die Pergamenische Sigillata aus der Stadtgrabung von Pergamon mitte 2 Jh. v. Chr. – mitte Jh. n. Chr.* (Pergamenische Forschungen Band 6, Berlin).

Moorey, P.R.S., 1980. *Cemeteries of the First Millennium BC at Deve Hüyük* (British Archaeological Reports International S87, Oxford).

Negev, A, 1974. *The Nabatean Potter's Workshop at Oboda* (Rei Cretariae Romanae Fautorvm Acta Supplementa 1, Bonn).

Negev, A., 1986. *The Late Hellenistic and Early Roman Pottery of Nabatean Oboda.* (Qedem 22, Jerusalem).

von Oppenheim, M.F., 1950. *Tell Halaf II* (Berlin).

Orssaud, P., 1980. 'La ceramique', *Syria*, 57, 234–272.

Peña, I., 1983. 'Las iglesias de Jebel Baricha (Siria) de los siglos IV, V y VI', *Liber Annuus 33*, 327–334.

Peña, I., 1990. 'Aspectos Peculiares del Monacato Sirio', In G.C. Bottini, L. di Segni, and E. Alliata (eds) *Christian Archaeology in the Holy Land. New Discoveries* (Studium Biblicum Franciscanum Collectio Maior 36, Jerusalem), 561–570.

Peña, I., Castellana, P., and Fernández, R., 1975. *Les Stylites Syriens* (Biblicum Franciscanum Collectio Minor No. 16, Milan).

Peña, I., Castellana, P., and Fernández, R., 1980. *Les Reclus Syriens* (Biblicum Franciscanum Collectio Minor No. 23, Milan).

Peña, I., Castellana, P., and Fernández, R., 1983. *Les Cénobites Syriens* (Biblicum Franciscanum Collectio Minor No. 28, Milan).

Peña, I., Castellana, P., and Fernández, R., 1987. *Inventaire du Jebel Baricha. Recherches archéologiques dans la région des Villes Mortes de la Syrie du Nord* (Biblicum Franciscanum Collectio Minor 33, Milan).

Peña, I., Castellana, P., and Fernández, R., 1990. *Inventaire du Jebel el-A'la. Recherches archéologiques dans la région des Villes Mortes de la Syrie du Nord* (Biblicum Franciscanum Collectio Minor 31, Milan).

Pucci, G., 1977. 'La terre sigillate italiche, galliche e orientali'. In R. Peroni, A. Carandini, and R. Francovich (eds) *L'instrumentum domesticum di Ercolano e Pompei nella prima età imperiale* (Roma), 9–22.

Reynolds, P., 1997–1998. 'Pottery Production and Economic Exchange in Second Century Berytus. Preliminary Observations of Ceramic Trends from Quantified Ceramic Deposits from the Souks Excavations in Beirut', *Berytus 42*, 35–110.

Robinson, E.S.G., 1937. 'Coins from the Excavations at Al-Mina (1936)', *Numismatic Chronicle, 5th Series*, 17, 182–196.

Robinson, H.S, 1959. *The Athenian Agora V: Pottery of the Roman Period* (Princeton).

Schäfer, J., 1962. 'Terra Sigillata aus Pergamon', *Archäologischer Anzeiger*, 778–802.

Scherrer, P., 1995. 'The City of Ephesos from the Roman Period to Late Antiquity'. In H. Koester (ed.) *Ephesos Metropolis of Asia: An Interdisciplinary Approach to its Archaeology, Religion, and Culture* (Harvard Theological Studies 41, Valley Forge, (PA), 1–26.

Schmidt-Colinet, A., 1997. 'Aspects of 'Romanization': The Tomb Architecture at Palmyra and its Decoration'. In S. Alcock (ed.) *The Roman Empire in the East* (Oxbow Monograph 95, Oxford), 157–177.

Sheehan, M.M., 1985. 'Religious Life and Monastic Organization at Alahan'. In M. Gough (ed.) *Alahan: An Early Christian Monastery in Southern Turkey* (Studies and Texts 73, Canada), 197–220.

Slane, K.W., 1990. *Corinth XVII. Part II. The Sanctuary of Demeter and Kore. The Roman Pottery and Lamps.* (Princeton).

Slane, K.W., 1997. 'The Fine Wares'. In S.C. Herbert (ed.) *Tel Anafa II, i: The Hellenistic and Roman Pottery* (Journal of Roman Archaeology Supplementary Series, 10, Ann Arbor), 252–394.

Smith, R.R.R., 1998. 'Cultural Choice and Political Identity in Honorific Portrait Statues in Greek East in the Second Century A.D.', *Journal of Roman Studies* 88, 56–93.

Sodini, J.-P., 1989. 'Les églises de Syrie du Nord'. In J.-M. Dentzer and W. Orthmann (eds) *Archeologie et histoire de la Syrie II. La Syrie de l'époque achéménide à l'avènement de l'Islam* (Saarbrücken), 347–384.

Sodini, J.-P., Tate, G., Bauvant, B., Bauvant, S., Biscop, J.L., and Orssaud, P., 1980. 'Déhès (Syrie du nord), Campagnes I–III (1976–1978): recherches sur l'habitat rural', *Syria* 57, 1–304.

Stillwell, R. (ed.), 1938. *Antioch-on-the-Orontes II: The Excavations of 1933–1936* (Princeton).

Stillwell, R. (ed.), 1941. *Antioch-on-the-Orontes III: The Excavations of 1937–1939* (Princeton).

Stucky, R.A., 1983. *Ras Shamra Leukos Liman. Die Nach-Ugaritische Besiedlung von Ras Shamra* (Paris).

Tate, G., 1992. *Les Campagnes de la Syrie du nord I du IIe au VIIe siècle: un exemple d'expansion démographie et économique à la fin de l'antiquité* (Bibliothèque archéologique et historique 133, Paris).

Tchalenko, G., 1953–1958. *Villages Antiques de la Syrie du Nord: Le Massif du Bélus a l'époque Romaine* (Bibliothèque archéologique et historique 50, Paris).

Touma, M., 1984. *La ceramique byzantine de la Syrie du Nord du IV au VI siecle.* (DPhil. Thesis, Université de Paris I).

Tushingham, A.D., 1985. 'Excavations in the Armenian Garden on the Western Hill'. In *Excavations in Jerusalem 1961–1967. Volume 1* (Toronto), 2–155.

Unterkircher, E., 1983. 'Terra Sigillata aus dem Heraion von Samos', *Mitteilungen des deutschen Archäologischen Instituts Athenische Abteilung* 98, 173–214.

Vööbus, A., 1960. *History of Asceticism in the Syrian Orient: A Contribution to the History and Culture in the Near East. II. Early Monasticism in Mesopotamia and Syria* (Corpus Scriptorum Christianorum Orientalium 197, Louvain).

Waagé, D.B., 1952. *Antioch-on-the-Orontes IV. Part 2. Greek, Roman, Byzantine, and Crusaders' Coins* (Princeton).

Waagé, F.O., 1934. 'Lamps'. In G.W. Elderkin (ed.) *Antioch-on-the-Orontes 1: The Excavations of 1932* (Princeton), 58–66.

Waagé, F.O., 1941. 'Lamps'. In R. Stillwell (ed.) *Antioch-on-the-Orontes III: The Excavations of 1937–1939* (Princeton), 55–82.

Waagé, F.O., 1948. 'Hellenistic and Roman Tableware of North Syria', In F.O. Waagé (ed.) *Antioch-on- the-Orontes IV. Part One: Ceramics and Islamic Coins* (Princeton), 1–60.

Winstone, H.V.F., 1990. *Woolley of Ur: The Life of Sir Leonard Woolley* (London).

Woolf, G., 1993–1994. 'Becoming Roman, Staying Greek: Culture, Identity, and the Civilizing Process in the Roman East', *Proceedings of the Cambridge Philological Society* 40, 116–143.

Woolf, G., 1997. 'Roman Urbanization of the East', In S. Alcock (ed.) *The Roman Empire in the East* (Oxbow Monograph 95, Oxford), 1–14.

Woolley, C.L., 1937. 'Excavations Near Antioch in 1936', *The Antiquaries' Journal* 17, 1–15.

Woolley, C.L., 1938. 'The Excavations at Al Mina, Sueidia. II', *Journal of the Hellenic Society* 53, 133–170.

Woolley, C.L., 1953. *A Forgotten Kingdom: Being a Result of the Results Obtained from the Excavations of Two Mounds Atchana and Al Mina in the Turkish Hatay* (London).

Zorolu, L., 1989. 'Some Roman Names on Eastern Sigillata A from Samosata'. In D.H. French (ed.) *The Eastern Frontier of the Roman Empire. Proceedings of a Colloquium Held at Ankara in September 1988* (British Archaeological Reports International S553 ii, Oxford), 573–579.

6. The Archaeological Landscape of Late Roman Antioch

Jesse Casana

Recent archaeological survey by the Oriental Institute's Amuq Valley Regional Project has begun to document extensive remains of the Late Roman landscape in the plains and hills around Antioch helping to transform our understanding of issues ranging from the distribution of population and wealth in the countryside to the organization of specialized production and exchange in the northern Levant. Considering the size and importance of Antioch in late antiquity, it is not surprising that its immediate agricultural hinterland in the Amuq Valley was densely occupied, and yet previous archaeological investigations found little evidence of Late Roman settlement.[1] The paucity of archaeological data from the region has led many discussions to focus attention myopically on the Dead Cities of the *massif calcaire*, treating these settlements as though they were historically unique and geographically isolated. In fact, they are simply the best preserved and therefore most obvious features within a much more extensive settled landscape of which the Amuq Valley is a part.[2] Unlike the Dead Cities, settlements that were located in the lowland plains and the western highlands were constructed primarily of mudbrick and wood, and are often evidenced today only by scatters of sherds, tile and stone. Contrary to the popularly held belief that late antique settlements in the Amuq Valley are forever lost because "the locals lived in houses of reeds and mudbrick that have left no trace",[3] these sites can be located using intensive survey strategies. Ball recently argues that intensive archaeological surveys of regions like the Amuq Valley are critical if we are to contextualize our understanding of the Dead Cities.[4] Moreover, the survey data are essential in order to situate Antioch within a larger framework of rural settlement.

In 1995 the University of Chicago's Oriental Institute initiated the Amuq Valley Regional Project (AVRP), a coordinated regional research programme designed to integrate archaeological survey, geomorphological and palaeo-environmental investigations, and targeted excavations in order to build a comprehensive under-standing of the cultural history and archaeological sequences in this important region.[5] As the archaeological survey strategy has moved from an extensive, full-coverage survey of the entire region (1995–1998) towards more intensive investigations of specific areas (2000–2001), our knowledge of the Hellenistic, Roman and Late Roman landscapes has been enormously improved.[6] In particular, the introduction of very high-resolution Corona satellite imagery,[7] and the extension of the survey into the

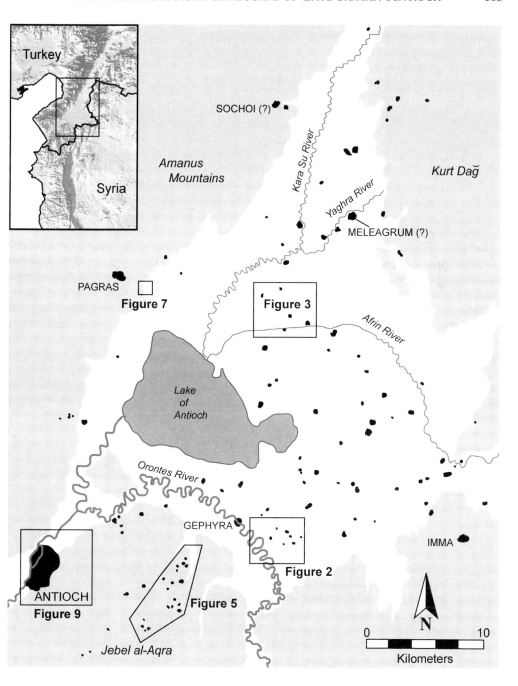

Figure 6.1: Map of the Amuq Valley showing archaeological sites with documented evidence of Late Roman or late antique occupation. Recent work both on the plain (Figure 6.2) and in the uplands (Figure 6.5) suggests that there are many more small Late Roman sites in the Amuq Valley that have not yet been recorded.

uplands have resulted in the discovery of many previously unknown Late Roman settlements and other features including canals, roads, mines and quarries. Our understanding of Late Roman settlement and economy is enhanced by contemporary historical sources.[8] In particular, Libanius' *In praise of Antioch* (*Or.* II), a panegyric delivered as part of the Olympic festival held in Antioch in AD 356, provides detailed descriptions of many aspects pertinent to the rural landscape.[9] In addition to its main research goals, the AVRP has also recorded many areas where important archaeological remains are threatened by the growth of modern cities and industrial/agricultural development in the region. While the archaeological survey is far from complete, the interim results presented here provide a clear picture of the general nature of Late Roman settlement in the Amuq Valley. These findings offer new insights into many issues including the organization of agricultural production, the locations of transportation and communication networks, and the relationship between an intensification of land use and local environmental change, as well as highlighting the need for continued salvage and preservation work in the region.

SETTLEMENTS IN THE PLAIN

Antioch (modern Antakya) is located at the southwestern corner of the fertile and well-watered Amuq Plain, which today is in the province of Hatay, Turkey (Figure 6.1). The plain, measuring approximately 30x40 km, has been a centre of dense human settlement from the Neolithic to the modern era, and this rich cultural history attracted many archaeologists to the region in the 1920s and 1930s. An Oriental Institute team excavated several large Bronze and Iron Age tells, and Robert Braidwood conducted a pioneering archaeological survey of the plain.[10] In addition, Sir Leonard Woolley led excavations at the site of Alalakh (Tell Atchana), the capital of the Middle and Late Bronze Age kingdom of Mukish that was centreed in the Amuq Valley.[11] However, these projects documented little Late Roman occupation. Excavations at Chatal Höyük and Tell Judaidah found a minor late antique village and a small church, while the survey by Braidwood recorded surprisingly few Late Roman sites. These ephemeral remains and a handful of inscriptions and monuments recorded primarily by earlier French epigraphers[12] constitute the bulk of what has been known of the Late Roman Antiochene landscape until recently.

Results of the AVRP archaeological survey have made it apparent that the late first millennium BC witnessed the beginning of a profound structural transformation in settlement that helps to explain the dearth of Late Roman remains found by earlier projects. For most of the history of human occupation in the Amuq Valley, from the Chalcolithic through the Iron Age (6000–500 BC), virtually all settlement was concentrated at large, nucleated tell sites located in the lowland plains and river valleys, as was the case throughout much of the Near East.[13] However, beginning in the Hellenistic period and peaking in the Late Roman period, there was an increasing emphasis on settlement in small, dispersed villages that were spread across all parts of the plain and into surrounding highlands. The reason Braidwood found little evidence of Late Roman settlement in his original survey of the plain is actually

Figure 6.2: A Corona image of the southern Amuq Plain, around Tell Tayinat and Tell Atchana (Alalakh). All Early Bronze Age through Iron Age occupation was concentrated at these two major tells, while Hellenistic through Early Islamic occupation was located at numerous small sites (indicated by arrows) on the surrounding plain. Other features, including the ancient Orontes River channel, are also visible).

because he was mainly concerned with recording tell sites, as is indicated by the title of his monograph, *Mounds in the Plain of Antioch*.[14] In fact, during the Late Roman period the plain was probably more densely occupied than at any other time in its history, but because the large majority of sites in that period are very small with little topographic relief, they are largely invisible to tell-based surveys.[15]

The use of high-resolution Corona satellite imagery has proved to be a tremendously valuable tool in locating the many small, dispersed archaeological sites that typify the Late Roman period. For example, in the region around Tells Tayinat and Atchana in the southern plain, all Early Bronze Age through Iron Age occupation is concentrated at these two large tells. However, examination of a Corona image reveals the location of many other very small, previously unrecorded sites in the vicinity (Figure 6.2). Further examination of the satellite imagery has shown that the situation appears to be similar throughout the Amuq Plain, and nearly 100 previously unrecorded small sites have been identified. The sample of these small sites that has been visited were all occupied at some time in the Roman-Late Roman period, suggesting that the AVRP settlement map (Figure 6.1) may severely under-represent the intensity of Late Roman settlement on the plain. In upcoming seasons we plan to continue recording more of these small sites, and to refine their dating criteria as much as possible.

While settlement away from tells was very common in the Late Roman period, there also appears to have been small settlements on many tell sites, although they were usually very minor in comparison to much larger earlier components. The situation of late antique tell settlement is probably well illustrated by the excavations at Chatal Höyük, where a large, walled Iron Age city was abandoned in the late first millennium BC, and replaced by a very small village nestled on the northern spur of the site that was occupied in the Late Roman period.[16] Recent survey work shows that elsewhere in the valley, evidence of Late Roman settlement on tells can be even more elusive. However, at any site that has been intensively surveyed, at least some small indication of late antique settlement has been found. For instance, at Alalakh (Tell Atchana), excavations recorded no architectural features dating to after the Late Bronze Age,[17] but a recent systematic surface collection of the site found a handful of late antique ceramics and roof tiles on the mound and a contemporary field scatter northeast of the site.[18] Similarly, at the Chalcolithic site of Tell Kurdu, excavations revealed no evidence of later architecture.[19] However, several roof tiles and late antique sherds were found on the site and in surrounding fields, while excavations recovered one 6th century coin. The evidence suggests that there may have been small villages, or at least isolated buildings, on many tells in the Amuq at some time during the Late Roman period.

RIVERS AND CANALS

The very large number of small settlements both on and off tells was probably part of a region-wide system of intensive agricultural production that fed the seemingly large rural population as well as the major urban centres of Antioch and Seleucia Pieria. Agricultural production was made possible by an abundant water supply, both from the Lake of Antioch in the centre of the plain, and several rivers that flow into the Amuq, including the Orontes River from the south, the Kara Su river from the north, and the Afrin River from the east (Figure 6.1), as Libanius described:

> Who could enumerate the streams which irrigate the land, whether they be great or small, perennial or seasonal, they are all equally beneficial whether they have their source in the mountains, or rise in the plain, whether they unite with each other, or flow into the lake, or into the sea (*Or.*11.27).

The Orontes is by far the largest of these rivers and was a critically important resource as a reliable supply of water (Libanius *In praise of Antioch* 244), but also for the ease by which it facilitated transport of agricultural products and bulk goods to Antioch and further to the Mediterranean coast at Seleucia Pieria. As early as the first century BC Strabo reports that the voyage from the Mediterranean coast to Antioch was made in one day (*Geography* 16.2.7).[20] In the Late Roman period, Libanius reports similarly that, "the intervening distance [between Antioch and the coast] is 120 stades, so that a well-girt man setting off from the coast at sunrise will carry goods from there and arrive here by noon" (*In praise of Antioch* 41). Later he remarks that, "most important of all [the Orontes'] course below the city is navigable. It is not impassable because of rocks as much even of the Nile is" (*In Praise of Antioch* 262). However, the Orontes required maintenance to ensure that river traffic could pass its length unobstructed, as is indicated by a law known from the Theodosian Code mandating that the fleet of Seleucia was responsible for clearing the river.[21] Moreover, by the eleventh century the Islamic geographer Muqqaddasī (170) comments that the Orontes between Antioch and the coast was no longer navigable,[22] presumably because the maintenance of the river had ceased.

Similarly, it has often been suggested that agricultural products of the *massif calcaire* would have been transported down the Orontes River to Antioch, yet the northern Ghab Valley through which the Orontes flows has traditionally been an extensive shallow marsh, and would have been impassable to river traffic without considerable maintenance. A reference in Abu al-Fida suggests that in the Islamic period, river transport was facilitated in the Ghab through a canalized waterway:

> The second great lagoon, which is to the north of the first, is separated from
> it by the marshy land covered with reeds, through which runs a waterway,
> whereby boats go from the southern to the northern lagoon. (Abu al-Fida,
> 40)[23]

Examination of Corona imagery in the region has revealed the presence of a very large canalized feature that runs through the entire northern Ghab Valley, which is probably the very waterway that is described by al-Fida (Figure 6.3). Many archaeological sites are visible along the waterway, and the dating of these sites by a recent archaeological survey suggests that the same channel was in use from at least the Late Roman period,[24] making river transport possible.

The importance of the Orontes River to the transport network in late antiquity is clear, but there was also an extensive system of smaller canals and rivers in the Amuq. In the central plain, analysis of Corona imagery reveals the presence of a large Late Roman-Early Islamic canal network, tapping the waters of the Kara Su and Afrin Rivers (Figure 6.4). Today the Afrin River, flowing from the east, runs through the central plain, and emptied into the Lake of Antioch until the lake was drained in the 1960s. However, in the Roman-Middle Islamic periods, the Afrin flowed along a more northerly course.[25] Major upcast mounds attest that this older course had been canalized, and the presence of numerous archaeological sites along it helps to date the feature. On the lower course of this ancient, canalized portion of the Afrin, there was once an extensive network of smaller canals, irrigating a large part of the central plain. Associated with the canal network, there were many small settlements fairly evenly spaced throughout the irrigated landscape. Interestingly, the northern half of this irrigation and settlement system was eventually submerged below the extensive marshland that covered much of the plain until the 1960s, and even the southern portion of the system is in an area that was seasonally inundated.

A coring project has shown that the Lake of Antioch did not begin to form until the

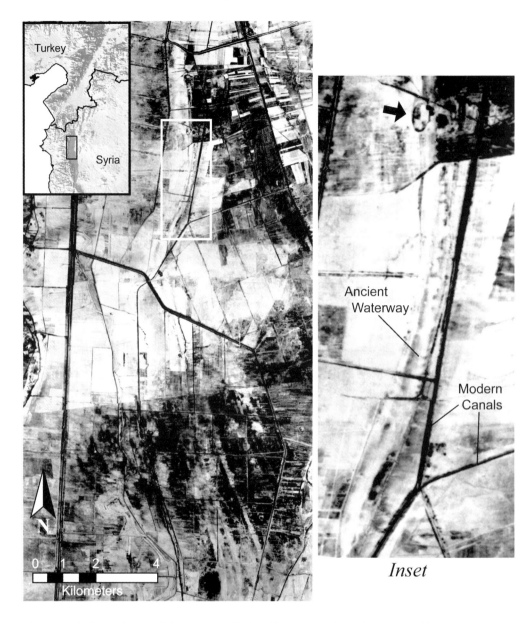

Figure 6.3: A Corona image of the northern Ghab Valley, upriver from the Amuq Valley in Syria. Major linear features running through this area of traditional marshland are the remnants of a waterway that facilitated river traffic. Numerous archaeological sites located along the waterway, one visible at the top of the inset (indicated by arrow), date the feature from the Late Roman to Middle Islamic period).

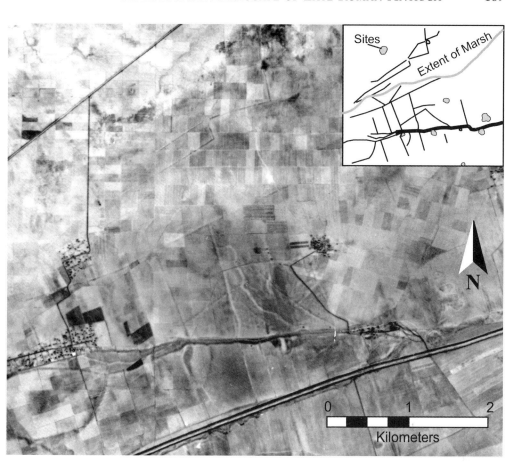

Figure 6.4: A Corona image of the central Amuq Plain. Linear features visible throughout the image are Late Roman-Early Islamic canals. In the Islamic period, the northern part of this irrigation network was inundated by the expansion of marshland, which appears as a light-toned feature in the upper left of the image.

late first millennium BC, and that it continued to grow in size through the Islamic period.[26] Geomorphological evidence alone makes a determination of the precise timing of the formation of the lake difficult, but John Malalas reports from a secondary Hellenistic source that the city of Antigonia, founded in the late fourth century BC, was located near the shores of the lake (*Chronicle* 8.198).[27] By the Late Roman period, the lake formed a prominent geographical feature in the plain and an important part of the local economy (Libanius, *In praise of Antioch* 260–262). In the fourteenth century, Abu al-Fida[28] describes the Lake of Antioch as an extensive marsh, saying: "It is covered with reeds, and there are fish and birds here like to which we have mentioned in describing the Lake of Afâmiyyah" (Abu al-Fida, 41). In this way the geomorphological and historical evidence complement one another in building a history of the lake, in which it began to form in the late first millennium BC, was an important feature by the early Hellenistic period, and continued to grow in size through the Islamic period.[29] With the inundation of large areas of the Amuq Plain in the Islamic period, much of the settlement and agricultural landscape that is visible on the Corona imagery was lost, but in the Late Roman period the system was at its heyday.

These river and canal systems provided water to irrigate the plain, but also played a critical role in the transport of agricultural products from the entire Amuq Valley into Antioch in the Late Roman period. The system of transport facilitated by the rivers is described by Libanius:

> The river and the lake are a source of profit to the city not merely in that they provide fare for our tables, but also because all the produce of the soil comes into the city's possession through the ease by which it is transported, for the import of grain is not reduced to the meagre amount brought in by pack animals. The countryside is divided up between them; the river flows through areas which derive no assistance from the lake; similarly the lake extends over those areas where there is no aid from the river. By lake and river craft they empty the countryside of its produce and transport it to our town (*In praise of Antioch* 260).

Waterborne transport was fundamental to the movement of large quantities of bulk goods everywhere in the ancient world, and the importance of the river and canal networks in the Amuq Valley is highlighted by the severe grain shortage that occurred in Antioch in AD 362–3.[30] There was a drought in the Amuq Valley that led to a very poor spring grain harvest in AD 362, and at the same time, there was a very large contingent of troops in Antioch preparing to march against Persia under Julian. The increased demand for grain combined with a poor harvest led to skyrocketing prices and widespread famine during Julian's visit to the city. Only when the situation was on the brink of crisis in late October did Julian issue an order to import 400,000 *modii* of grain from Chalcis and Hieropolis (*Misopogon* 368).[31] What is striking from a modern perspective is that these cities were not far from Antioch, and yet only as a last resort and under imperial edict was any grain transported overland. In spite of very high inflation of prices and rampant speculation and profiteering by local businessmen, grain was not imported from beyond the limits of the riverine network.

HIGHLAND SETTLEMENT

The highlands surrounding the Amuq Plain also formed an important component of the Late Roman landscape, and in those areas there is a stark contrast between settlement in the Bronze Age and that in the Roman-Late Roman period. Surveys of selected areas in the Amanus Mountains to the west of the plain, and in the low hills of the Jebel al-Aqra to the south, have found little evidence of upland occupation after the Neolithic and before the Hellenistic period. However, beginning in the late first millennium BC there was a rapid movement of settlements into the hills, and by the

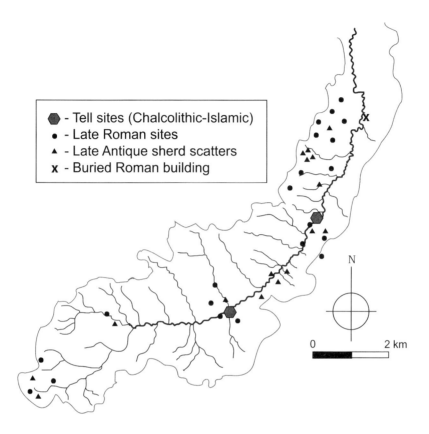

Figure 6.5: A map of a valley in the Jebel al-Aqra showing the distribution of archaeological sites. All pre-Hellenistic occupation was concentrated at two tell sites on the valley floor. However, by the Late Roman period, small, dispersed settlements were located on hills throughout the valley.

Late Roman period, the uplands were very densely settled. A small side valley to the south of the Amuq Plain in the Jebel al-Aqra clearly illustrates this pattern of increased and dispersed upland settlement (Figure 6.5). In this area, all Chalcolithic through Iron Age settlement was located at two tell sites on the valley floor. However, beginning in the Hellenistic period and peaking in the Late Roman period, new settlements appear on almost every hill that has been surveyed, providing a virtual microcosm of the general transformation in settlement that has been documented on a regional scale. Similarly, exploratory surveys of the Amanus foothills to the west of the plain have found many small Roman and Late Roman sites. Following a description of the rich and fertile Amuq Plain and the abundance of its agricultural production, Libanius mentions the agricultural production of the highlands that was undoubtedly associated with the many settlements:

> We have hills either in our own territory or around it; some bisect the plain,
> others with a broad sweep enclose the entrance and bar it in at the outer
> limits. Some of them differ in appearance from the level plains for they are
> raised aloft, yet they vie in fertility with the lands at their feet. Farmers work
> there, in land no less desirable, driving their ploughs to the summits. In
> short, whatever the level plain alone produces elsewhere, here is produced
> by the mountain districts also. (*In praise of Antioch* 22).

The Amanus Mountains are well known for their rich metallurgical, stone and timber resources, and some of the highland settlements were likely to have been partially devoted to their exploitation as well as to farming. For instance a late antique copper mine and a nearby Late Roman settlement were found by the AVRP in the region of Kisicik in the Amanus Mountains, and ancient gold mines have been documented as well.[32] To the north, near the Beylan Pass, a Hellenistic-Roman site and a late antique site were found in association with an ancient limestone quarry. Similar but much larger limestone quarries were found in the hills to the northeast of Antioch, some of which may have provided stone for the nearby city wall and for major building projects within the city itself. Libanius also describes these kinds of extractive industries in the mountains:

> The more infertile of the mountain districts make their contributions in other
> ways. Either from their quarries, they provide stone for the city walls, or
> timber for roofing and other purposes…Flocks of sheep and goats make
> their contribution to human welfare: no part of the land is cast off as useless
> (*In praise of Antioch* 25–26).

The extension of agricultural settlements into the highlands, deforestation associated both with farmland clearance and timbering, and the consequential movement of pastoral grazing into increasingly marginal areas all probably contributed to episodes of severe soil erosion that occurred in the Late Roman period. The best evidence is found in the Jebel al-Aqra, where at the mouth of the intensively surveyed valley (Figure 6.5), a section in a modern streambed exposed a Roman building buried by over four meters of sediment (Figure 6.6).

The deposition of the sediments occurred in the late antique period, indicated by many sherds contained within the strata overlying the building, contemporary with the phase of peak settlement on surrounding hills. Similar evidence of extreme erosion has been found on the fringes of the Amanus as well,[33] and one securely dated section appears to relate to intensive settlement in the valley above, around a large Late Roman town probably identified as Sochoi (see below). These episodes of severe erosion contributed to rapid aggradation of the Orontes River levee. Flood-borne sediments buried much of the southern Amuq Plain and also covered large parts of Roman Antioch below as many as six meters of alluvium, hindering excavations of the city.[34]

Figure 6.6: A section exposed in the modern streambed at the mouth of the valley shown in Figure 6.5. A Roman building seen at the base of the section was buried by over 4 meters of sediment in the late antique period, suggesting extreme erosion of nearby slopes.

The Productive Economy

The erosion of the hills in the Late Roman period is probably related in part to extensive farming around the many settlements located there, but to understand better the processes involved requires some knowledge of what was being produced and where. There is a long debate regarding the nature of agricultural production in the Dead Cities, and because the sites in the Amuq Valley are part of the same settlement system, the arguments are relevant here. The discussion has been divided between two basic perspectives. On the one hand, Tchalenko argues in his original publication of the Dead Cities that they were specialized producers of cash crops, primarily olive oil. Conversely, Tate, on the basis of further survey and excavation, maintains that there is no evidence for this kind of mono-cropping horticulture, but that the Dead Cities were largely self-sufficient villages.[35] The question of production and exchange in the Dead Cities plays into a larger debate regarding the degree to which the ancient world can be understood through the lens of market-capitalism. It is undoubtedly wrong to assume, as is often the case in archaeological literature, that the movement of objects constitutes evidence of market-based trade. On the other hand, to disregard the operation of some monetarized, profit-driven trade in the Late Roman period would ignore a large body of evidence to the contrary.[36]

In the Amuq Valley there is a very long tradition of mixed agricultural production both in the highland and the plain, and therefore there is little reason to infer the cash crop, mono-culture suggested by Tchalenko. As far back as the Late Bronze Age there is clear evidence for mixed agricultural production in the Alalakh census lists, where many settlements are recorded as having fields, orchards and vineyards together in the same areas.[37] In the Late Roman period, the same system of mixed agricultural production that appears to have been in operation since at least the Bronze Age is described by Libanius:

> The land, for instance, is as level as the sea. It is deep, fertile and friable…it is good for sowing and planting alike and is well adapted for crops of either kind (*In praise of Antioch* 19)

> (The hills) vie in fertility with the lands at their feet…in short, whatever the level plain alone produces elsewhere, here is produced by the mountain districts also; whatever the mountain districts usually provide elsewhere, here is produced by the plains also. It has not been divided up to grow either plants or seed. You can see in one and the same place, trees growing and corn beneath them. In fact, though it shows these crops separately, it produces them all together, for their part of our domain is rich in barley and in wine, and partakes in everything (*In praise of Antioch* 22–23)

Mixed agricultural production appears to have continued to be the norm in the Islamic period,[38] and as recently as the 1930s, Weulersse describes the same mixed agricultural economy.[39] Even today, while much of the plain has been given over to industrialized cotton production, in areas around villages in the hills unsuited for cotton, mixed agricultural and horticultural production is still common.

Nevertheless, it is probably wrong to view the many rural settlements of the Amuq Valley as entirely self-sufficient and somehow disconnected from regional and global market-oriented trading networks. The sheer volume of amphorae that originate in the northern Levant and appear at sites throughout the Mediterranean and beyond, particularly the "Late-Roman 1" amphorae, attest to the movement of massive quantities of olive oil and/or wine from the Antiochene region. These amphorae became extremely common at sites throughout the Roman world in the fourth to sixth centuries,[40] contemporary with the phase of peak settlement in the Amuq Valley. The fact that the rural settlements of the Amuq were involved in the production of olive oil and wine is further suggested by the numerous presses found in the region. Better preserved oil and wine presses from the Dead Cities suggest very large-scale production, far beyond the needs of local communities.[41] Additionally, palynological evidence from Lake Hula in the southern Levant, where there is a similar intensification of rural settlement, and from the Ghab valley below the *massif calcaire*, both show a major peak in olive pollen in the Late Roman period.[42] These palynological data suggest an increase in the cultivation of olive by orders of magnitude. Perhaps most telling is the description of the exportation of olive oil and wine by Libanius:

> If you mention Dionysus, he revels in our midst; if Athena, the earth is luxuriant with her olives. So wine in plenty is exported to our neighbours, and a still greater quantity of olive oil is transported to all quarters in merchant ships (*In praise of Antioch* 20)

Libanius goes on to describe in detail the process by which these products were transported into the city centre in Antioch, and from there sent down the Orontes River to Seleucia Pieria on the coast to be exported throughout the Mediterranean.

The co-occurrence of an intensification in rural settlement with a proliferation of exported amphorae has been argued to be related to market-based trade in products such as oil and wine.[43] There is certainly at least some evidence for a mercantile trade in agricultural products in Antioch during the Late Roman period. For instance, we learn of many profiteering landholders in Julian's account of his visit to Antioch in AD 362–3 who took advantage of famine and inflated grain prices to gouge the urban population of Antioch.[44] A thriving trade in both grains and cash crops could have generated substantial wealth. If Ward-Perkins is correct in his assessment that villages in northwest Syria and much of the eastern Empire were largely populated by independent landowners,[45] then much of this wealth may have fed the rural economy as well as that in Antioch.

Virtually all scholars agree that there is evidence of substantial rural wealth in the Dead Cities, seen in the monumentality of the architecture and the fineries recovered in excavation. Furthermore, inscriptions from within the Dead Cities suggest that indigenous rural landowners may have paid for these luxuries.[46] Because of the close parallels between settlements in the *massif calcaire* and those in the Amuq Valley, it is likely that the latter were comparably wealthy. However, because the settlements in the Amuq are not well preserved, it is far more difficult to determine how wealthy they might have been. Nevertheless, the limited evidence that can be derived from survey does support the view that the villages of the Amuq Valley were also centres of rural wealth. For instance, even the smallest sites routinely contain fine, imported ceramics and glass, mosaic floor tesserae, and occasional coins.[47] Some sites also show evidence of monumental stone architecture, and others are associated with elaborate rock-cut tombs. Finally, Libanius reports that the rural settlements were indeed very wealthy and prosperous, asserting, "there are large towns and populous villages with a larger population than many towns; they employ craftsmen, just as happens in cities…they buy and sell, and are far more prosperous than merchant venturers" (*In praise of Antioch* 230).

TOWNS AND CITIES

Although small village sites were very common in the Late Roman period throughout the Amuq Valley, there were also several larger towns and cities in the region, some of which have been identified with historically known toponyms (Figure 6.1). For example, the Late Roman towns of Imma and Pagras are firmly identified with the modern towns of Yeni Sehir and Bakras. Other ancient towns, including Meleagrum and Sochoi, have been tentatively identified with Murat Pasa and Ceylanli, respectively. Still other major settlements that are known historically, notably Antigonia, the Hellenistic predecessor to Antioch, have not been located on the ground. Finally, several very large sites recorded by the AVRP do not seem to appear in any extant historical sources, such as Tell Sultan (AS 32).

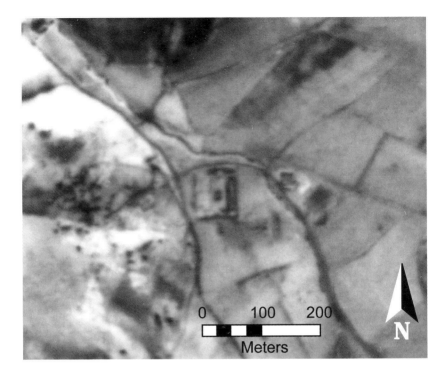

Figure 6.7: A Corona image of the valley below the fort at Bakras in the Amanus foothills, where there are extensive remains of a large town, with historically attested occupation from the Hellenistic period. The rectilinear feature at the center of the image is an Early-Middle Islamic caravansary. While the building complex is clearly visible in this 1970 image, today only a few walls are extant.

While many of these larger sites are known exclusively from occasional standing architectural remains or monumental inscriptions, recent work by the AVRP demonstrated the quantity of other archaeological remains at these sites and the need for more intensive investigations of the urban landscape. For example, at Bakras, the presence of a large fort is well known and appears in tour guides and academic works alike. However, the survey documented a very large town in the valley below the castle that dates from the Hellenistic period, as well as numerous water mills, terrace walls and bridges in the vicinity. There is a caravansary at the entrance to the Beylan pass near the mouth of the valley, but today the building complex is only preserved as a few fragmentary stone walls.[48] However, its plan is clearly visible on Corona imagery of the area (Figure 6.7).

Further north in the Amanus foothills, the town of Ceylanli (or Gunduzlu), probably ancient Sochoi, was known only from a Roman tomb complex and several inscriptions recorded there in the 1890s[49] (Figure 6.1). The AVRP investigated the area in 2001 and began to document the rich urban landscape related to the site. In the modern village of Ceylanli, the Late Roman settlement is most evident in the reused column fragments

Figure 6.8: A small Hellenistic and early Roman temple situated on a mountain top above the large Roman-Late Roman town at Ceylanli, possibly ancient Sochoi.

and other monumental architectural pieces that are built into modern houses. Additionally, the streets of the village are on a rough grid plan, suggesting that it has maintained the original Roman plan. Interestingly, at the base of the mountain upon which Ceylanli is situated, a very large, orthogonally planned Hellenistic site was found, which is likely the Hellenistic forerunner of the Late Roman settlement above. Cut into a cliff overlooking the town there is a series of monumental tombs and on top of this mountain, the survey found a small Hellenistic-Roman temple complex (Figure 6.8). The temple appears to have been demolished in antiquity and a stone fortification wall was later built around the complex. The settlement is located at the junction of the north-south road through the Amuq plain and a traditional road leading west to Alexandretta (Iskenderun). Evidence of the ancient road and several other features including numerous watermills were recorded as well. More investigations at the larger Late Roman towns in the Amuq Valley are planned in future seasons, and will help to further document the complex urban landscapes in the region.

ANTIOCH

In the Late Roman period, Antioch dwarfed all other settlements in the northern Levant, both in terms of its political, religious and economic importance, as well as in size and population. However, accepted wisdom holds that the majority of the ancient city is either deeply buried below alluvium or is obscured by the modern city of Antakya.[50] Neither is entirely true.[51] Some parts of the ancient city are deeply buried, but in other areas remains are clearly visible at the surface. Moreover, while Antakya

Figure 6.9: Corona image of Antakya (Antioch). The modern city (A) covers only the southern portion of Late Roman Antioch because most recent urban growth has been on the west bank of the Orontes. Several features important features are visible on the image including: (B) the city walls, (C) the former island where the imperial palace and cathedral were located, and preserved portions of the Roman street plan. (D) Sections exposed to the northeast of the city at are illustrated in Figures 6.10–6.11.[52]

covers much of the southern end of the ancient city, most of the modern city's growth has been on the west bank of the Orontes, while the ancient city was on the east bank. Today, large parts of the ancient city, including much of the central island, are covered only by agricultural fields. Nevertheless, since the close of the Princeton-led excavations in the 1930s, little if any systematic archaeological work has been done in the city.

Beginning in 2001, the AVRP undertook a preliminary survey of areas along the modern Antakya-Reyhanli road, in an area once probably covered by Antioch's northern suburbs. Archaeological excavations in the 1930s focused on the central part of the city and in the suburb of Daphne (modern Harbiye) to the south. However, in the Late Roman period Antioch extended very far to the north along the road to Imma and Beroea, and Libanius comments that in these suburbs the "buildings now before the city gates would suffice to form a city in themselves" (*In praise of Antioch* 231) and that, "when you drive out, you will swear you are seeing what you have left behind, but in miniature" (*In praise of Antioch* 232).

Recent construction, earthmoving and severe flooding in the spring of 2001 have exposed many sections along the modern Antakya-Reyhanli road, which roughly

Figure 6.10: A section excavated into a hillside north of Antakya that has exposed many Late Roman buildings.

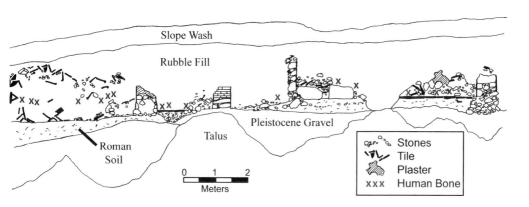

Figure 6.11: A drawing of the left part of the section seen in Figure 10. Well-preserved Late Roman buildings are constructed on top of an earlier Roman soil, and are buried by 2–3 meters of rubble. Human skeletal remains are found beneath the rubble and roof collapse throughout the section.

follows the ancient road to Imma. And, as Libanius almost seems to foretell, "now, as you dig the ground to lay foundations, everywhere you find traces of the past" (*In praise of Antioch* 229). In these sections, many fragments of ancient architecture were recorded, the majority of which appear to have been small houses or terrace walls. However, several much more impressive and important finds were made. For example, in one area, an excavated hillside behind modern houses has exposed a very large building constructed of well-dressed limestone blocks, the plan of which suggests it may have been a bathhouse. Nearby a large mosaic floor seen in section, and marble column fragments found in rubble washed down the drainage, attest to the scale of the building complex.

Space prevents a detailed presentation of all finds from the ongoing survey, however one area is of particular interest and warrants discussion. Along the road north of Antakya, recent earthmoving has exposed a 10 meter-high x 150 meter-long section in a hillside (Figure 6.10 and 6.11). The area provides a cross-sectional view of many buildings dating to the 5th or 6th centuries. The buildings, probably houses, are very well preserved with intact wall and floor plaster, and appear to have been destroyed in a landslide event that covered the structures by several meters of rubble. On the floors of most of the houses there are many human skeletons, which appear to be buried beneath roof collapse. Whole vessels eroding out of the section, the well-preserved nature of the houses, and the characteristics of the rubble fill above the buildings all suggest that they were destroyed suddenly, and therefore that the human remains may be *in-situ* victims of a landslide. Ceramics date the buildings to the fifth or sixth century, raising the possibility that they were destroyed in the great earthquake of AD 526. The account of the earthquake by John Malalas, who was probably an eyewitness, details the extensive destruction of most of Antioch and puts the death toll at 250,000. Considering the scale of the catastrophe it certainly would not be surprising to find some archaeological evidence of the event. Of course, it is impossible to be certain without further investigations whether this particular section is the product of the 526 earthquake, one of the other many calamities that befell Antioch in the sixth century, or unrelated entirely. But the section does demonstrate that there is tremendous potential throughout Antioch and its suburbs to uncover sealed, *in-situ* destruction deposits. Moreover, because there was no reoccupation of the area subsequent to the destruction, it provides good archaeological evidence for the decline of Antioch following the disastrous sixth century.

CONCLUSIONS

The results presented here are preliminary, but they greatly improve our under-standing of the cultural landscape of Late Roman Antioch. It is now clear that the plains and highlands throughout the Amuq Valley were densely occupied by small village sites interspersed by occasional large towns. These settlements were part of a region-wide system of intensive agricultural production and exploitation of natural resources that was facilitated by an extensive network of rivers and canals. It appears that the dispersal of settlement away from traditional tell sites and the movement of settlements into the highlands contributed to a series of severe environmental changes including extreme upland erosion, flooding and sedimentation on the Orontes River, and the growth of the Lake of Antioch. While many of the sites recorded by the survey are evidenced only by small artifact scatters, more substantial remains have been found, and others likely lie undiscovered at the larger towns and in the extensive suburbs of Antioch.

The Oriental Institute's Amuq Valley Regional Project is ongoing, and our primary goals in upcoming seasons will be: 1) to expand intensive survey to more upland areas, 2) to visit and record more of the small sites that have been located on Corona imagery, and 3) to further investigate the relationship between changing land use and environmental systems. These efforts will help to clarify many questions that are raised by our current understanding of the late antique landscape. For instance, while it is evident that the Late Roman period witnessed an overall peak in dispersed, rural settlement, the timing and nature of the movement away from tell sites in the later first millennium BC remains poorly understood. Furthermore, it appears that the system of rural settlement was once again transformed in the Islamic period, as many small village sites were abandoned, although it remains unclear precisely when and how this change occurred. Finally, the intensification of upland settlement seems to have been the primary cause of erosion in some areas, but it remains possible that a change in climate, such as an increase in storminess, might have also contributed to the series of environmental changes that have been documented in the Amuq. In addition to these main ongoing research goals, the AVRP will continue its efforts to record threatened remains throughout the Amuq Valley, and as always, to work with the Turkish Ministry of Culture and our colleagues both at the Antakya Archaeological Museum and at Mustafa Kemal University to preserve and protect important finds wherever possible.

Notes

Acknowledgements

The fieldwork discussed in this paper was conducted as part of the University of Chicago Oriental Institute Amuq Valley Regional Project (AVRP) under the auspices of the Turkish Ministry of Culture and the Directorate Generale of Monuments and Museums, Kenan Yurttagül. The AVRP works in partnership with The Mustafa Kemal University, as well as with the Antakya Archaeological Museum and its director Aslı Tütüncü. I must thank K. Aslihan Yener, the director of the AVRP, and T.J. Wilkinson, the director of the archaeological survey, for making the fieldwork possible and for their ongoing academic support and guidance. Fieldwork has been supported by grants from the National Geographic Society, the Institute for Aegean Prehistory, the Kress Foundation, the Oriental Institute and the University of Chicago. Special thanks must be given to Dr. Hatice Pamir for the many ways she provides assistance in Turkey, as well as to The Mustafa Kemal University and its Rector Professor Haluk Ipek for providing personnel, facilities and accommodations in Antakya. I also owe a debt of gratitude to all the survey staff members who have worked on the project since 1995, and especially to Asa Eger for his able assistance in the 2001 season. Work on the remote sensing portion of this project was begun at the Center for Earth Observation at Yale University, and I must thank the staff there as well as Nicholas Kouchoukos for facilitating the collaboration. The ongoing remote sensing and GIS-based modeling project is being conducted at the Center for Archaeology of the Middle East Landscape (CAMEL) at the Oriental Institute. Finally, I must thank Walter Kaegi and T.J. Wilkinson for giving comments and helpful suggestions on early drafts of this paper.

1 Haines, 1971; Braidwood, 1937.
2 Due to the fact that their preservation is strictly a taphonomic issue, the Dead Cities are probably not historically anomalous; more likely they are analogous to the general nature of late antique settlement in the region. Therefore, many of the questions that have been

raised in past treatments of the Dead Cities, such as why they were located in such a marginal area, or how agricultural products could have been transported from them to major urban centres, are probably over-emphasized. Evidence from the Amuq Valley suggests that there were likely to have been equally impressive settlements throughout the northern Levant, in areas that are more agriculturally productive and that had easier access to transportation and communication networks.

3   Foss, 1997:197.

4   Ball, 2000: 234.

5   Yener *et al.*, 2000a.

6   Because of frequently imprecise dating evidence and the incongruities between archaeologically and historically defined phases, it is difficult to find consensus regarding period terminology, especially when dealing primarily with survey data. "Late Roman" is used here and throughout to refer to Amuq Phases S and T (see Haines, 1971; Braidwood, 1937). The phase post-dates the presence of *terra sigillata*, and other wares, such as African red-slipped wares, become common. Because some types that occur in the historically defined Late Roman or Early Byzantine period, such as corrugated brittle wares, continue into the seventh and even eighth centuries, the date of some sites and features where other evidence is lacking is sometimes ambiguous. In these cases I have used the term "late antique". More detailed discussion of ceramic dating criteria can be found in Verstraete and Wilkinson, 2000; and Wilkinson and Casana, *forthcoming*.

7   "Corona" images were taken by a series of military imaging satellites that operated from the 1960s to early 1970s. The enormous archive of images produced by these satellites was declassified by the United States Government in 1995, and has since been made publicly available. The archive contains high-resolution, black-and-white photographic images of many parts of the world. As part of an ongoing programme of regional, landscape archaeology at the Oriental Institute, we have developed techniques to enlarge, digitize and rectify these photographs to produce extremely accurate, "image maps". Precise real-world coordinates of features, such as archaeological sites, can then be derived from the digital image. Using hand-held GPS units, we are then able to navigate to the exact location of the features in the field. Because the Corona images are 30+ years old, they predate many of the landscape modifications that have come with modernization and urban development, and therefore also provide a detailed photographic record of many features that today are totally obscured.

8   I am grateful to Asa Eger for bringing many of the historical references noted throughout this discussion to my attention. He has also provided a useful synthetic treatment of the Late Roman and Islamic sources pertinent to the settlement and geography of the Amuq Valley in his recent master's thesis (Eger, 2002).

9   Translation from Norman, 2000 are used with permission from Liverpool University Press.

10 Haines, 1971; Braidwood, 1937.

11 Woolley, 1955.

12 *IGLS* I; Chapot, 1902; Jacquot, 1931.

13 Movement of settlement away from tells and towards small, dispersed sites occurs in many regions of the Near East, although the timing of this transformation ranges from as early as the eighth-seventh centuries BC in the Jezireh and the Judean hills of southern Palestine, to the fourth-fifth centuries AD in other places. For a detailed discussion see Wilkinson, *forthcoming*: "The Great Dispersal" (Chapter 7).

14 Braidwood, 1937.

15 To be fair, Braidwood's survey was one of the most sophisticated of its day, and he did locate and record a significant number of small sites in addition to major tells.

16   Haines, 1971.
17   Woolley, 1955.
18   Casana and Dhesi, *forthcoming*.
19   Yener *et al.*, 2000b.
20   Translation in Jones, 1917.
21   10.24.3, Translation in Pharr, 1952.
22   Translation in Collins, 1994.
23   Translation in Le Strange, 1890.
24   I am grateful to Sarah Graff for providing information regarding the dating of the Ghab sites. The dating evidence comes from an ongoing archaeological survey of the northern Ghab Valley, see: Graff, *forthcoming*.
25   Wilkinson, 2000.
26   Wilkinson, 1997.
27   Translation in Jefferys *et al.*, 1986.
28   Translation in Le Strange, 1890.
29   For a more detailed discussion of the history of the Lake of Antioch see: Wilkinson, 1997; Wilkinson *et al.*, 2001.
30   Downey, 1961: 350ff.
31   Translation by Wright, 1949.
32   Wilkinson and Casana, *forthcoming*; also see Yener and Wilkinson, 1996.
33   Wilkinson, 2000.
34   *Antioch-on-the-Orontes I–IV*.
35   Tchalenko, 1953:372ff; Tate, 1992:220; 1997:64–66.
36   Kingsley and Decker, 2001; Ward-Perkins 2001a.
37   Wiseman, 1953:10-12; Dietrich and Loretz, 1970.
38   Eger, 2002.
39   Weulersse, 1940.
40   Decker, 2001.
41   i.e. Tchalenko, 1953:368, pl.CXVIII–CXX.
42   Baruch and Bottema, 1999; Yasuda *et al.*, 2000.
43   Ward-Perkins, 2001b.
44   Downey, 1965; see also Ward-Perkins, 2001a and 2001b for an extended discussion of other examples.
45   Ward-Perkins, 2001a.
46   *IGLS* IV, no.1490.
47   Coins, glass and imported ceramics alone do not alone suggest much in terms of the relative wealth of settlements, because they are commonly found in the most humble contexts. However, the very fact of their ubiquity is not insignificant, but rather provides evidence that even the smallest settlements were integrated to some degree within a larger trading network.
48   For Bakras see Sinclair, 1990:266–271; caravansary Sinclair, 1990:270; Jacquot, 1931:197
49   Perdrizet and Fossey, 1897.
50   Foss, 1997:190ff; Kondoleon, 2000a:7.
51   The recent beautifully presented exhibition and accompanying catalogue entitled "Antioch: The Lost Ancient City" (Kondoleon, 2000b) help to underscore the attitude of most modern scholarship regarding the potential for archaeological investigations in Antioch. But in what sense is the city lost?
52   For a detailed discussion of the urban geography of late antique Antioch based on analysis of aerial photographs from the 1930s, see Poccardi, 2001; Leblanc and Poccardi, 1999.

Bibliography

Ball, W., 2000. *Rome in the East: The Transformation of an Empire.* (London and New York).

Baruch, U. and Bottema, S., 1999. 'A new pollen diagram from lake Hula'. In H. Kawanabe, G.W. Coulter and A.C. Roosevelt (eds), *Ancient Lakes: their cultural and biological diversity* (Kenboi Production, Belgium).

Braidwood, R.J., 1937. *Mounds in the Plain of Antioch: An Archaeological Survey.* Oriental Institute Publication 48. (Chicago).

Casana, J. and Dhesi, S., *Forthcoming.* 'Surface collection, off-site survey, and geophysical remote sensing at Tell Atchana'. In K.A. Yener (ed.) *The Amuq Valley Regional Project, 1995–2001.* Institute for Aegean Prehistory Publication.

Collins, B.A. (trans.), 1994. *The Best Divisions for Knowledge of the Regions. (al-Muqadassī)* (Reading).

Chapot, V., 1902. 'Antiquités de la Syrie du Nord', *Bulletin de Correspondance Hellénique* 26, 187–190.

Dietrich, M. and Loretz, O., 1970. 'Die soziale Struktur von Alalah und Ugarit IV: Die É=*bitu* Listen aus Alalah IV als Quelle für die Erforschung der gesellschaftlichen Schichtung von Alalah im 15. Jh.v.Chr.' *Zeitschrift für Assyriologie und vorderasiatische Archäologie 60,* 88–123.

Decker, M., 2001. 'Food for an Empire: Wine and Oil Production in North Syria'. In S. Kingsley and M. Decker (eds) *Economy and Exchange in the East Mediterranean during Late Antiquity* (Oxford), 69–86.

Downey, G., 1961. *A History of Antioch in Syria from Seleucus to the Arab Conquest* (Princeton).

Eger, A., 2002. *Rural Settlement and Land Use in the Amuq (Antiochene) Plain: A Historical Geography of the Byzantine and Islamic Periods.* Unpublished master's thesis submitted to the Department of Near Eastern Languages and Civilizations, University of Chicago.

Elderkin, G.W. (ed.), 1934. *Antioch-on-the-Orontes I: The Excavations of 1932.* (Princeton).

Foss, C., 1997. 'Syria in Transition, AD 550–750: An Archaeological Approach' *Dumbarton Oaks Papers* 51, 189–269.

Graff, S.R., *forthcoming.* 'Report on the Second Season of the Northern Ghab Regional Survey 2001', *Chronique Archologique en Syrie.* (Directorate General of Antiquities and Museums, Damascus).

Haines, R.C., 1971. *Excavations in the Plain of Antioch. Vol. 2. The Structural Remains of the Later Phases: Chatal Hoyuk, Tell al-Judaidah, and Tell Ta'yinat.* Oriental Institute Publication 95 (Chicago).

IGLS Inscriptions grecques et latines de la Syrie. Ed L.Jalabert, R.Mouterde etalii 1–7 (Paris 1929,–70).

Jacquot, P., 1931. *Antioche, centre de tourisme.* (Paris: Comité de tourisme d'Antioch).

Jalabert, L. and Mouterde, R., 1929. *Inscriptions Grecques et Latines de la Syrie 1.* Bibliothèque Archéologique et Historique 12 (Paris).

Jefferys, E., Jefferys , M., and Scott, R., (trans.), 1986. *The Chronicle of John Malalas. Byzantina Australiensia* 4. (Melbourne).

Jones, H.L. (trans.), 1917. *The Geography of Strabo vol. 8.* (New York).

Kingsley, S. and Decker, M., 2001. 'New Rome, New Theories on Inter-Regional Exchange. An Introduction to the East Mediterranean Economy in Late Antiquity'. In S. Kingsley and M. Decker (eds) *Economy and Exchange in the East Mediterranean during Late Antiquity* (Oxford), 1–27.

Kondoleon, C., 2000a. 'The City of Antioch: An Introduction'. In Kondoleon, 2000b, 3–11.

Kondoleon, C. (ed.), 2000b. *Antioch: The Lost Ancient City* (Princeton and Worcester).

Leblanc, J. and Poccardi, G., 1999. 'Étude de la permanence de traces antiques à Antioche-sur-l'Oronte', *Syria* 76, 91–126.

Le Strange, G., 1890. *Palestine under the Moslems : a description of Syria and the Holy Land from A.D. 650 to 1500* (Boston).

Norman, A.F., 2000, *Antioch as a Centre of Hellenic Culture as Observed by Libanius* (Liverpool).

Perdrizet, P. and Fossey, C., 1897. 'Voyage dans la Syrie du Nord', *Bulletin de Correspondance Hellénique* 21, 87–89.

Pharr, C. (trans.), 1952. *The Theodosian Code and Novels and the Sirmondian Constitutions* (Princeton).

Poccardi, G., 2001. 'L'île d'Antioche à la fin de l'antiquité: histoire et problème de topographie urbaine'. In L. Lavan (ed.) *Recent research in late-antique urbanism (Journal of Roman Archaeology. Supplementary Series 42)*, 155–172.

Sinclair, T.A., 1990. *Eastern Turkey: An Architectural and Archaeological Survey vol 4* (London).

Stillwell, R. (ed.), 1937. *Antioch-on-the-Orontes II: The Excavations of 1933–1936* (Princeton).

Tate, G., 1992, *Les Campagnes de la Syrie du Nord : un exemple d'expansion démographie et économique à la fin de l'antiquité* (Bibliothèque archéologique et historique 133, Paris).

Tate, G., 1997. 'The Syrian Countryside during the Roman Era'. In S. Alcock (ed.) *The Early Roman Empire in the East. Oxbow Monograph 95* (Oxford), 55–71.

Tchalenko, G., 1953–7. *Villages antiques de la Syrie du nord. I–III* (Paris).

Verstraete, J. and Wilkinson, T.J., 2000. 'The Amuq Regional Archaeological Survey'. In K.A. Yener *et al.* 'The Amuq Valley Regional Project, 1995–1998', *American Journal of Archaeology* 104, 163–220.

Ward-Perkins, B., 2001a. 'Land, Labour and Settlement'. In A. Cameron, B. Ward-Perkins and M. Whitby (eds) *Cambridge Ancient History* 14 (Cambridge), 315–345.

Ward-Perkins, B., 2001b. 'Specialised Production and Exchange'. In A. Cameron, B. Ward-Perkins and M. Whitby (eds) *Cambridge Ancient History* 14. (Cambridge), 346–391.

Weulersse, J., 1940. *L' Oronte: étude de fleuve* (Tours).

Wilkinson, T.J., 1997. 'The History of the Lake of Antioch: A Preliminary Note'. In G. Young, M. Chavalas and R.E. Averbeck (eds) *Crossing Boundaries and Linking Horizons: Studies in Honor of Michael C. Astour* (Bethesda).

Wilkinson, T.J., 2000. 'Geoarchaeology of the Amuq Plain'. In K.A. Yener *et al.* 'The Amuq Valley Regional Project, 1995–1998', American Journal of Archaeology *104, 163–220.*

Wilkinson, T.J and Casana, J. *forthcoming.* 'The Amuq Valley Archaeological Survey: Interim Report'. In K.A. Yener (ed.) T*he Amuq Valley Regional Project, 1995–2001.* Institute for Aegean Prehistory Publication.

Wiseman, D.J., 1953. *The Alalakh Tablets* (London: British Institute of Archaeology at Ankara).

Woolley, C.L., 1955. *Alalakh: An Account of the Excavations at Tell Atchana in the Hatay, 1937–1949.* London: The Society of Antiquaries of London.

Wright, W.C. (trans.), 1949. *The Works of Emperor Julian.* Loeb Classical Library.

Yasuda, Y., Kitagawa, H., and Nakagawa, T., 1999. 'The earliest record of major anthropogenic deforestation in the Ghab Valley, northwest Syria: a palynological study', *Quaternary International* 73/74, 127–136.

Yener, A., Edens, C., Harrison, T.P., Verstraete, J., and Wilkinson, T.J., 2000a. 'The Amuq Valley Regional Project, 1995–1998', *American Journal of Archaeology,* 104, 163–220.

Yener, K.A., Edens, C., Casana, J., Diebold, B., Ekstrom, H., Loyet, M. and Özbal, R. 2000b. 'Tell Kurdu Excavations 1999', *Anatolica* 26, 32–117.

Yener, K.A. and Wilkinson, T. J., 1996. 'The Amuq Valley Projects' *Oriental Institute 1995–1996 Annual Report* (Chicago).

7. The Seedier Side of Antioch

Simon Ellis

Introduction

Antioch would normally be considered as a wealthy city of riches and mosaics – home to the glitterati of late antiquity. I will use texts and archaeology to demonstrate a different side to the city – the seedy side of Antioch. I will consider two types of housing, shops and subdivision, which are normally overlooked by archaeologists and historians alike.

The wealth of Antioch, in terms of late antique domestic architecture can be seen from the houses known from the suburb of Daphne 7km to the south of the city. Private houses of the fifth century AD such as the House of the Buffet Supper had fine reception suites and private baths.

The main archaeological evidence for Antioch comes from the Princeton excavations of the 1930s.[1] The Princeton excavations were very advanced in terms of both recording and publication. Using their excavation notebooks in Princeton University it is possible to identify stratigraphic sequences, including for example stratified Islamic coins. Stratigraphic sequences were also published, especially for the Atrium House and the House of the Buffet Supper. A subsequent report could be written on Middle Byzantine and Islamic Antioch. Even today few excavations in the Mediterranean, and especially modern Turkey, have met such standards.

The excavations were recorded on a grid that covered the whole of Antioch and Daphne. For ease of reference I will either refer to these grid squares (*e.g.* 19 M) or the name applied to the House concerned. In dealing with both shops and subdivision I have divided my narrative into three sections – an introduction on the significance of this type of housing, a brief mention of relevant texts, and an analysis of the archaeology.

Shops

Shops as housing

Publication of the line of 32 shops at Sardis by Crawford[2] provided definitive evidence of how people lived in shops in late antiquity. They lived in a second room, either behind or above the shop itself. They could also bed down adjacent to the counter if need be. Several 'shops' at Sardis present no sign of artisanal production.[3] This is particularly significant given Sardis' excellent preservation. If these shops were not producing material goods, they may have been offices, perhaps for scribes. Alternatively they may have been purely residential (even a peristyle house operated as a business base for the owner). Given the choice between a shack, sleeping on the streets, or a shop, the latter must have been a very desirable, solid, residence. The shop must therefore be given an important place in a typology of houses, as the smallest form of house with substantial architecture.

Texts

The shops at Antioch, especially those uncovered on the city's main street during the Princeton campaigns, may have been more luxurious than in other cities, but they were not significantly different in form. The writings of Libanius talk about shopkeepers as poor people struggling to make ends meet and to honour their civic obligations; one of which was to keep lamps burning in the street porticoes.[4]

The street lighting in Antioch was famous even in late antiquity. It is assumed to have been the duty of shopkeepers to maintain it, indicating that they perhaps were in overall terms somewhat wealthier class than in other cities. Libanius, *Oration* 33.6, describes the plaintive cry of a widow upstairs above a shop when asked to carry out her duty. 'How can I light them [the lamps in the street]? Where do I get oil?' Characteristically living in the floor above the shop, whence she could hear the shout of the official, she was clearly reluctant or incapable of leaving to obtain oil. Perhaps she had an absent landlord, or perhaps she had rented the shop below to an absentee commercial tenant after her husband's death. Her seeming lack of oil also raises the question of how or whether she lit her own property.

Remains[5]

During the 1930s a complete shop plan was found at Main Street Dig V 16-P where the shop was 4 x 4.7m in plan. This is similar to the size of late antique shops found at Sardis and Carthage.[6] It is sometimes hard to distinguish between shops and house vestibules when excavating in small trenches, which do not provide a complete plan of the remains. Vestibules are likely to have a rear door, whereas shops may not if living quarters were above rather than behind them.

One shop at 19-M level 3 (Lassus, 1971: 26–7) lay within street porticos of basalt blocks, which were said to be of Justinianic date. Later, in Middle Byzantine times the street porticos and the shops were walled in. This continued occupation might reflect its city centre location where land was at a premium. The presence of many lines of ceramic pipe suggested that the porticoes remained in use for common drainage of properties to the rear. Liebeschuetz gives the impression from Libanius' writings that spaces in the porticoes were much in demand by shopkeepers.[7]

At MSD8 16-O (Lassus, 1971: 104–6) a rectangular building was erected right on the Justinianic street between the two stylobates, with walls just inside the street front and another wall at 90' to street. These walls did not seem to relate to higher mediaeval or post mediaeval occupation, and thus they could be of sixth to seventh century date.

The most significant discovery was made at MSD9 17-P (Lassus, 1971:122–3). There were 2 shops with a simple mosaic, and a circle design, cut by 2 drains. A flagged floor at a higher level sealed the drains. Lassus says that a silver candelabra with monogram of Phocas (?) together with some gold plaques were found 'sous'/under the mosaic, but he then says this deposit is later than the mosaic so 'sous' must mean 'at a lower level', for instance in a pit. The shop was then covered with a fine 'intermediate' flagged floor 30cm higher before being resurfaced again, probably in the eleventh century.

A final unanswerable stratigraphic question is whether the drains were associated with the intermediate flagged floor, or if filled in, whether they were associated with an unrecorded earth floor.

Conclusions

The Princeton excavations uncovered extensive evidence for conventional shops opening onto porticoed streets, especially on the main street through the city. The last conventional makeover of the street was dated to Justinianic times. There is some evidence for reflooring and rebuilding within the ancient structures, which by reason of the stratigraphic sequence is likely to be post Justinianic but pre Middle Byzantine in date. Walls of the late antique period respect earlier structures, whereas Middle Byzantine remains do not. On the basis of finds from MSD9 17-P these refurbishments might be dated to the seventh century AD. The nature of the finds – gold and silver – as well as the use of stone flags suggest such changes should not be lightly dismissed as 'squatters' and should rather be interpreted as a continuing urban presence in the ancient city.

Archaeological evidence from Carthage and Sardis suggests that shop counters were placed inside their front doors. There is further evidence from many sites such as Antioch that shop counters were also frequent in street porticoes. In the classic theory of Sauvaget [8] such street counters and subdivision were the precursor to blocked streets. Indeed later, probably in Islamic and Middle Byzantine times, buildings blocked the streets of Antioch completely, but they followed irregular alignments suggesting the break down of the ancient urban street plan, whereas shop constructions in porticoes respect ancient alignments. The positioning of shop counters is more likely to represent a 'natural' commercial practice of trying to attract customers by putting displays in their path rather than any real breakdown of public order. There is no reason to assume that such practices were a new development in late antiquity. The positioning of goods inside a shop is more of a modern tradition than one stemming from the ancient world.

SUBDIVISION

Subdivision as housing

Subdivision represents a definitive architectural style. It does not represent a random distribution of walls above an older building. Instead walls are built in specific locations that relate to the architecture of the previous building. There is a definite attempt to *use* the earlier architecture to create a new context, and in housing terms new living space.

Some of the principles involved are

1. Walls in intercolumniations leaving standing columns in place.
2. Divide *triclinia* in half, perpendicular to the entrance with a low wall topped with re-used dressed stone. This wall will also follow principles 3 and 4.
3. Walls are built of coarse unplastered rubble, reusing architectural fragments
4. Walls are built on top of existing mosaic floors rather than destroying them.
5. The original, exterior, façade of the building is left untouched.

The best example of these principles remains the House of the Frescoes at Tipasa, which divides an existing peristyle house into four apartments.[9] This can be dated broadly to the fifth century AD by an adjacent coin hoard. The apartments can be identified on the basis of access patterns. Some subdividing walls were placed so as to create separate external access to each apartment, while others were built to limit access from one apartment to another.

The literary evidence for subdivision demonstrates the economic and social basis for the transformation of public buildings in this fashion.[10] The aristocrat was able to buy up abandoned public buildings, of which there were many in late antiquity.[11] The interests of the town council were that the derelict space was reused and that the façade of classical monuments extolling the early greatness of the city were maintained. Imperial rescripts demonstrate the importance of the façade. The aristocrat could ransack the *inside* of the building for art works for his own house, and laws tried to limit the removal of decorative stonework or sculptures. He could then install a number of poor people within this shell. They obtained housing in the centre of the city. He obtained their allegiance in elections, political riots, and other activity. The best textual evidence for this comes from Rome in the eighth and ninth centuries where several imperial buildings are attested as fortified bases for prominent families.

While subdivision of a house did not hold as many benefits for an aristocrat as subdivision of a public building, it certainly provided the same degree of political support through tenancies. The general pattern of subdivision and abandonment suggests that the last great period of suburban development was during the Theodosian period, but that already traditional peristyle houses were being abandoned in increasing numbers. This may have created a supply of cheap urban land ready for redevelopment, or exploitation by subdivision.

Texts

Libanius in his panegyric *In praise of Antioch* 254 mentions wooden shacks/shops with branch roofs between columns. It seems strange that regular shops in a portico would require branch roofs instead of the regular tiled roof of a colonnade. It may be instead that this is a description of a later re-use of the street portico by houses or shacks with brush roofs.

Remains

House of Menander The columns in front of the *nymphaeum* were blocked with rubble walls, re-using large stone blocks. These walls were associated with a shallow drain cut into the mosaic. There were also traces of blocking in adjacent rooms (4). The excavators dated all this work to the sixth century. These walls conform to the characteristics of subdivision – walls re-using blocks, structures founded on earlier mosaic, and blocking of colonnades. The adjacent street also had a blocked colonnade.

Both the *Atrium House* and the *House of Buffet Supper* had upper levels that included complex small rooms re-using earlier remains. The peristyle colonnade of the *Atrium House* was subdivided, reusing columns in some places. Two adjacent *triclinia* had characteristic subdivisions across middle of room. There were perhaps three separate apartments. One was in a yard to the rear of the *triclinia* consisting of five rooms (numbered 92, 98, 99, 100 in Figure 7.1, which is a plan of the site in various earlier building stages). One was created from the east portico of the peristyle, with about six rooms (rooms 130, 85, 86, 101, 62/3, 106, and portico 83/84). Dating evidence (pottery) suggests a sixth to seventh century date. The third to the south west of the peristyle (87 and 89 on the plan) looks as if it went through two phases; first a typical subdivision of the peristyle portico into rooms , then a rebuilding rather than subdivision of much of this corner of the house (rooms 114 to 120). The subdivion of the west portico is not shown in Figure 7.1 as it was associated with a so-called 'upper level' but since it follows in every respect the intercolumniations of the portico it should be regarded as subdivision of the original building. This second phase was not subdivision, as it did not take place *within* the earlier structure.[12]

The *House of Buffet Supper* is named after a fine fourth century dining room mosaic in the south-east wing of the house (see Figure 8.2). However the whole house was rebuilt and reoriented by 90° in the fifth century with a *triclinium* to the north-east and a characteristic *nymphaeum* on the opposite side of the peristyle. Most of the subdivision seems to have occurred in the south-east wing of the house. One Justinianic coin was found within a subdivision wall, and the coin sequence continues to Heraclius. A Byzantine sword was also recorded.[13]

Some late subdivision walls also existed in the *House of the Boat of Psyches*, but the plan of these is difficult to interpret and their date cannot be established with any certainty.

Conclusion

Several houses at Daphne, and the Atrium house at Antioch itself, demonstrate that some of the rich mosaic houses were already in terminal decline in the sixth century. Whilst more precise dating would clearly be desirable this picture conforms to that of

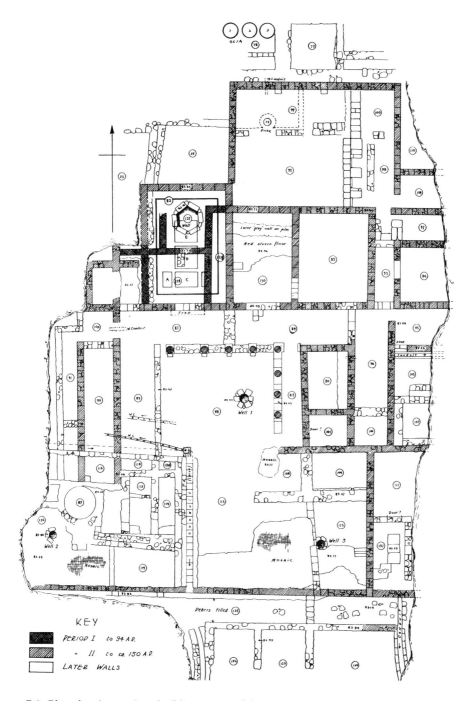

Figure 7.1: Plan showing various building stages of the Atrium House: Fisher, 1934, 19, pl. 1V, 'The Roman Villa under House A'. Reproduced by kind permission of the Department of Art and Archaeology, Princeton University.

other Mediterranean sites. No new peristyle houses were built anywhere after the mid sixth century, but already in the fifth century AD peristyle houses were going out of use and not being rebuilt.[14] The House of the Buffet Supper with its substantial fifth century rebuilding and re-orientation by 90° is probably to be associated with what may be the last *floruit* of aristocratic house building in Asia under Theodosius II, which can also be identified at the Sardis suburb of Pactolus North.[15]

GRAVES

Sporadic graves within the urban circuit are another characteristic of the degradation of the late antique urban fabric. Such graves, including small cemeteries, were found throughout the 1930s Princeton excavations. However the dating evidence suggests they were of the Arab or Middle Byzantine periods. Although it is possible that some were of an earlier date, uncertainty suggests prudence in interpretation, and I have preferred to leave analysis to a consideration of the mediaeval remains.

CONCLUSION

This paper has set out the evidence for poorer forms of housing in Antioch. It has presented evidence for the life of shopkeepers, some of which were perhaps more wealthy than their counterparts in other cities, and indeed were not the poorest citizens of Antioch itself. It has demonstrated that houses in Antioch were subject to subdivision and re-occupation by poorer inhabitants during late antiquity. This process of subdivision has been linked to wider social trends in which the older building in late antique cities became alienated and exploited by aristocrats seeking to establish a wider clientele.

It is easy to conclude that all these degradations happened because of depopulation of the city after Persian sack in the sixth century, but there is no evidence on which to base such an association other than a general dating to the sixth or seventh century. The writings of Libanius suggest that many of the developments identified here were, at the latest, beginning to take place by the end of the fourth century AD. Indeed the picture of Antioch presented here is similar to other cities of the Mediterranean at the same time, such as Ephesus, Carthage, and Rome. This paper demonstrates the existence of a wider civil society in Antioch that does not present the city as privileged in late antiquity, but rather places it within the regular currents of late antique urbanism. Daphne was not the Eden of late antiquity. The recorded remains span a period of several centuries. By the time the last figured mosaics were laid in some peristyle houses, communities of inhabitants with a much poorer lifestyle already occupied others.

Archaeologists need to pay more attention to shops and subdivision as types of housing. An examination of their place within the urban fabric offers an understanding of the lower classes of late antique society. Subdivision especially was a new form of architecture. It created a new class, or a new social milieu, which did not exist in the earlier imperial period.

Notes

1 The Princeton excavations mainly worked outside the city in suburban areas such as Daphne. Only the street trenches reported by Lassus, 1971 represent a substantial campaign within the city walls. This paper is more concerned with stratigraphy rather than mosaics and so the most relevant texts are Elderkin, 1934; Stillwell, 1941; and Lassus, 1971. The excavation reports should be read with Stillwell, 1961: 45–57, which remains the best analytical study of the architectural development. This paper also profited from a visit to the Princeton University archives of the excavations in 1983, for which the author is very grateful to the Department of Classics.
2 Crawford, 1990.
3 E2A, E3, E16, E18, E19.
4 Liebeschuetz, 1972 : 55–9, and Petit, 1955.
5 References in this section to Lassus, 1971.
6 See Crawford, 1990 and Ellis, 2000: 78–80.
7 Liebeschuetz, 1972.
8 Sauvaget, 1941.
9 Baradez, 1961 : 49–199.
10 Ellis, 1998.
11 Janvier, 1969.
12 For the Atrium House see Elderkin, 1934.
13 For the House of the Buffet Supper see Stillwell, 1941.
14 Ellis, 1988: 565–76.
15 Foss, 1976, and Ellis, 1997.

Bibliography

Baradez, J., 1961. 'La maison des fresques et la voie la limitant', *Libyca* 9, 49–199.
Crawford, J.S., 1990. *The Byzantine Shops at Sardis*, (Harvard).
Elderkin, G., (ed.), 1934. *Antioch-on-the-Orontes I The Excavations of 1932* (Princeton).
Ellis, S., 1988. 'The End of the Roman House', *American Journal of Archaeology* 92, 565–76.
Ellis, S., 1997. 'Late Antique Houses in Asia Minor'. In S. Isager and B.Poulsen, *Patron and Pavements in Late Antiquity, Halicarnassian Studies* 2 (Odense): 38–50.
Ellis, S., 1998. 'Power-broking and the re-use of public buildings in late antiquity', *Acts of the 13th Congress of Early Christian Archaeology Split 1994*, III, 233–239 (Vatican and Split).
Ellis, S., 2000. *Roman Housing*, (London).
Fisher, C.S., 1934. 'Bath B, House A and the Roman Villa'. In Elderkin, 1934, 8–18.
Foss, C., 1976. *Late antique and Byzantine Sardis* (Harvard).
Janvier,Y., 1969. *La législation du Bas Empire romain sur les édifices publics* (Aix-en-Provence).
Lassus, J., 1971. *Antioch-on-the-Orontes V: Les portiques d'Antioche* (Princeton).
Liebeschuetz, J.H.W.G., 1972. *Antioch City and Imperial Administration in the Later Roman Empire*, (Oxford).
Petit, P., 1955. *Libanius et la vie municipale à Antioche au quatrième siècle après J-C.* (Paris).
Sauvaget, J., 1941. *Alep* (Paris).
Stillwell, R., (ed.) 1941. *Antioch-on -the-Orontes III The Excavations 1937–1939* (Princeton).
Stillwell, R., 1961. 'Houses of Antioch', *Dumbarton Oaks Papers* 15, 45–57.

8. SURVEYING THE SCENE: ANTIOCH MOSAIC PAVEMENTS AS A SOURCE OF HISTORICAL EVIDENCE

Janet Huskinson

Perhaps the most famous artefacts to survive from Roman Antioch are its floor-mosaics. These are regularly cited in all kinds of art-historical and archaeological enquiries, and no study of the city would seem complete without some discussion of them. Undoubtedly their attractiveness and sheer number make them such a popular source of reference, but an even more important factor has been their accessible publication. The earliest discussions tended to emphasise their art-historical value, in terms which have tended to dominate later debates, yet the pavements' function as high-profile decoration in houses of the well-to-do means that they have a lot to offer as evidence for the cultural and social life of the city. This is so well documented in the literature of later Roman Antioch, and it is the aim of this paper to survey how floor-mosaics may also contribute.[1]

Reports of the campaigns carried out between 1932 and 1939 by the Committee for the Excavation of Antioch and its Vicinity show that the discovery of so many mosaics was a surprise outcome.[2] Whereas the excavators were disappointed in their original goal of locating some of the city's major buildings, they discovered around three hundred floor-mosaics in Antioch, its suburb of Daphne and in the nearby port of Seleucia Pieria (with more found since.[3]) Most came from private and domestic buildings, of the early second to the mid sixth century AD; and even these are likely to have been 'only a fraction' of the original number.[4] Here perhaps is some tangible evidence to confirm Libanius' fulsome praise of the many magnificent houses of Antioch and its suburbs, since the splendour of these mosaics must have made them indeed 'the pride of householders and the envy of their guests'.[5]

Most of the pavements (or the figured ones, at least) were published soon after their discovery. Details of sites and findspots were recorded in the series of *Antioch Excavation Reports*, along with initial descriptions of individual pavements and papers discussing particular images.[6] In 1938 C.R. Morey presented a selection of mosaics in a short book which also included a brief history of the city, but their most comprehensive – and influential – publication was to come in 1947 with Doro Levi's *Antioch Mosaic Pavements*. This aimed to describe individual pavements from the excavations and then '… to sketch the history of mosaic art at Antioch, and to bring mosaic art as a whole into the wider picture of the history of art in antiquity'.[7] Levi's work has had an enduring impact on the study of Roman mosaic in general, and of the

Antioch pavements in particular. His detailed analysis of style and iconography created a deeper understanding of how mosaic developed as an art form during the Roman empire, and also established a line of approach which was followed in many studies which looked at form or content in mosaics from Antioch and beyond: Lavin, for instance, began his paper (1963) on stylistic transformation in late antique mosaic with an analysis of the later hunting scenes from Antioch.

In the last twenty years or so the Antioch pavements have been studied in various other contexts. For instance they have been included in regional studies of floor-mosaic which have taken various geographical and methodological standpoints. Campbell's catalogue of floor-mosaics from the city of Antioch was part of a *Corpus of Mosaic Pavements from Asia Minor* and as such recorded basic information (including clear dating criteria) for every pavement, figured and geometric from the city.[8] By contrast Dauphin considered Antioch examples in the context of the Near East, and analysed them as indicators of social and economic developments in the area.[9] In numerous papers Balty has discussed them in their Syrian setting; and most recently, Dunbabin treats them in a regional context in her survey of mosaics of the Greek and Roman world.[10]

In another, more recent development the mosaics have been investigated as part of the city's cultural and social history. This reflects the 'cultural turn' in scholarship at large and the recognition that visual arts can serve to construct the values of society as well as passively reflecting them. It is also an attempt to approach the various historic sources for Antioch – literary and material – in an holistic and interdisciplinary way. A good idea of what is to be gained from this can be found in Kondoleon's catalogue for the exhibition 'Antioch, the lost ancient city', which toured American cities in 2000 to 2001.[11] Here the pavements are presented alongside other material evidence for the city and are also discussed in a separate essay in which Kondoleon analyses how viewers might have read and responded to the cultural allusions in mosaics from three particular houses.[12] Other recent studies also attempt to link the visual imagery of the mosaics to specific aspects of the city's culture: Leyerle, for example, shows how scenes in a single pavement can be used to frame a much wider question (in this case, the 'Megalopsychia' pavement from Daphne (see Figure 8.3) for a study of Chrysostom), and in another paper I look at scenes of performance in the mosaics and how these might be read in the context of contemporary cultural interests.[13]

This paper will concentrate on this line of approach, but alongside discussion of some stylistic developments. The aim is a broad survey of how and how far the mosaics can contribute to our understanding of the culture and society of later Roman Antioch.

ANTIOCH PAVEMENTS AND THE HISTORY OF MOSAIC

The starting-point has to be their contribution to the study of mosaic. Thanks particularly to Levi, Antioch pavements occupy a prime place in the historiography of Roman floor-mosaic. Although this primacy may sometimes prove distorting, the pavements provide crucial evidence for one of the most profound changes in later

Roman art, from Hellenistic traditions to the late antique.[14] Their long sequence makes clearly visible this shift from pictorial illusionism, with framed three-dimensional figured scenes, contained in panels, to all-over designs which treated the floor as a flat, continuous surface.[15] It shows too how this change affected not only style, but also the relationship of the pavements to the rooms they decorated, their composition, and their subject-matter, with mythology giving way to generic themes such as the hunt. Antioch mosaics document all these developments and, even more important, help to address some major questions that they raise.

One of these questions concerns the transmission of style and subject-matter in floor-mosaics across the region. It is still unclear how workshops were organized in Antioch itself, but the pavements they produced provide useful comparison for studies of mosaic in the area. Because of their range they have been included in various kinds of regional analysis: similarities of style and subject-matter have revealed links between Antioch and mosaics from Cilicia and Cyprus, for example, and 'cluster analysis' of motifs has been used to identify schools and travel patterns of mosaicists in the Levant.[16] There is also evidence that Antiochene mosaicists worked even further afield, outside the region: a mosaic inscription from Chania in Crete records the work of an artist from Daphne, while stylistic features in pavements at Bishapur in Iran suggest that Sapor I took back captive mosaicists back to work for him there when he sacked Antioch in AD 253 and 256.[17] New finds at Zeugma may reveal more links.

On a wider level there are also questions about artistic tradition and forces for change – a major theme in the stylistic studies of Levi and Lavin. The change from illusionism to 'carpet-style' patterns can be described in terms of a move from Hellenistic artistic traditions, with their pictorial and mythological interests, to a style and motifs which show influences from other parts of the Roman world and from outside it. Yet it is also linked to some fundamental conceptual questions about floor-mosaics and about figured scenes within them – should they emphasise the solidity of the floor, or suggest space beyond it? – which were played out across the empire in different ways and at different times. In Italy, for instance, black and white mosaics, which also stressed the two dimensionality of the floor, were popular until the late third century AD, while North African pavements had been moving towards all-over designs and a flat background from the second.[18] In Antioch, however, the development towards all-over designs with a flat background began in the late fourth century with the geometric 'carpets' in the church of Kaoussie Church and Apolausis baths (see Figure 8.1) and moved into hunting scenes and animal pavements in the fifth century.[19] In the timing of this change Antioch shows itself typical of its eastern locality: like other centres in this part of Syria it had adhered to Hellenistic traditions well into the fourth century.[20] But the influences that appear from the late fourth century bring in elements that have been attributed to North Africa and the west, and also to Sassanian Persia (particularly in the small patterns used as background motifs in 'carpet' pavements).[21] How far these 'oriental' elements represent a direct import from the contemporary art of the Near East has long been the subject of debate, and often as part of a larger discussion about factors in the development of late antique and early medieval art.[22] But even if it is the case, as Levi argued, that many of these eastern motifs had long been present in Graeco-Roman art, Sassanian art clearly exercised a

Figure 8.1: Baths of Apolausis, Room 10.

strong attraction at this time, and could well have influenced Antiochene taste through imported silverware and textiles.[23] There were obviously various long-term contacts between Antioch and Persia, instances of the kind of social and cultural factors that may have contributed to this stylistic change, as will be discussed again later.[24]

Finally, there is the question of how pavements related to the rooms they decorate. At Antioch the major stylistic change can be closely linked with changes in domestic architecture that can be documented from the early fifth century AD on: reception rooms show a tendency to increase in size, requiring a larger expanse of mosaic flooring.[25] This kind of connection is a reminder of the role mosaic decoration played in the structuring of social space, and the various lines of enquiry that this involves. It also points to the link with economic development in the city and surrounding region: mosaics are anyway a sign of affluence, and at Antioch the increase in their size (and number, compared to the pre-Constantinian examples) may be taken as evidence for increasing economic prosperity in this later period.[26]

CONTEXTS OF TIME AND PLACE

Although Antioch mosaics fit well into the general framework of this major stylistic change, for many individual examples there are real problems in placing them in even the most basic contexts of time and space. The reasons for this are essentially practical: a large number were discovered on sites where little of the original building remained or which could not be properly excavated.[27] Many were then exported among various museums in Europe and the United States, often divided up into separate sections and to be displayed as art objects.[28]

In developing a chronology little explicit information is given by the mosaics themselves: only a very few contain details which date them with any reliability. An inscription in a pavement from Kaoussie Church dates it to AD 387, while a *terminus post quem* is provided for the 'Megalopsychia' mosaic (Figure 8.3) by the depiction in its border of a building labelled as the private bath of Ardaburius, who lived in Antioch as *magister militum per Orientem* in the 450s and 460s.[29] On the other hand, the mosaics' long time-span provides an opportunity to build up a chronology based on detailed observation of stylistic change. This was Levi's approach in developing his dating scheme, which is still generally accepted.[30] But he also drew on external evidence where it existed. This more often took the form of finds associated with particular pavements, which he carefully evaluated, but occasionally he gave *termini post* or *ante quem* based on external events, such as earthquakes or incursions (notably the Persian Sack of 540 which concluded mosaic production at Antioch).[31] Since he was concerned with the individual mosaics, this dearth of references to the outside world is not surprising; but a glance at histories of the area is enough to show what important, often turbulent events occurred at Antioch during this period. Even if there is no overt trace in the mosaics of imperial visits, military presence, invasions by Persia and Palmyra, or the innumerable internal factions and riots in the city, these happenings are integral to the social context in which the pavements were produced.

As for a spatial context, most of the mosaics seem to have come from residential sites, although some decorated baths, tombs or religious buildings.[32] These houses were obviously attractive and well-appointed, but it is not known what proportion of the total housing they comprised, or anything specific about the social background of their owners.[33] Again, lack of detailed information can make the houses hard to use as a context for studying the pavements: like the mosaics themselves, many were found poorly preserved and – rather surprisingly – have received little systematic study since.[34] In this situation, in which neither mosaics nor their architectural context is fully understood, there is a real danger of circular argument, and of explaining one in the light of the other. To quote Dobbins, 'in the publications [that is, the excavation volumes and Doro Levi's *Antioch Mosaic Pavements*] the houses are merely the framework for the mosaics and never form the center of an architectural discussion'.[35] Yet other studies show the reverse, noting how pavements became by default crucial evidence for the design of houses: as flooring they survived whereas wall-painting and domestic sculpture (so valuable in reconstructing the domestic setting in Campanian houses, for example) did not.[36]

Mosaics can suggest the layout and chronological development of particular houses as well as general hierarchies of social space.[37] For dining rooms (*triclinia*) the pavement's distinctive arrangement is a clear signifier of room function: the three couches were set out on an area of plainer mosaic, with a figured scene at the centre which diners could view as they reclined at their meal. In the simpler examples the plainer areas were shaped like a rectilinear U, and enclosed a single figured scene; but in more expansive versions the figured decoration comprised several panels arranged like a (rather squat) letter T. There are many examples of these designs at Antioch, and one pavement which shows the later horseshoe layout for the sigma couch. (Figure 8.2)[38] It is also quite common to find *triclinia* set behind a colonnade or near a courtyard with a pool, creating a welcoming setting for the diners, often with attractive views across the house.[39] This arrangement of couches, with its hierarchy of diners, was typical of Roman dining rooms in the western empire, so on the face of it there is a interesting cultural contrast to be explored between the 'Roman' layout of the room and its decoration with traditional Hellenistic styles and subjects.[40]

MOSAICS AND THE REPRESENTATION OF SOCIAL ACTIVITIES IN ANTIOCH

Triclinia can offer some important evidence since their identifiable shape and function allow the subjects of their mosaics to be read in the specific social context of dining, making them a particularly rich source for the culture of Roman Antioch. Dining – the dinner and the drinking-party which followed – would have been a very important social activity in the wealthy houses of Antioch and its environs (as it was for the elite across the empire): it was a chance for householders to impress visitors with their lavish generosity and (alleged) high-brow cultural tastes. This is more than apparent from the subjects they chose for the floors of their dining rooms.

Perhaps the most famous dining-room pavement in Antioch is from the 'House of the Buffet Supper' (Figure 8.2).[41] Here, made permanent in mosaic, are courses of a lavish meal, set out in order and with magnificent tableware. Evidence this may be for contemporary gastronomy and silverware, but it is also a testimony to contemporary aspiration: the meal itself is a spectacle of the ideal, and at its centre is depicted Ganymede, the cupbearer of the gods come, as it were, to adminster to the Antiochene guests, whose convivial wreaths are shown tossed on to the table.[42]

As well as wining and dining the occasion expected entertainment and good conversation, to judge from contemporary literary sources such as Plutarch's *Convivial Questions*. Many *triclinia* mosaics, (especially of the second and third centuries) depict subjects which also suggest this. In the 'House of Menander', for instance, there is a musical performance and a scene of Menander himself reclining on a couch, with Glykera and a personification of Comedy , which recalls Plutarch's comments on the popularity of his plays for recitations at dinner.[43] Many other mosaics have subjects which may have been performed or discussed at dinner. A scene in the *triclinium* of the 'House of Iphigeneia' has been identified as an episode from Euripides' tragedy *Iphigeneia in Aulis*, and may well allude to highlights of the drama recited in the dining-room after dinner.[44] This may also explain literary subjects taken from Homer or from novels; and even well-known mythological stories such as Aphrodite and

Figure 8.2: Detail of the mosaic showing the 'Buffet Supper' from the 'House of the Buffet Supper'.

Adonis and the Judgement of Paris could offer a wealth of philosophical issues to stimulate high-minded debate after dinner, as Kondoleon has suggested for the scenes in the *triclinium* of the 'Atrium House'.[45]

Dionysiac figures and myths are, not surprisingly, common in the decoration of *triclinia* and adjacent rooms where they help to set the mood for festivity, 'loosened' by the god of wine. Guests to the *triclinium* could be greeted by images of drinking and dancing, or even by a sobering vision of the drinking contest between Heracles and Dionysus with its warning against excess.[46] Yet Dionysiac subjects in at least some of the mosaics are also open to a more spiritual or cultic interpretation: Dionysus was the great deity of the later Greek east, and his engagement with humanity is spelled out in mythological events such as his union with Ariadne which could symbolise the mystic joining of human and divine.[47] This subject is depicted in a *triclinium* of the 'House of Dionysus and Ariadne' at Seleucia, and the mosaic suggests something of this significance through the attendant figures of a satyr and maenad who stand quietly at the sides, half-turned as if to invite the diners to gaze upon this spiritual event.[48] Similar interpretations are raised by the group of Dionysiac figures in the 'House of the Triumph of Dionysus', which has been seen as evidence for a 'real' cultic procession of the kind known from Hellenistic literary sources.[49] Although its linear arrangement of figures is more likely to be explained by the narrow shape of the panel at the entrance to the dining-room, this example shows yet again how Dionysiac imagery in pavements is often polyvalent, offering several different levels of meaning to the viewer.

The subjects described here, and the ancient interpretations they invited, clearly belong to a Greek world, and especially to the educated world of Greek *paideia*: they are evidence for the cultural identity that the wealthy patrons claimed for themselves and chose to display through this luxury art form to their guests. The mosaics show that much: but what they cannot really clarify is how far this was a superficial learning, a token gesture in the decoration of the house towards the 'right' kind of interests. These Hellenic themes are particularly prominent in Antioch pavements of the second and third centuries. There are no depictions of 'Roman' activities, such as the gladiator combats which were popular in the city, or of the hunt or arena which patrons in North Africa were using so much to represent their interests.[50] A contemporary-style hunt first appears in the pavement of Room One in the 'Constantinian Villa', and though never hugely popular (to judge from surviving examples) it recurs in fifth century pavements such as the 'Worcester' and 'Honolulu Hunts'. Once again, the setting is a reception room, where the scene can be read as symbolizing the interests and values of the influential patrons: perhaps there is some allusion to wild beast displays they had sponsored, as in the mid-fifth century 'Megalopsychia' pavement where the personified virtue, handing out coins, presides over scenes of *venatores* in combat with animals (Figure 8.3).[51]

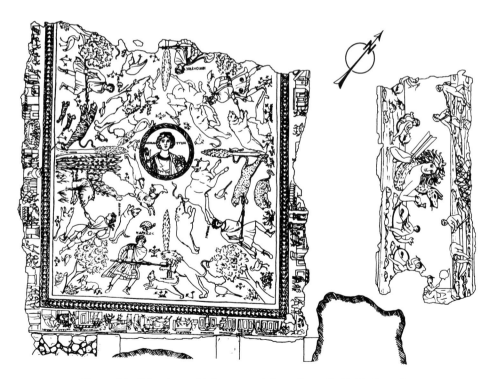

Figure 8.3: 'Megalopsychia' pavement from Room B, Yakto Complex.

In this pavement the townscape border (see below) constructs a public context for the activities at its centre, and is therefore unlike most of the images discussed so far which have revolved around activities within the private house and the social interactions between householder and guests. In general, events with a public or civic context are far less frequently represented in surviving mosaics from Antioch, as is shown by a review of other performance themes in mosaics from Antioch.[52] Most of these appear to relate to religious cult, if their fragmentary scenes have been reliably interpreted. Local religious festivals have been suggested as the subjects of pavements from the 'House of the Calendar' and the 'House of Menander' , but they have proved hard to recognize.[53] Levi identified scenes of Isiac rituals in two badly damaged mosaics in the 'House of the Mysteries of Isis'; but although they appear to depict more private moments, including initiation, these images should be used with caution as evidence for the house owner's personal beliefs (Figure 8.4).[54] Of contemporary Christianity, there are few substantial signs in the mosaics: apart from the pavements of religious buildings at Kaoussie, Machouka, and Seleucia, its only other possible traces are in the iconography of the 'Philia' mosaic and in the inscription in the 'Mosaic of the Biblical Quotation'.[55] As for the games and other public entertainments, there are a few (fragmentary) scenes to do with athletics.[56] Other activities said to have been hugely popular at Antioch are not represented in (surviving) mosaics at all: horse-racing is an obvious example, and mime and pantomime another (although it is quite likely that various mythological and literary subjects depicted in Antioch pavements reflect subjects performed in dance or recitation).[57]

Figure 8.4: 'Isiac' scene from the 'House of the Mysteries of Isis'.

MOSAICS AND LOCAL INTERESTS

Most of the subjects just described belong to a repertory common to mosaics across the eastern Mediterranean; but some themes are particularly popular or are specially treated at Antioch, and these are worth looking at more closely for the particular local significance they may have held.

Oceanus and Tethys (or Thetis, as Levi identified her) are amongst the most popular mythological subjects at Antioch (Figure 8.3). Along with other aquatic imagery (such as fish, and cupids fishing) they regularly appear in mosaics decorating pools and *nymphaea* in the houses. Their popularity is surely explained by the great pride that Antioch took in its abundant water supply, and in the high quality of life it provided for the population. Libanius boasted of this in his eulogy *In Praise of Antioch* and these images provide some visual support to his claims.[58]

Other myths depicted in the mosaics had a local significance because they had supposedly happened in the area. The most famous of these was Apollo's meeting with Daphne and her subsequent metamorphosis, which tradition had located at Daphne. This is represented by two mosaics in the 'House of Menander': one shows Daphne pursued by a richly dressed Apollo, and the other includes a named personification of the river Ladon, who in the Antiochene version of the myth was Daphne's father.[59] In these cases the dress and inscription stress the local value of these scenes, but in other instances it is far less clear. For example, the Judgment of Paris was also supposed to have taken place near Antioch, but its depiction in the *triclinium* of the 'Atrium House' has no special iconographical pointers, raising the question of just how much local interest should be read into the image which, after all, was quite common in ancient art.[60] The same problem recurs for the representation of characters linked with myths about the earliest days of Antioch: Perseus (who figures in aetiological legends connected with the earliest settlements) is depicted with Andromeda at the' House of Dionysus and Ariadne', while mythological characters mentioned in John Malalas' history of the foundation, have given their names to hunters in the 'Megalopsychia' pavement (Figure 8.3).[61] They all *could* be cited as evidence of Antiochene interest in references to their past, but whether they *should* be is another matter.

Antioch differed from other cities in the locality through its great importance as a Roman administrative and operational centre. During its long history many emperors resided there and there was a strong military presence, especially during the third century. Yet there seems to be little sign in the mosaics of this Roman interest, with the arguable exception of a late second century pavement from a *triclinium* in the 'House of Cilicia' (Figure 8.5).[62] Even though damaged in antiquity it can be reconstructed as an outer border, containing busts of rivers, and a central panel with two (or perhaps three) female figures in a landscape. Inscriptions in the mosaic identify the rivers as the Pyramus and Tigris, and the women as personifications of the nearby regions of Cilicia and Mesopotamia. Although clearly based on Hellenistic *tychai* figures (such as the famous Tyche of Antioch, as depicted in Figure 0.1), the figures have strong connections with Roman official art where personifications of territories and rivers were often used to commemorate the location of Roman triumphs.[63]

Figure 8.5: Pavement from the triclinium of the 'House of Cilicia'.

Although personifications of place are rare in Antioch mosaics, personifications of abstract qualities first occur in the 'Constantinian Villa' and then become quite frequent.[64] They are usually shown as busts of young women, richly adorned, and are often set at the centre of pavements 'carpeted' with geometric or hunting scenes. These personifications are found in many eastern mosaics of this time, but are particularly popular at Antioch and cover quite a wide range of qualities.[65] Many can be related without too much difficulty to the buildings which they decorate, or to other nearby images in the pavement. For instance, *Bios* (life) and *Tryphe* (luxury) greeted visitors to the 'House of the Drunken Dionysus'; *Apolausis* (enjoyment) (Figure 8.1) and *Soteria* (health) decorated pavements in baths; while *Ananeosis* (renewal) and *Ktisis* (foundation, or possession) may possibly represent buildings completed or restored.[66] Other personifications give moral value to the activities depicted in scenes around them; in particular the qualities from the 'Constantinian Villa' and *Megalo-psychia* in a pavement from Yakto (Figure 8.3), are all juxtaposed with scenes of the hunt, and can be read in that specific context.[67] Yet it is also true that many of the personifications depicted in Antioch pavements have an ambiguity derived from multiple meanings or associations – *Ananeosis*, for instance, can symbolise seasonal renewal (also represented by *Ge*, the personification of Earth), while *Ktisis* can be read as possesssion (with the suggestion, according to Levi, that right usage of possessions leads to enjoyment).[68] Thus they offer ideas for viewers to ponder, morals for contemplation or even for emulation through the activities depicted alongside them. Downey described them as providing 'precise formulations of contemporary thought' which 'in their directness will often go far beyond literary treatments'.[69] It is certainly the case that like the mythological scenes, which by and large preceded them in the Antiochene repertory, they represent cultural values espoused by the patrons; and in these later mosaics they do so alongside other symbolic images such as the hunt or the seasons.[70]

Townscape, exemplified in the border of the 'Megalopsychia' pavement (Figure 8.3), is another subject which becomes of particular interest in later mosaics in the Levant.[71] A second example from Antioch comprises two fragments showing generic rural activities and a walled building inscribed with the owner's name (?); but the 'Megalopsychia' border survives to such an extent that it has been subjected to extensive analysis as a source of evidence for the appearance of contemporary Antioch.[72] Much of its detail is schematically rendered, but even so there are many buildings that can be identified from their general architectural forms and from the accompanying inscriptions. Here is an opportunity to relate image to external history, such as the residence of Ardaburius (whose property is indicated in the border), and perhaps to the restoration of buildings after earthquake damage. It is also an opportunity to explore the relationship between text and image, and there have been various attempts to link the order of the buildings in the border with written descriptions of parts of the city.[73] Like these literary pieces the townscape testifies to a sense of place; and furthermore, in this pavement it serves to represent Antioch as the particular spatial context in which other depicted activities should be read.[74] The imagery of this pavement is so rich and flexible that it can support many possible readings, through the combination of depicted virtue (of a benefactor perhaps?), hunters with contemporary dress and mythological names (foundation heroes?), and 'real' city. Here local and wider influences (Hellenistic and late antique), the material and literary seem to converge.

CONCLUSIONS

On the face of it this survey suggests that the mosaics are a rich source of evidence in some fields, but less so in many others. They have a clear potential to contribute to the cultural and social history of Antioch, but – perhaps not surprisingly – reveal little of its politics or economic state, apart from existing as tangible evidence for the affluence enjoyed by its wealthier inhabitants over a long period in the empire. There is a similar distinction on the artistic side: the Antioch mosaics are excellent for studies of iconography and style, but provide patchy information on questions to do with the decoration of buildings or with precise chronology, because so many were found without other contextualizing material.

But these conclusions can be pushed a little further, particularly by turning to look at literary sources which help to shed some more light on the mosaics' imagery.

One important question which the written sources help to answer is how the major stylistic changes that happened in mosaic from the fourth century may relate to social developments in contemporary Antioch. As described above, the pavements provide unrivalled evidence for the move from Hellenistic traditions towards features characteristic of late Roman and early Byzantine art; and to a similiar degree the

written record for the city provides evidence for substantial changes in its culture and
social structures, particularly during the fourth century. Yet to date there has been
little attempt to look at the two together, and to see what impetus may have been
created by the new social order for the much discussed changes in art. To some extent
this lack is understandable, since for the earlier period at least the links between the
mosaics and the city's cultural life are easy to see. The illusionistic style and classical
subject-matter of pavements dated to the second and third centuries can be easily
explained by the Hellenistic culture which continued to prevail: this was both a source
of personal pride for the local elites, and also a cohesive factor in the city as a whole.

But although the later period initially presents a more complex picture, it is not
hard to see in it some general social trends which may have contributed to the artistic
change.[75] One was the declining influence of the city's council and its patronage:
although Antioch as a whole seems to have prospered in the fourth century, many
curiales felt increasingly pressurized in performing their traditional civic duties and
economic and social power moved towards a small group of wealthy people, a 'new
aristocracy' composed of people linked with imperial service, whose interests often
lay beyond the city.[76] Another major factor was the rise of Christians to prominence in
the local community. Christians too had an organization and attitudes which went
beyond civic boundaries; after Constantine they had emerged as new empire-wide
elite (and patrons of the arts), and also drew together people from the town and
country (as is particularly evident in Antioch and its hinterland). By the late fourth
century Libanius and John Chrysostom show between them how this change had
meant the end of the city as a cohesive community, bound by the old pagan civic
religion. Although many traditional cultural activities, like dining, pantomime, and
indeed the ownership of fine houses, continued to be enjoyed, they were strongly
attacked by Christian leaders, while the new Christian ascetic rejected mimesis and
tryphe (luxury), for the 'propagation of a non-classical and other-worldly ideal'.[77]

Since this period saw such change in the traditional urban values of Antioch (as
well as in the range of people likely to have commissioned mosaics), it seems
unsurprising that the Hellenistic imagery which had for so long been their natural
form of expression disappeared from use, or that it was replaced by symbols which
were more cosmopolitan and polyvalent. These might still express the patrons' values
but in terms which could support differing religious readings or which signified ideals
to which no-one could take exception. This would explain the popularity of the
personified virtues and the development of townscape which, as in the 'Megalopsychia'
pavement (Figure 8.3), could be used to represent the actual locality.[78] The hunt is an
example par excellence of this new terminology, as it is universally recognizable and
has connotations of domination and success that could be used for various contexts
and interpretations. It also leads stylistically and conceptually to the 'animal carpets'
which were used to decorate at least two Christian buildings in the vicinity of Antioch:
as Kondoleon says of the example in the church building at Seleucia, these represent
'a rather seamless transition of the hunt theme from the house of the Roman *dominus*
to the house of the Christian Lord'.[79]

So in the end we may conclude that artistic tradition and social change were finely
balanced as factors governing the production of floor-mosaics in Antioch, and that

this needs to be taken into consideration in any evaluation of them as a source of historical evidence. Yet at the end of the day artistic tradition perhaps had the upper hand. For even the major changes just described resulted in only a restricted number of new subjects, centring around personifications and images of the hunt and 'animal carpets'. There is little indication from surviving pavements that Christianity had much impact on mosaic at Antioch, while Persian influence is restricted mainly to individual motifs. And further back, in the second and third centuries, the traditions of Hellenistic art had been so entrenched as to exclude any subjects which reflected Roman cultural activities, even the gladiatorial games which (as we know from other sources) were hugely popular in the 'real life' of the city. The inevitable mismatch between the life of Antioch as documented in written sources and the world conjured up by the visual images makes it inappropriate to use the mosaics as literal evidence for everyday existence. We must not forget that in Antioch, as elsewhere in this part of Syria, mosaic was an imported art form, adopted by a relatively small group of educated and wealthy people to decorate their houses with symbols of an elite Greek culture they shared with their peers across the eastern Mediterranean. [80] It had no real roots in the everyday culture of the country, or scope for articulating the particular interests of other sections of the local community, such as Roman or Syrian. [81] Its social usage was limited, although the artistic traditions which underpin it are themselves extensive and long-established.

So while Antioch pavements are an invaluable source of evidence for aspects of the city's history – notably its culture and society – what they perhaps illustrate best are the strengths of mosaic as an art-form and in particular, its powers of renewal over time.

Notes

1   This replaces the paper I gave at the Colloquium on performance themes in the House of Menander (published in Huskinson 2003). Figures reproduced here by kind permission of the Dept. of Art and Archaeology, Princeton University.
2   *e.g.* Levi, 1947:1. For a succinct record of the excavation campaigns see Najbjerg in Padgett, 2001: 178–181; Kondoleon, 2000: 5–8.
3   More recent discoveries: *e.g.* Campbell, 1983: 143; 1994 : 55, pl XVI, 1. NB unless otherwise specified this paper will use 'Antioch' as a general term for the locality.
4   Kondoleon, 2000a: 63.
5   Libanius *In Praise of Antioch* 221, 238–9 etc.; Kondoleon, 2000a:76
6   *e.g.* Friend, 1941 on representations of Menander and Glykera; and Weitzmann, 1941 on scenes which he identified as coming from Homer and Euripides.
7   See Levi, 1947 : 10.
8   Campbell, 1988: xiii; for reviews cf. Dunbabin, 1999: 160, no.3.
9   Dauphin, 1976 and 1980.
10 *e.g.* Balty, 1981 and 1995; Dunbabin, 1999.
11 Kondoleon, 2000.
12 Kondoleon, 2000a: 65–76.
13 Huskinson, 2003; Leyerle, 2001.
14 Re distortion: Campbell (1983: 143 and 1988: xiii) has observed, for instance, how wrong conclusions drawn at Antioch can adversely affect the comparative dating of mosaics

found elsewhere, while Kondoleon (2000a:64) notes how even in studies of local Syrian mosaics the Antiochene examples may stand apart as 'somewhat isolated' and with 'a false impression of singularity'.

15 Especially Lavin, 1963. For a summary Dauphin, 1980: 132–3; Balty, 1995: 30–1; Dunbabin, 1999: 176. NB virtually all the framed scenes at Antioch were pseudo-emblemata (but cf. Levi, 1947: 25).

16 *e.g.* Cilicia: Balty, 1995: 31–33. Cyprus: *e.g.* Kondoleon, 1995: 30,147–8,156. Dauphin, 1976: 135–37 (links Antioch with Misis, Urfa, and Serdjilla); but cf. Balty, 1995: 24–5 on this.

17 Crete: Kondoleon, 2000a: 64–65. For Bishapur: Balty, 1995:17; 149–152; Dunbabin, 1999:174.

18 Dunbabin, 1999: 58–65; 111–15.

19 Kaoussie: Levi, 1947: 283–285. Apolausis baths: Levi, 1947: 304–07. For late hunt mosaics: Levi, 1947, 357–59; 363–65; and Lavin, 1963.

20 Balty, 1995: 153–4.

21 Cf. also Lavin, 1963: 182–183 and 184; Dunbabin, 1999: 178; Kondoleon 2000a: 65; also Gonosová, 2000.

22 For summary see *e.g.* Lavin, 1963: 196–98.

23 Gonosová, 2000.

24 Ball, 2000, 153 for long tradition of Iranophilism amongst the Syrians.

25 Stillwell, 1961: 54–55; Dauphin, 1980: 116–17. Cf. Dunbabin, 1999: 176–77 who adds the influence of church architecture with similar demands of size.

26 According to Dauphin, 1980:113.

27 For these problems see Lassus, 1984: 361; cf. Kondoleon, 2000: 7–8 for summary.

28 Cf. Jones, 1981: 16–26.

29 Kaoussie: Lassus, 1938: 38–39; Levi, 1947: 283–5. For Ardaburius: Downey, 1961: 471–72.

30 Balty, 1981: 348–350; Dunbabin, 1999: 160, note 3. Also Balty, 1995:15–30 for problem of dating Middle eastern mosaics in general.

31 Re 'associated finds': Levi himself was quick to point out caveats (Levi, 1947:5–6); and some of his 'external' evidence has since been challenged as unreliable: cf. debate over the coin dating 'the Constantinian Villa': Levi, 1947: 226 and Campbell, 1983. Earthquakes: Levi, 1947: 6 for a list of dates and possible damage. For examples of their use for dating: *e.g.* Levi, 1947: 16 (cf. also Campbell, 1988: 22), 25, 34, 257, 311, 359. For Persian Sack: *e.g.* Levi, 1947: 366–67.

32 *e.g.* Baths: Levi, 1947: 260–77; 285–91. Tomb of Mnemosyne: Levi, 1947: 291–304. Portico of theatre at Daphne: Levi, 1947: 223; Churches: Levi, 1947: 283–5 and 368–9. NB some sites originally described as 'houses' are now not thought to be so.

33 Re social status of the householders: cf. Pollard, 2000: 238 who cites the later mosaics as evidence which counters *curiales'* claims to be hard-up, and Liebeschuetz, 1972: 134 who suggests that these were houses of former imperial officials who had made their home in Antioch.

34 Stillwell, 1961; Lassus, 1984; Dobbins, 2000: 51–3; cf.also Ellis this volume.

35 Dobbins, 2000: 51.

36 *e.g.* Lassus, 1984: 362. Cf. Levi, 1947: 45 for fragments of wall-painting (subsequently lost) in the House of the Bacchic Thiasos. For sculptures: Padgett, 2001; and a cache from Building 25-H (Levi, 1947: 316) : Brinkerhoff, 1970.

37 Suggesting alterations in particular houses: *e.g.* House of Cilicia (Levi, 1947: 57) ; House of the Red Pavement (Levi, 1947: 68) ; Ellis, this volume. For increase in room size and its relation to changes in mosaic design: Stillwell, 1961: 54–55; Dunbabin, 1999: 176. For indicating orientation of room: *e.g.* Stillwell, 1961: 52–3; 55–56. For spatial hierarchies: Dobbins, 2000.

38 Dunbabin, 1991: 126 and 130 for examples. Cf. here figure 8.5 (House of Cilicia) with figure 8.2 (House of Buffet Supper).

39 Stillwell, 1961: 48; Dobbins, 2000: 53.

40 Dunbabin, 1998: 95–98: the Roman form was itself influenced by Hellenistic palatial halls.

41 Levi 1947: 127–136.

42 For the mosaic as reliable evidence for contemporary silverware: Dunbabin, 1993: 120.

43 Plutarch *Convivial Questions* 712B. Cf. Jones, 1991: 191–194.

44 Levi, 1947: 119–126.

45 *e.g.* Achilles and Briseis (House of Aion); Levi, 1947: 195–96. Novels: *e.g.* Ninus and Semiramis and Metiochus and Parthenope (House of the Man of Letters) : Levi, 1947: 117–19. Abstract topics: *e.g.* Aion and the Chronoi: Levi, 1947: 197. Plutarch *Convivial Questions* 716D. Atrium House: Kondoleon, 2000a: 68–71.

46 *e.g.* the Atrium House: Kondoleon, 2000a: 68; and the House of the Drunken Dionysus: Levi, 1947: 223.

47 Bowersock, 1990: 41–53.

48 Levi, 1947: 141–56; Huskinson, 2003.

49 Levi, 1947: 93–99; Geyer, 1977, 113–18.

50 Kondoleon, 2000a: 65; cf. Dunbabin, 1978.

51 Cf. Kondoleon, 2000: 159–60; Dunbabin, 1999: 181–83. Cf. also Downey,1938: 359 for the owner's desire to associate himself with this abstract quality.

52 Huskinson, 2003.

53 House of Calendar: Levi, 1947: 36–38; Parrish 1994: 388; 'Dioskouria' in the House of Menander: Levi, 2000: 215.

54 Cf. Levi, 1947: 37, 163–66.

55 For churches : Levi, 1947: 283–5 and 368-9; Martyrion of Seleucia: Levi, 1947: 359–363; also Kondoleon, 2000b. For Philia mosaic: Levi, 1947: 318; 'Mosaic of the Biblical Quotation (or Inscription)': Levi, 1947: 320.

56 *e.g.* in House of the Porticoes': Levi, 1947: 106–8; House of Menander: Levi, 1947: 200.

57 Horse-racing: Libanius *In Praise of Antioch* 218, 268. For mime and pantomime: e.g Judgment of Paris (as in the Atrium House), Europa and the Bull (in the House of the Boat of Psyches), Achilles with Briseis and on Scyros (as in the House of the Porticoes) were all recorded as performed in pantomime (though not all necessarily in Antioch): Molloy, 1996: 277–287.

58 Libanius *In Praise of Antioch* 244 –248; and 258–260. Popularity of water-motifs at Antioch: Levi, 1947: 2, 168–9; Downey, 1961: 23,n.47; Kondoleon, 2000: nos 38, 39; 2000a: 74–76.

59 For the myth, Downey, 1961: 83–84. For House of Menander: Levi, 1947: 205, 211–14; pl.XLVII a and b. For Ladon: Kondoleon, 2000a: 75.

60 Downey, 1961: 84; Levi, 1947: 21.

61 For the myth Downey, 1961: 50; also Nonnos, *Dionysiaka* 47: 498ff for the account of hostility between Dionysus and Perseus. For the mosaics: Levi, 1947: 150–156. For the mythological heroes and possible links with Antioch's legendary beginnings: Malalas 13–14 (Adonis, a philosopher); 40–42 (Teiresias, a Boeotian philosopher and hunter exiled to the Temple of Apollo at Daphne); 88–90 (Hippolytus); 164–6 (Meleager). See also Mango, 1995.

62 Levi, 1947: 57–9, fig. 21, pl. IX b-d. For dating: Levi, 1947: 625; cf. Kondoleon, 2000: 152. Roman imperial themes occur in other mosaics from the area: *e.g.* provinces, from Belkis/ Zeugma (Ostrowski,1990; 218 no. 5); and Euphrates with provinces from Mas'Udiye, dated AD 227/8 (Balty, 1981: 369).

63 For coinage of Trajan grouping together river gods and a female territorial personification

to commemorate his original annexation of the area: *LIMC* VIII,1 1997, 28 cf. nos 3 and 4:, for coins of Hadrian recording his visit to Cilicia in AD 129, showing the personified province, with helmet and standard: *LIMC* VI,1, 1992, 45–6.

64   Levi, 1947: 227–56.

65   For discussions *e.g.* Downey, 1938 and 1941; Levi, 1947: 253–6; Campbell, 1994.

66   For *Bios* and *Tryphe* (here as reclining figures, with cups raised): Levi 1947: 223–24. Baths: Dunbabin, 1989: 19–20; cf. Downey, 1938:359 on healing waters. For *Ktisis*: Levi, 1947: 255.

67   From the 'Constantinian Villa' *Ktisis*, *Euandria*, *Dynamis* and *Ananeosis* survive. For *Megalopsychia*: Levi, 1947: 338–345.

68   For Ananeosis with seasonal attributes: Levi, 1947: 320–21. See also Levi, 1947: 254, note 199 and 350 for suggestion that the four virtues found in the Constantinian Villa and in the House of the Sea Goddess might symbolize the seasons, and the ages of man.

69   Downey, 1938: 360.

70   For hunt, moral and seasonal themes, and associations with the householder: Downey, 1938; Ellis, 1991: 122–26.

71   Levi, 1947: 326–337, 324, fig. 136; pls. LXXIX–LXXX. For some other late antique townscapes: *e.g.* Bertelli, 1999.

72   Levi, 1947: 345–6, pls. LXXIV b and c .

73   *e.g.* Downey, 1961: 659–664 for how the order of scenes may relate to specific itineraries between Antioch and Daphne, and for dating from various depicted buildings.

74   Bertelli, 1999: 145–46 notes that figurative representations of towns are preceded by a literary interest in the same theme; cf. Libanius *In Praise of Antioch.*

75   The major study of these social and cultural changes is Liebeschuetz, 1972.

76   For this 'new aristocracy' *e.g.* Liebeschuetz, 1972: 258–9; Meeks, 1978: 25–27.

77   Liebeschuetz, 1972: 259. Also Sandwell in this volume. Cf. also Goody, 1997: 105–8, more generally, for the link between the rise of Christianity and the decline in representational arts. Re some Antiochene priorities at this time: Dauphin, 1980: 125 notes how wealthy Antiochenes 'invested their capital in private buildings, villae and baths whereas the Palestinians spent theirs on ecclesiastical buildings'.

78   Campbell, 1994: 57–9 suggests that the personifications, with their imperial-like adornments may have had an apotropaic value, and as secularized themes were acceptable to Christians for decorating floors (whereas specifically religious images were not).

79   Kondoleon , 2000b: 219. The other example is the 'Philia' mosaic.

80   Balty, 1995: 159.

81   For cultural make-up of Antioch: Ball, 2000: 150–56.

Bibliography

Ball, W., 2000. *Rome in the east. The Transformation of an empire* (London).

Balty, J., 1981. 'La mosaïque antique au proche orient. I Des origines à la Tetrarchie'. In H. Temporini and W. Haase (eds) *Aufstieg und Niedergang der römischen Welt* (Berlin, New York), 12, 2: 347–429.

Balty, J., 1995. *Mosaïques antiques du proche-orient. Chronologie, iconographie, interprétation* (Annales littéraires de l'Université de Besancon 550). (Paris).

Bertelli, C., 1999.'Visual images of the town in late antiquity and the early Middle Ages'. In G.P. Brogiolo and B. Ward-Perkins (eds) *The Idea and Ideal of the Town between Late Antiquity and the early Middle Ages,* (Leiden), 127–146.

Bowersock, G., 1990. *Hellenism in Late Antiquity* (Cambridge).

Brinkerhoff, D.M., 1970. *A Collection of Sculpture in Classical and early Christian Antioch* (New York).

Campbell, S., 1983. 'Antioch and the Corpus of Mosaics in Southern Turkey'. In R. F. Campanati (ed.) III *Colloquio internazionale sul mosaico antico Ravenna. 6–10 settembre 1980* (Bologna), 143–8.

Campbell, S., 1988. *The Mosaics of Antioch* (Subsidia Mediaevalia 15) (Toronto).

Campbell, S., 1994. 'Enhanced images: the Power of gems in abstract personifications'. In J.-P. Darmon and A. Rebourg (eds) *La mosaïque gréco-romaine IVe colloque international pour l'Étude de la mosaïque antique, Trèves 1984* (Paris), 55–59.

Campbell, W.A. and Stillwell, R., 1941. 'Catalogue of Mosaics'. In Stillwell, 1941: 171–219.

Cimok, F., 2000. *Antioch Mosaics. A Corpus* (Istanbul).

Dauphin, C., 1976. 'A new method of studying early Byzantine pavements (coding and a computed cluster analysis) with special reference to the Levant', *Levant* 8, 113–149.

Dauphin, C., 1980. 'Mosaic pavements as an index of prosperity and fashion', *Levant* 12, 112–134.

Dobbins, J.J., 2000. 'The houses of Antioch'. In Kondoleon, 2000: 51–61.

Downey, G., 1938. 'Personifications of abstract ideas in the Antioch Mosaics' *Transactions of the American Philological Association* 69, 349–363.

Downey, G., 1941. 'Ethical themes in the Antioch Mosaics', *Church History* 10, 367–376.

Downey, G., 1961. *A History of Antioch in Syria from Seleucus to the Arab Conquest* (Princeton).

Dunbabin, K.M.D., 1978. *The Mosaics of Roman North Africa. Studies in Iconography and Patronage.* (Oxford).

Dunbabin, K.M.D., 1989. 'Baiarum Grata Voluptas: Pleasures and dangers of the baths', *Papers of the British School at Rome* 57, 6–46.

Dunbabin, K.M.D., 1991. 'Triclinium and Stibadium'. In Slater, 1991:121–148.

Dunbabin, K.M.D., 1993. ' Wine and water at the Roman *convivium*', *Journal of Roman Archaeology* 6, 116–41.

Dunbabin, K.M.D., 1996. 'Convivial spaces: dining and entertainment in the Roman Villa' *Journal of Roman archaeology* 9, 66–80.

Dunbabin, K.M.D., 1998. 'Ut Graeco more biberetur: Greeks and Romans on the Dining Couch'. In I. Nielsen and H.S. Nielsen (eds) *Meals in a social context. Aspects of the Communal Meal in the Hellenistic and Roman World* (Aarhus), 81–101.

Dunbabin, K.M.D., 1999. *Mosaics of the Greek and Roman world* (Cambridge).

Ellis, S., 1991. 'Power, Architecture and Decor: How the late Roman Aristocrat appeared to his Guests'. In E. Gazda (ed.) *Roman Art in the Private Sphere.* (Ann Arbor), 117–134.

Friend, A.M., 1941. 'Menander and Glykera in the Mosaics of Antioch' . In Stillwell, 1941: 248–251.

Geyer, A., 1977. *Das Problem des Realitätsbezuges in der Dionysischen Bildkunst der Kaiserzeit* (Beiträge zur Archäologie) (Würzburg).

Gonosová, A., 2000. 'Exotic taste: the Lure of Sasanian Persia'. In Kondoleon, 2000: 130–133.

Goody, J., 1997. *Representations and contradictions. Ambivalence towards images, theatre, fiction, relics and sexuality* (Oxford).

Huskinson, J., 2003. 'Theatre, performance and theatricality in some mosaic pavements from Antioch' in *Bulletin of the Institute of Classical Studies* 46 forthcoming.

Jones, C.P., 1991. 'Dinner Theater'. In Slater, 1991: 185–198.

Jones, F. F., 1981. 'Antioch Mosaics in Princeton', *Record of the Art Museum, Princeton University* 40, no. 2, 2–27.

Kondoleon, C., 1995. *Domestic and Divine. Roman Mosaics in the House of Dionysos.* (Ithaca and London).

Kondoleon, C., 2000. *Antioch The Lost Ancient City.* (Princeton, in association with the Worcester Art Museum).

Kondoleon, C., 2000a. 'Mosaics of Antioch'. In Kondoleon, 2000: 63–77.

Kondoleon , C., 2000b. 'The mosaic of the Church building of Seleucia Pieria'. In Kondoleon, 2000: 218–219.

Lassus, J., 1938. 'L'église cruciforme. Antioche – Kaoussié 12-F'. In R. Stillwell (ed.) *Antioch-on-the-Orontes II The Excavations 1933–1936* (Princeton), 5–44.

Lassus, J., 1984. 'Sur les maisons d'Antioche' *Apamée de Syrie. Bilan des recherches archéologiques 1973–1979. Aspects de l'architecture domestique d' Apamée. Actes du colloque tenu à Bruxelles les 29, 30, et 31 mai 1980.* (Fouilles d'Apamée de Syrie. Miscellanea, fasc 13) (Brussels), 361–372.

Lavin, I., 1963. 'The Hunting Mosaics of Antioch and their sources. A study of Compositional Principles in the development of early medieval style', *Dumbarton Oaks Papers* 17, 179–286.

Levi, D., 1947. *Antioch Mosaic Pavements, I and II* (Princeton).

Leyerle, B., 2001. *Theatrical Shows and Ascetic Lives. John Chrysostom's Attack on Spiritual Marriage* (Berkeley, Los Angeles, London).

Libanius, *Oration 11: The Antiochikos: In praise of Antioch* in M. Whitby (ed.), *Antioch as a Centre of Hellenic Culture as Observed by Libanius.* Translated by A.F. Norman (Translated texts for historians 34: Liverpool, 2000).

Liebeschuetz, J.H.W.G., 1972. *Antioch. City and imperial administration in the Later Roman Empire.* (Oxford).

LIMC: Lexicon Iconographicum Mythologiae Classicae , I,1- Zürich and Düsseldorf, 1981–

Malalas, *The chronicle of John Malalas. A translation.* Translated by E. Jeffreys, M. Jeffreys and R. Scott (Melbourne: Australian Association for Byzantine Studies 1986).

Mango, M., 1995. 'Artemis in Daphne', *Byzantinische Forschungen* 21, 263-283.

Meeks, W.A. and Wilken, R.L., 1978. *Jews and Christians in Antioch in the first four centuries of the Common Era,* (SBL Sources for Biblical Study 13). (Missoula).

Millar, F., 1993. *The Roman Near East 31 BC–AD 337.* (Cambridge, Mass.).

Molloy, M., 1996. *Libanius and the dancers.* Altertumswissenschaftliche Texte und Studien Band 31 (Hildesheim, Zürich, New York).

Morey, C.R., 1938. *The Mosaics of Antioch* (London, New York, Toronto).

Ostrowski, J.A., 1990. *Les personnifications des provinces dans l'art romain.* Travaux du centre d' archéologie méditerranéenne de l'Académie polonaise des sciences 27 (Warsaw).

Padgett, J.M., 2001. *Roman sculpture in the Art Museum Princeton University* (Princeton).

Parrish, D., 1994. 'The Calendar Mosaic from Antioch: a new interpretation of its illustrations of the months'. In C.M. Batalla (ed.) *VI Coloquio internacional sobre mosaico antiguo. Palencia-Mérida. Octubre 1990* (no place of publication given), 383–389.

Pollard, N., 2000. *Soldiers, Cities and Civilians in Roman Syria* (Ann Arbor).

Slater, W. (ed.), 1991. *Dining in a Classical Context* (Ann Arbor).

Stillwell, R., (ed.) 1941. *Antioch-on -the- Orontes III The Excavations 1937–1939* (Princeton).

Stillwell R., 1941a. ' Outline of the campaigns'. In Stillwell, 1941: 1–34.

Stillwell, R., 1961. 'Houses of Antioch', *Dumbarton Oaks Papers* 15, 47–57.

Weitzmann, K., 1941. 'Illustrations of Euripides and Homer in the mosaics of Antioch'. In Stillwell, 1941: 233–247.

Yegül, F., 2000. 'Baths and Bathing in Roman Antioch'. In Kondoleon, 2000: 146–151.